THE GOLDEN RETRIEVER

POPULAR DOGS' BREED SERIES

THE
GOLDEN
RETRIEVER

JOAN TUDOR

Popular Dogs

London   Sydney   Auckland   Johannesburg

Popular Dogs Publishing Co. Ltd

An imprint of Century Hutchinson Ltd
Brookmount House, 62–65 Chandos Place,
Covent Garden, London WC2N 4NW

Century Hutchinson Australia (Pty) Ltd
20 Alfred Street, Milsons Point, Sydney 2061, Australia

Century Hutchinson New Zealand Limited
191 Archers Road, PO Box 40–086, Glenfield, Auckland 10

Century Hutchinson South Africa (Pty) Ltd
PO Box 337, Bergvlei 2012, South Africa

First published 1966
Revised editions 1968, 1970, 1972, 1974, 1977, 1980, 1981, 1983
Reprinted 1984
Revised edition 1987, 1989

Set in Baskerville by BookEns, Saffron Walden, Essex

Printed and bound in Great Britain by Mackays of Chatham PLC, Chatham, Kent

British Library Cataloguing in Publication Data

Tudor, Joan
The golden retriever.——11th ed.——
(Popular Dogs' breed series).
1. Golden retrievers
1. Title
636.7'52   SF429.G63

ISBN 0 09 174385 0

CONTENTS

ILLUSTRATIONS

Between pages 48 and 49

Between pages 80 and 81

THE GOLDEN RETRIEVER

IN THE TEXT

ACKNOWLEDGEMENTS

I gratefully acknowledge the help of all those who have been kind enough to provide me with information which has gone towards the writing of this book. I wish particularly to express my sincere thanks to Mrs Elma Stonex, who has so generously made available to me the results of her research into the origin of the breed, and also the photos of the early dogs, some of which were given to her by Lady Pentland.

I wish also to express my gratitude to a veterinary surgeon friend, who kindly gave so much of his valuable time to assist with the technical side of the chapter on 'Ailments'. Also to those many people overseas who have taken the trouble to send me information about the breed in their countries, I am most grateful. I especially acknowledge the help of Mrs Rachel Elliott of the U.S.A., Mr Christopher Burton (Canada), Mrs D. Sprunt (Secretary of the Golden Retriever Club of Canada), Mrs C. van Crevel (Holland), Mrs J. Tucker (New Zealand), Mrs Lilliehöök (Sweden) and Mrs C. Twist (Eire), who all put in a great deal of work to ensure that I had accurate information from their countries.

To Mr C. A. Binney, who so kindly made the Kennel Club Library available to me, thus enabling me to look at Lord Tweedmouth's records, I express my sincere thanks, as well as to the other members of the Kennel Club staff who have kindly answered my many queries from time to time.

I am most grateful also to all those who have provided me with such beautiful photographs of their dogs. I only wish it had been possible to publish all of them, but, alas, there is only space for those selected in an endeavour to give a picture of the breed from its early days right up to the present time.

Lastly, I express my appreciation of a very long-suffering husband, who has so unstintingly given of his time by taking over many of my kennel chores to allow me to get on with my writing, and has also spent many hours checking and rechecking with me.

J.T.

AUTHOR'S INTRODUCTIONS

To the First Edition
In this book I have tried to deal with all aspects of the breed in as much detail as space will allow. It is hoped that all Golden Retriever lovers will find something of interest therein, and that it may be of help to those wishing to learn about the breed.

The first three chapters give an outline of the breed from its early days right up to the present day. From this part of the book those interested in the study of pedigrees should find help, for as well as telling of the outstanding dogs of their respective times, I have also mentioned those dogs and bitches which have proved influential on the breed through their descendants. I have also told of those owners and breeders in this country and abroad who have contributed much towards establishing the breed as it is today – for it is through their efforts in maintaining the high standard of the breed that it owes its present popularity.

The book also endeavours to give guidance to those desirous of producing the correct conformation, and to afford help to owners – whether of pet dogs, show stock or of working dogs – on how to rear, care for, breed, show and train their Golden Retrievers.

The true Golden is one which looks typical and has a temperament which makes it equally suitable for working with the gun and of being the ideal family companion. It would be detrimental to the breed were we to concentrate solely on one aspect, and thereby to lose its other qualities. To produce outstanding show specimens, incapable of being taught to work with the gun, is no more desirable than to breed the brilliant gundog without regard to his looks – a Golden is not typical of its breed unless it looks and acts like one!

Having had Golden Retrievers in the family since my early teens, my admiration of their great qualities is boundless, consequently there can be no other breed for me! They look beautiful, have the most delightful temperaments, and are ready to do whatever is required of them – they are truly 'all purpose', so let us endeavour to keep them that way!

1966   J.T.

To the Second Edition

I am delighted that the first edition of *The Golden Retriever* has been so well received. Nothing has happened in the past two years to change my opinion of this breed. If you want the ideal show dog, shooting dog and companion, then you cannot do better than to have a Golden Retriever. I would just like to stress the fact that though Goldens were specifically evolved as gundogs, there is no point in breeding those which perform superbly in the shooting field if they do not also resemble the breed they represent. We must always endeavour to keep type, working ability and the breed's delightful temperament in mind when breeding.

1968   J.T.

To the Third Edition

It is gratifying to me to learn that there is a need for a third edition of *The Golden Retriever*, and the appendices, which include records of the breed, have been brought up to date in this.

1970   J.T.

To the Fourth Edition

In this edition I have been able to bring the text of Chapter 3 up to date, so that influences on the breed up to the early 1970s are shown. The Breed Standard and appendices have also been brought up to date.

1972   J.T.

To the Fifth Edition

Golden Retrievers become more popular each year all over the world, and this is not surprising, for their beauty and brains abound, and their well-feathered, dense coats, of a variety of colours – from palest cream to deep golden – look a picture in the show ring. This edition brings the book up to date, in an endeavour to help novice and experienced Golden lovers.

1974   J.T.

To the Sixth Edition
I am delighted to find that another edition of this book is now necessary. In this I have made more amendments, and brought the appendices up to date yet again.

1977   J.T.

To the Seventh Edition
Various parts of this edition have been brought up to date, including additions to the lists of champions, etc. This time I have amended the Goldens Overseas chapter to make the information more recent. I am particularly indebted to Mrs Wymann (Switzerland), Mrs van Rhijn (Holland), Mr Fryck-strand (Sweden) and Mr Curry (New Zealand) for their help with their countries. Unfortunately, some other countries, which had expressed a desire for this updating, did not let me have information in time for this new edition.

1980   J.T.

To the Eighth Edition
As the eighth edition is appearing so soon after the seventh it has not been necessary for me to make many revisions to the text. However, I have brought the appendices up to date once again and replaced one of the photographs.

1981   J.T.

To the Ninth Edition
Since this book was first published over sixteen years ago, the breed's popularity has continued to increase until now it has the fourth highest number of registrations of all breeds at the Kennel Club. This can become a danger to the breed, as it means that too many people are breeding these lovely dogs and, inevitably, many bad dogs must be produced. We must keep a careful watch to ensure the beautiful temperament and good looks of the Golden are retained. In this edition, I have

once again updated parts of the text and added to and amended the appendices.

1982
Burstow, Surrey   J.T.

To the Tenth Edition

I am delighted that the tenth edition of this book has once again gone into hardback. This time I have been able to completely amend the text and to alter where this has been necessary to bring it up to date, including the amended Standards for the United Kingdom, the United States of America and Canada – the three Standards which apply in different parts of the world. Once again some of the photographs have been altered, and some of the present-day dogs inserted instead of some of those of the past. It is a sad thing to have to say that, through the increasing popularity of this lovely breed – which ranks as the fourth most popular of all breeds – there are some quite untypical Goldens appearing, and temperament has suffered as well. Please do keep this in mind when planning future matings. The Golden, as stressed in this book, is a dog which must be able to mix happily with adults, children and other animals alike, and this is how we must endeavour to keep it.

My thanks go to Miss Lucy Tucker for the line drawing of 'The typical Golden outline'.

1987   J.T.

CHAPTER 1

THE ORIGIN OF THE BREED

The history of the breed, as officially recognised by the Kennel Club, in 1960 is recorded annually in Crufts Catalogues under the heading 'Description of the Golden Retriever', and reads as follows:

> 'The origin of the Golden Retriever is less obscure than most of the Retriever varieties, as the breed was definitely started by the first Lord Tweedmouth last century, as shown in his carefully kept private stud book and notes, first brought to light by his great-nephew, the Earl of Ilchester, in 1952. In 1868 Lord Tweedmouth mated a yellow Wavy-Coated Retriever (Nous) he had bought from a cobbler in Brighton (bred by Lord Chichester) to a Tweed Water-Spaniel (Belle) from Ladykirk on the Tweed. These Tweed Water-Spaniels, rare except in the Border Country, are described by authorities of the times as like a small Retriever, liver-coloured and curly-coated. Lord Tweedmouth methodically line-bred down from this mating between 1868 and 1890, using another Tweed Water-Spaniel, and outcrosses of two black Retrievers, an Irish Setter and a sandy coloured Bloodhound. (It is now known that one of the most influential Kennels in the first part of the century which lies behind all present day Golden Retrievers was founded on stock bred by Lord Tweedmouth.)'

The recognition of this origin as authentic must have been very rewarding to the sixth Lord Ilchester (Lord Tweedmouth's great-nephew), but even more so to Mrs Elma Stonex, who put in nearly ten years of research to find out all the true facts, piecing them together bit by bit to ensure a complete picture, from the first dogs bred at Guisachan (Gaelic for 'Place of the Firs'), the Scottish seat of Lord Tweedmouth (formerly Sir Dudley Coutts Marjoribanks), to those of the present day. The culmination of all this hard work was when Lord

Ilchester suggested in 1959 that Mrs Stonex and he should put these facts to the Kennel Club for its approval, and the result was this official recognition. This origin was also officially recognised a year earlier by the American Golden Retriever Club and the American Kennel Club through the efforts of Mrs Rachel Elliott, a one-time President of the American Golden Retriever Club.

Prior to the true origin of the breed becoming known, many people believed that the original yellow Retrievers were 'sports' of that colour, bred from other coloured Retrievers, for during the latter half of the last century long-coated Retrievers of sandy, liver, brown and yellow colours were well known, and yellow-coloured puppies were quite often bred from black parents. In *The Illustrated Book of the Dog* (1882) Vero Shaw mentions seeing some of these in Dr Bond Moore's Retriever kennel and was told that they were not rare. Rawdon Lee in his *Modern Dogs* (1893) also alludes to 'Brown Retrievers . . . some curly-coated, some wavy or straight-coated. The latter are repeatedly produced from black parents. . . . Personally I have quite a fancy for this pale or chocolate-brown coloured Retriever.' (In a later edition of this book Lee also mentions Tweed Water-Spaniels as coming into Retriever ancestry.) There is also Sir Francis Grant's 1840 painting of *The Earl of Lichfield's Shooting Party* which shows a yellow Retriever carrying a pheasant, and this gave support to their theory, as did an article in *The Field* in 1922 which said: '. . . the valued strain of yellow labradors in possession of Captain Radclyffe at Wareham . . . is not to be confused with the yellow retrievers which have existed for many years on the Border'.

There were, however, others who believed that the Golden Retriever originated from a troupe of six or eight Russian circus-dogs supposed to have been bought by Lord Tweedmouth during a visit to Brighton and taken back to Guisachan. This Russian circus-dog origin appeared in Crufts Catalogues until 1960 when the new facts were put to the Kennel Club and the now proven origin accepted. One wonders how this myth started and how it became recognised as the authentic history of the breed for so many years without tangible evidence to substantiate it, for nowhere in the first Lord Tweedmouth's records is there any mention of any Russian circus-dogs. One strong supporter of this theory was Colonel le Poer Trench, who had his first yellow Retriever, Andy (who is supposed to have been descended from Lord Tweedmouth's dogs), as early as 1883, and on whom he founded his St Huberts' strain. He later registered his dogs with the Kennel Club as Retrievers (Russian Yellow). He seems to have believed this 'Russian' theory without any apparent evidence to support it, and seems to have fired all the earlier breeders and descendants of the early keepers at Guisachan with enthusiasm for it, so that, over the years, it became accepted, by many, as fact. There is a possibility that Lord Chichester (from whose kennel Nous originated) may have been to the Crimea and could have brought a dog from there home with him, which Colonel le Poer Trench may have known about, but there is no real evidence of this.

Undoubtedly dogs with some similarity of type to the old yellow Retrievers have been known in Russia for over a century. There they are reported to have been used as sheepdogs in the Caucasus and as gundogs in Siberia and southern Manchuria. But how this idea of the circus-dogs could get mixed up with the recorded fact of Lord Tweedmouth's purchase of Nous is a mystery which will ever be with us.

In his *Dogs Since 1900* Mr Croxton Smith relates that he was told Colonel le Poer Trench's 'Russian' version of the origin of the Guisachan dogs. After seeing the later dogs he rather doubted his theory, and during talks he had with the first Lord Tweedmouth's grandson he was told the true story – namely, that in the late 1860s Lord Tweedmouth and his son encountered a cobbler at Brighton who had a good-looking yellow Retriever. This he said he had got from a neighbouring keeper (who was, presumably, in Lord Chichester's employ), and it was bought and taken back to Guisachan, and this dog, supposedly the only yellow puppy out of a black wavy-coated Retriever litter, was to be known as Nous.

Articles and other early books on the breed had previously maintained the Russian theory, and in 1926 the Year Book of the Golden Retriever Club contained an article reprinted from *The Field* on 24th June 1922, in which the author says: 'The Golden Retriever is identified with the breed which was known for some time as the Marjoribanks and Ilchester

Trackers, brought to public notice by Colonel le Poer Trench of "St Hubert's", Gerrards Cross', and goes on to give the Russian circus-dog origin, and tells that 'they breed absolutely true to their fixed type and colour'.

These strong adherents to this circus-dog theory went to great lengths to prove their ideas, seeking confirmation from the descendants of the early keepers at Guisachan, who, it seems, had also been told this story by Colonel le Poer Trench. An article in the 1932 Year Book of the Golden Retriever Club, which sought to dispel the doubts of others, says:

'In recent years there have been those who have endeavoured to prove that the story of the purchase of some performing dogs of the Golden Retriever type at a Brighton Circus by Sir Dudley Marjoribanks, afterwards the first Lord Tweedmouth, is a myth. We, however, prefer to accept in full the truth of the story of origin.'

This article goes on to mention letters and photos from Duncan MacLennan, a descendant of an early keeper. One of these letters states:

'My mother has got an old photograph of the first dog, and the finest, of the group of dogs bought by the first Lord Tweedmouth between 1860 and 1870, from a party of Russians who were performing with them at Brighton. . . . The Golden Retriever in this photograph is the first dog, and the finest, called Nous.'

Mrs Charlesworth, who did so much to help establish the breed as it stands today, and with a few others formed the Golden Retriever Club in 1913, upheld the Russian origin theory throughout her life, and it is given as the history of the breed in her *Book of the Golden Retriever* published in 1932, and in her later book *Golden Retrievers*, 1952, as well as in an article written by her in *Hutchinson's Dog Encyclopaedia*.

As mentioned earlier, the true facts were brought to light in 1952 by Lord Ilchester in an article published in *Country Life* entitled 'The Origin of the Yellow Retriever'. In this he revealed that his great-uncle, the first Lord Tweedmouth, had meticulously kept a stud book in which was recorded every dog in his kennel, and the matings which took place from 1835 to 1890. From these records Lord Ilchester concluded that this Russian circus-dog ancestry theory must have been quite false, for there was no reference in these records to such a dog or dogs. Thus, as Lord Tweedmouth is indisputably acknowledged as having founded Golden Retrievers as a definite breed, it follows that the forbears of our breed, which were bred at Guisachan, all stem from the original mating recorded by Lord Tweedmouth in 1868 of the yellow Retriever (Nous) and the Tweed Water-Spaniel (Belle). In this *Country Life* article Lord Ilchester stated that neither the Kennel Club nor the Natural History Museum could tell him what these Tweed Water-Spaniels were, but whilst carrying out research for her book *The Golden Retriever Handbook* (Nicholson & Watson) Mrs Stonex found a reference to a Water-dog in a book (*The Complete Farrier and British Sportsman*) written in 1815 by Richard Lawrence which says:

> 'Along the rocky shores and dreadful declivities beyond the junction of the Tweed with the sea of Berwick, Water dogs have received an addition of strength from the experimental introductions of a cross with a Newfoundland dog.'

He went on to say that its descendant, the Water-Spaniel, was of different colours but 'the liver coloured is the most rapid of swimmers, and the most eager in pursuit'.

Another reference is made to Tweed Spaniels in Dalziel's *British Dogs*, 1881, which reads:

> 'When I first commenced to keep Irish Water-Spaniels, many years ago, there were three strains, or rather varieties – one was known as the Tweed Spaniel, having its origin in the neighbourhood of the river of that name. They were very light liver-colour, so close in curl as to give me the idea that they had originally been a cross from a smooth haired dog.'

A final piece of information in her search for knowledge of the Tweed Water-Spaniel came to Mrs Stonex from Mr Stanley O'Neill, the Flat-Coated Retriever authority, who told her that he came into contact with this breed as early as 1903. On the Northumbrian coast he saw a tawny coloured 'Water-dog' owned by fishermen netting salmon, and when asked about the dog they told him that it was a Tweed Water-Spaniel and came from Berwick. He said that the dog was 'Retrieverish' and not at all like a Spaniel. In the 1920s Mr O'Neill made enquiries about these Tweed Water-Spaniels and was told by

Berwick people that they were practically the same as the east coast Water-dogs, but in those bred on the Border the browns and yellows predominated.

The results of Mrs Stonex's research have filled, to a considerable extent, the gaps in the factual knowledge of the history of the breed, and the discoveries she made have been recounted in full in an article in the Golden Retriever Club of Scotland's 1964 Handbook, entitled 'Ten Years Research into Golden Retriever Ancestry'. In 1959 she was lent Lord Tweedmouth's stud book and records by his grand-daughter, Lady Pentland, and from these and other papers she has traced the descent of virtually all our present-day Goldens, through Lord Harcourt's 'Culhams' – the 'influential kennel' referred to in the Crufts 'Description of the Golden Retriever' – to the early Guisachan dogs. Lord Tweedmouth's records, which I found fascinating reading, were later presented to the Kennel Club Library by Lady Pentland, where they are preserved for posterity.

In these records the first mention of Retrievers occurs in 1842, and there are several others mentioned over the next ten years, but the first yellow Retriever entered is the dog Nous, recorded as 'Lord Chichester's Breed. Pupped June, 1864. Purchased at Brighton.'

It is also recorded that in 1868 Nous was mated to a bitch called Belle entered as 'Ladykirk Breed. Pupped 1863' (a note in Lord Tweedmouth's handwriting on 'Guisachan' paper states that Belle was a Tweed Water-Spaniel). This mating produced four yellow puppies (Crocus, Cowslip, Ada and Primrose), and these laid the foundations of Goldens as a breed.

From this litter Lord Tweedmouth retained at Guisachan the two bitches Cowslip and Primrose. The other bitch, Ada, was given to the fifth Earl of Ilchester, and founded the Ilchester strain, in which black 'crosses' were often used. The only dog, Crocus, was given to the second Lord Tweedmouth, then the Hon. Edward Marjoribanks.

From the following pages it will be seen that Lord Tweedmouth consistently line-bred[1] his strain of yellow Retrievers

1. See Chapter 6 (Line-breeding).

back to this original mating, though he ocasionally resorted to an out-cross. Cowslip (whelped 1868) was mated to Tweed (whelped 1872 referred to also, on a separate piece of paper, as a Tweed Water-Spaniel), which also came from Ladykirk, and Topsy was retained from the resulting litter. Later, Topsy was mated to Sambo – presumed to be a black Flat- or Wavy-Coated Retriever – and Zoe (1877) was kept from this mating.

Subsequently, Cowslip was again mated, this time to Sampson, a Red Setter belonging to Lord Tweedmouth's son, and Jack and Gill resulted (1875). In 1884 the two Nous lines – through Cowslip – were combined by mating Jack, Cowslip's son, to Zoe, Cowslip's grand-daughter, and four yellow puppies were whelped, of which a dog, Nous II, and two bitches, Gill II and Tansey, were retained at Guisachan. Zoe also had two other litters to Sweep (referred to in the record as 'Bred by Lord Ilchester – Crocus Breed'), both of which produced yellow puppies.

In 1886 Gill II (line-bred to Cowslip) was mated to Tracer, a black Flat- or Wavy-Coated Retriever, full brother to Ch. Moonstone, also black (this line had frequently produced red puppies and Ch. Moonstone mated to his own dam produced Foxcote, who was red). The result of this mating must therefore have been most disappointing, for ten black puppies appeared. One of these black puppies (Queenie) was, however, retained and later mated back to Nous II (yellow) – this again was line-breeding, for Queenie's dam and Nous II were litter brother and sister (thus giving four lines back to the original Nous × Belle mating). This mating had the desired results, producing the last two yellow Retrievers recorded in Lord Tweedmouth's records, Prim and Rose, whelped 1889. (Pedigree given.)

During this period from the first recorded mating in 1868 to the last in 1889 some of the puppies bred were kept, others were given to keepers on neighbouring estates, and others given to friends and relations in England and Scotland.

Early in the 1890s Lord Tweedmouth used a sandy coloured Bloodhound as a cross. According to Lord Ilchester, this was recorded on a separate piece of paper in the records, but was subsequently lost. Lord Ilchester reported that the

early descendants of this cross at Guisachan were darker
coloured, very big, powerful and ugly and definitely'houndy',
and some inclined to be savage.

No records of the dogs bred at Guisachan were kept after
the death of the first Lord Tweedmouth, and Guisachan itself
was sold in 1905, and this left a complete gap in the knowledge
of the breed. There was thus no recorded information on the
breed from 1890 and 1901, when the first pedigrees were kept.
It was therefore a great day for her when Mrs Stonex found
amongst the papers lent her by Lady Pentland a letter written
in 1946 by John MacLennan, one of the family of Guisachan
keepers, which said that Viscount Harcount (of the Culham
kennel) 'got the foundation of his breed from two puppies he
bought from me when I was at Kerrow House' – Kerrow was
one of the neighbouring estates which Lord Tweedmouth had
leased – 'The mother of these puppies was out of a bitch called
Lady belonging to Archie Marjoribanks' (Lord Tweedmouth's
youngest son).

In her article 'Ten Years Research into Golden Retriever
Ancestry' Mrs Stonex writes:

> 'Lady could have been a daughter of Prim or Rose, the last
> puppies recorded by Lord Tweedmouth, but we can never be cer-
> tain, as all who might have known are dead. It is obvious that
> whoever her parents were, they were bred at Guisachan from the
> original Nous and Tweed Water-Spaniel blood. That letter gives
> the key to the whole breed's descent from Lord Tweedmouth's
> original matings.'

To elucidate, Lady was bred at Guisachan about 1891, and
from her was descended Viscount Harcourt's Culham Brass,
who is at the back of all early pedigrees.

In this article Mrs Stonex also points out that although Lady
is the biggest link with the past, several other Guisachan-bred
dogs are behind the early pedigrees, such as Conon – the sire
of Proud Ben (1900), who, through his grandchildren, Stella of
Fyning and Astley Storm, is a forbear of the Heydown
kennel.

Conon also sired several of the Culhams. Rock was another
Tweedmouth dog who has left his mark on the breed through
his son Wavertree Sam (1903). Sam was originally the unregis-
tered Faithful Sam, and both these names appear at the back

Pedigree of Prim and Rose (Whelped 1889)

Sire
Nous II (1884)
(yellow)

- Jack (1875)
  - Sampson (Red Setter)
  - Cowslip (1868) yellow
    - Nous I (yellow Retriever)
    - Belle (Tweed Water-Spaniel)
- Zoë (1877)
  - Sambo (presumed black Flat-
    or Wavy-Coated Retriever)
  - Topsy (1873)
    - Tweed (Tweed Water-Spaniel)
    - Cowslip (1868)
      - Nous I
      - Belle

Dam
Queenie (1887)
(black)

- Tracer (black Flat-
  or Wavy-Coated
  Retriever, brother to
  Ch. Moonstone)
  - Ch. Zelstone (1880) (black,
    said to be half-bred
    Labrador)
    - Ben (1877)
    - Bridget
  - Think (black)
    - Dusk (1877)
    - Ch. Wisdom (black, 1875)
- Gill II (1884)
  (yellow)
  - Jack (1875)
    - Sampson
    - Cowslip
      - Nous I
      - Belle
  - Zoë (1877)
    - Sambo (black)
    - Topsy (1873)
      - Tweed
      - Cowslip

of early pedigrees. Wavertree Sam was sire of Ingestre Tyne, one of Mr Macdonald's Ingestres (said to be started from a liver Flat-Coat bitch of close Guisachan blood). Tyne mated to Ingestre Scamp produced Yellow Nell, dam of Mrs Charlesworth's early dog, Normanby Sandy. All the Ingestres were closely line-bred to Tyne and Scamp, and many of the present-day Goldens stem from them.

To conclude, I can do no better than to quote again Mrs Stonex, but for whom many of these facts would remain undisclosed:

> 'The influential recorded links of Guisachan bred Lady, Conon and Rock, prove the descent of today's Goldens from the first Lord Tweedmouth's thoughtfully planned matings on a foundation of yellow retriever of unknown antecedents (Nous) and two Tweed Water-Spaniels (Belle and Tweed). The roots of the breed lie in Scotland and the Border Country.'

CHAPTER 2

THE BREED FROM 1900 to 1939

PART I (1900–20)

It was not until 1913 that Goldens were given a separate register at the Kennel Club. Until then they had been registered as Flat- or Wavy-Coated Retrievers, identifiable only by their colour, and entered thus at shows. In 1913, however, several enthusiasts of the breed applied for this separate register, and were granted the name Retrievers (Golden or Yellow). Only in 1920 was the 'Yellow' dropped and the present designation of Retrievers (Golden) adopted.

These pioneers of the breed, with Mrs W.M. Charlesworth at their head, founded the Golden Retriever Club in this same year, and drew up the Standard of Points, which, except for one or two minor modifications, has not varied through the years. Mrs Charlesworth became secretary of the Club, which office she held until 1921, and she took over again during the late 1930s until 1946.

It may be assumed that Lord Harcourt (Culham) was among those who formed the Golden Retriever Club, for in 1909 he and Mrs Charlesworth were the only people showing Goldens. Others who may have had a hand in the formation of the Club were Lady Harris, the Hon. Mrs R.M. Grigg (Kentford), Captain Hardy (Auchencheyne) and Mr Herman (Balcombe), for all of these had Goldens at about that time.

At about the same time Colonel le Poer Trench had his separate register of Retrievers (Russian Yellow) recognised, and one of his St Huberts is listed in the 1913 Stud Book under this name, and later they had their own classes at Crufts. Several other Retrievers (Russian Yellow) were entered under the St Huberts prefix in the Stud Book between then and 1917, when the last entry was made.

Some of the first Golden Retrievers to be shown were those of Lord Harcourt, and his Culham Copper is entered in the Kennel Club Stud Book of 1911 as winning a first at Crufts. He had successes too with Culham Brass, Culham Tip, Culham Rossa and Culham Flame, all of which were descended from Lord Tweedmouth's Guisachan dogs. Who could then have predicted the great influence that some of these would have on the formation of the breed as a whole?

Also during the same period the Ingestre kennel, owned by Mr D. Macdonald, was started. This kennel was founded on descendants of the original Guisachan dogs, and the mating of Ingestre Scamp and Ingestre Tyne plays a very big part in the history of the breed, for in three litters, in 1908, 1910 and 1911, they produced Yellow Nell (dam of Normanby Sandy), Beena (who, mated to Culham Copper, produced Culham Tip), Normany Dandelion, Ingestre Luna, Ingestre Dred, Ingestre Tweed and Ingestre Dolly (the latter three all being entered in the 1911 Stud Book).

In 1906 Mrs Charlesworth (Noranby) had her first Golden Retriever, Normanby Beauty, of unknown pedigree. (A little confusion arises from the fact that Mrs Charlesworth's early dogs were registered as 'Normanby', whereas those registered after about 1912 appeared as 'Noranby'.) In 1908 Normanby Beauty was mated to Culham Brass and produced Normanby Balfour (also to play a big part in future pedigrees), and in 1912 she was again mated, this time to Culham Brass's son, Culham Cooper, and produced the breed's first Champion – Noranby Campfire. In her *Book of the Golden Retriever* Mrs Charlesworth rightly says: 'These two litters laid the foundation of the breed. Culham Tip and Yellow Nell have done the rest, through Dual Ch. Balcombe Boy and Normanby Sandy.'

Yellow Nell, referred to above, was owned by Mr W. Hall, and in 1910 Mrs Charlesworth had one of Nell's sons (Normanby Sandy) from him. This dog comes into many early pedigrees, and he was one of the first Goldens to take an award at trials – this was a Certificate of Merit at the Kennel Club's All-Aged Stake, listed in the 1913 Stud Book. Another of Mrs Charlesworth's early dogs was Noranby Dandelion, bred by Mr D. Macdonald, and the result of an in-bred mating of full brother and sister (Ingestre Dred and Ingestre Luna, both being from the Ingestre Scamp × Ingestre Tyne mating). Noranby Dandelion was later mated to Ch. Noranby Campfire, and the resultant litter was to have a widespread effect on the breed, for it produced two very important progenitors, the first of which was Mrs Charlesworth's own Noranby Daybeak, from whom stems her line of famous bitch Champions, which continued until the 1950s. The second was Binks of Kentford, whose mating to Balvaig produced Ch. Cornelius and Ch. and Indian Dual Ch. Flight of Kentford.

The earliest entry in the Kennel Club Stud Book of a dog with any possible 'Golden' ancestry to win at trials is that of Don of Gerwyn (whelped 1899), who, in the ownership of Mr A. T. Williams, won the International Gundog League's Open Retriever Stake in 1904. Although he is himself registered as a liver-coloured Retriever (Flat-Coated) his sire is given on the card of the trial as being Lord Tweedmouth's golden Flat-Coat Lucifer (at this time Golden Retrievers were still classified as Flat- or Wavy-Coated), and his dam was Rust, another liver-coated Flat-Coat.

The early breeders worked hard to get recognition of their dogs at trials, but it was uphill work, for they were greatly outnumbered by the other Retriever varieties. The earliest win recorded in the Stud Book of a Golden Retriever is in 1913 of Blofield Rufus, who took a Certificate of Merit at the Eastern Counties Retriever Society's Trials. Rufus was sired by Ingestre Dred and out of Folda — Folda being whelped in 1906 by 'Ilchester's Melbury out of Tweedmouth's Lady Betty'. The 1914 Stud Book shows that Miss R. Crawshay gained a Certificate of Merit with Gosmore Freeman (Culham Copper × Yellow Nell) at the Herts, Beds and Bucks Trial and Reserve with Hayshaw Boy (Ingestre Dred × Harpenden Jessie) in the Irish Retriever Society's Non-Winners Stake. That same year Captain Hardy's Vixie became the first bitch to win in trials by taking second in the Gamekeepers' National Association's Trial.

Mr J. Eccles (Haulstone), who had his first three Goldens round about 1912, used them solely as working dogs. The first was a light golden colour and came from Northumberland, bought as the result of an advertisement which said the puppy

– a bitch – was of Tweedmouth strain. Later he acquired the other two, and I quote from an article written by him in the 1924 Golden Retriever Club Year Book: 'These three dogs were all of them very useful sporting dogs, with good noses and tender mouths, and good retrievers, possibly rather lacking the quick, non-stop retrieve of Field Trials, though in no sense of the word slow.' These dogs started a life-long interest in the breed for himself and his wife, and though none of the Haulstones were shown or trialled until the 1920s, later several Champions and Field Trial Champions were made-up, and Mrs Eccles (one time President of the Golden Retriever Club ran her dogs with great success in trials – thus the family interest in Golden Retrievers spanned more than half a century.

Another breeder whose dogs were to have a lasting effect on the breed was Mr W.S. Hunt (Ottershaw), who founded his strong, winning kennel during this era. He bought Normanby Balfour from Mrs Charlesworth in or about the year 1914, and this dog's blood is carried through his sons, Rory of Bentley (1915) and Glory of Fyning (1916), by most of today's Goldens, and he is a double great-grandsire of Balvaig (1920). Several other Ottershaw dogs are also to be found in early pedigrees.

Lieutenant-Colonel the Hon. D. Carnegie (Heydown) started his kennels in 1916 when he was given the dog puppy Glory of Fyning, who was to play such a great part in the dual-purpose Heydown kennel, which produced several Champions and the well-known Field Trial winners to be mentioned in Part II of this chapter.

Another significant name was that of Mr H. Jenner of the Abbots kennel, who had his first Golden in 1917 when he acquired Rory of Bentley from Mr W.S. Hunt. This dog has lasting fame as the sire of the great Ch. Michael of Moreton, winner of seventeen c.c.s. The Abbots kennel, which will also be mentioned in Part II, was later to own or breed no less than eleven Champions and four *Show Champions*.[1]

These, and the lesser-known kennels, continued to keep the Golden's good name as a gundog to the fore, and to set the seal on future generations of dual-purpose dogs. There were no trials and few shows during the 1914–18 War, but fortunately

1. This title was not introduced until 1958 (see footnote on page 32).

breeders kept a nucleus of good dogs with which to start again at the end of hostilities, and the breed was to go on from strength to strength. It was not, however, until the 1920s that Goldens began to make a real impact at shows and trials.

PART II (1920–39)

As mentioned in Part I, in the year 1920 the name of the breed was amended from Retriever (Golden or Yellow) to Retriever (Golden), and in the years following, many newcomers joined the ranks of Golden Retriever owners and breeders, for the intelligence, gentleness and good looks of the breed attracted much attention. Those who had founded their kennels before the 1914–18 War continued with their successful lines, and during the next two decades the breed became really established in its type and flourished at shows and in the trial world.

The earliest recorded information on the breed appeared in 1923 when the first Year Book was produced by the Golden Retriever Club, at which time the Club membership numbered forty-eight. The Club has certainly flourished since those early days, its membership soon after its Golden Jubilee in 1963 having reached the 500 mark. Mrs Charlesworth became the secretary from its formation until 1921, and after a gap of some sixteen years resumed this office in the late 1930s. During the intervening years others to hold this office were Major Bagnall, Mrs Cottingham, Mr P.H. Palmer, Captain Escombe and Mr L. Evers-Swindell. Those who served as chairman of the Club during this period were the Hon. Mrs Grigg, Mr Sidney Todd, Colonel the Hon. D. Carnegie, Mr A. W. Copeland and Captain H. Hardy.

It was stated in Part I of this chapter that the Club drew up its Standard of Points in 1913. There is no actual record of this original Standard, though it seems very unlikely that any alterations would have been made during the next decade, and it will be seen from a perusal of the Standard as published in the early Year Books that it differs little from that of today (as given in full in Chapter 4). The only significant differences are, firstly, that in those days each feature was allotted points, i.e.

Head, 20 points; Colour, 20; Coat, 5; Ears, 5; Feet, 10; Forelegs, 10; Hindlegs, 10; Nose, 5; Tail, 5; Body, 25; Total 115. Secondly, that no reference was made to weight and size, and thirdly that cream was not recognised as a colour.

It was not until 1930 that any consideration was given to weight and size, and in that year the Club instigated an enquiry into the average size of the best dogs and bitches in the breed. This enquiry was instituted when guidance was asked for by Mr B.M. Armstrong of Winnipeg, concerning the correct size of Goldens. The result of this survey was that the following year the Golden Retriever Club Year Book published a note at the bottom of the Standard, which reads: 'The ideal weight of adult dogs and bitches in good hard condition should be: Dogs 65–68 lb., Bitches 55–60 lb., and Height at shoulder, Dogs 23–24 in., Bitches 20½–22 in.' This was amended in 1936 to the present-day one, viz. 'Weight, Dogs 65–70 lb., Bitches 55–60 lb., and Height, Dogs 22–24 in., Bitches 20–22 in.' In this same year (1936) the Standard also was altered to include the colour cream, the wording being almost identical with that of today, i.e. 'Any shade of gold or cream, but neither red nor mahogany'.

The year 1921 saw the first Golden Champion, Mrs Charlesworth's Noranby Campfire, who was to become a great sire. Soon afterwards the Hon. Mrs Grigg's F.T. Ch. Eredine Rufus took his Field Trial title, and to her also goes the honour of producing the breed's first bitch Champion in Bess of Kentford. Mr Herman scored a notable success in producing the breed's first Dual Champion, Balcombe Boy. Other Champions and Field Trial Champions were to follow during the course of the next few years, some of which will live in the annals of the breed. Others, although they gained no title, will ever be remembered for the influence they have had on the breed throughout the years.

SOME INFLUENTIAL SIRES AND DAMS

The ancestry of almost the whole of the breed today has been traced by Mrs Elma Stonex, through extended pedigrees, to one or more of four matings which took place between 1920 and 1925, viz:

1. Glory of Fyning to Stagden Cross Pamela
2. Dual Ch. Balcombe Boy to Balcombe Bunty
3. Binks of Kentford to Balvaig
4. Rory of Bentley to Aurora.

These pedigrees show that all are descended from the early Culhams and Ingestres – both of which kennels were founded on Lord Tweedmouth's Guisachan dogs.

What a tremendous part these four matings were to play in Golden Retriever history! An extract from the Golden Retriever Club's Golden Jubilee Supplement of 1963 substantiates this when it says:

'Every Golden today undoubtedly goes back to more than one of these four tremendously important matings, and in all probability to all of them, many times over. From them breeders began to stamp type and dual purpose through the breed, which continued careful line-breeding has consolidated over forty years, and it is also worth remembering that they link the beginnings of the breed to the Goldens of 1963 over at least fourteen generations of recorded pedigrees.'

The records of these early years clearly demonstrate the tremendous influence these dogs had on the breed. The descent of some of the greatest sires of the era can be traced to one or more of the pedigrees given. The ancestry of Gilder – the greatest of them all – who sired eight Champions, can be traced to both Pedigrees 1 and 2. Another great dog, Ch. Michael of Moreton, who sired seven Champions and one *Show Champion*, was a product of Pedigree 4; Ch. Heydown Grip, also sire of seven Champions (including a Dual Champion), emanates from Pedigree 1; Ch. Cubbington Diver, sire of five Champions, combines both Pedigrees 1 and 2; Ch. Diver of Woolley, sire of four Champions and one *Show Champion*, Pedigrees 1 and 2; the litter brothers Ch. Cornelius (sire of three Champions, two *Show Champions* and one Field Trial Champion) and Ch. and Indian Dual Ch. Flight of Kentford (sire of two Champions and one *Show Champion*) are both the result of the mating of Binks of Kentford with Balvaig, Pedigree 3.

There were also some outstanding brood bitches during this period, the foremost being Mr Jenner's Sewardstone Tess

(*Sh. Ch.*),[1] who was the dam of four Champions and one *Show Champion*. Others who produced three Champion offspring each were Mrs Charlesworth's Noranby Judith, Mrs Cottingham's Ch. Vic of Woolley and the Hon. Mrs Carnegie's Heydown Bertha.

The foregoing are just a few of those who were to leave their mark on the breed of the present day.

Some Successful Kennels And Dogs At Shows[2]

As has been mentioned, Mr H. Jenner (Abbots) started in 1917 with Rory of Bentley, and was most successful during this period. He owned or bred fifteen title-holders, as well as other Challenge Certificate winners. Mr Jenner restricted his numbers, and at no time kept a large kennel, so his achievements are accordingly perhaps all the more meritorious. The most famous dog bred in the Abbots kennel was Mr R.L. Kirk's dual-purpose Ch. Michael of Moreton. He won more Challenge Certificates than any other pre-war dog (seventeen), and had a good career in trials, and was a most successful sire. Another outstanding dog from Mr Jenner's kennel was one of Ch. Michael's sons, Ch. Haulstone Marker, who was also a good dual-purpose sire. Further, Ch. Davie of Yelme was the winner of ten Challenge Certificates, and other Champions from this famous kennel were Dr T. Wilshaw's Ch. Goldgleam of Aldgrove, Ch. Abbots Music, Mr Kirk's Ch. Abbots Winkle, Ch. Abbots Daisy (twelve c.c.s), Mrs Annesley's Ch. Abbots Flight, Ch. Tickencote Jennie, Mrs I. Parson's Ch. Dukeries Dancing Lady and Mrs Kirk's Ch. Abbots Trust. The most notable of the multiple c.c. winners was Sewardstone Tess (*Sh. Ch.*), already mentioned as an outstanding matron, who was also the winner of six Challenge Certificates. Though Mr Jenner did not breed Goldens after the Second World War, he con-

1. Dogs referred to in italics as '*Sh. Ch.*' are those which have won three c.c.s or more under three different judges, and are, therefore, entitled to be called Sh. Chs., but, as they won these prior to November 1958, they are not officially recorded as such in the Kennel Club records.

2. For easier reference, show and trial records are given under separate headings.

Pedigree 1

- **Glory of Fyning**
  - Normanby Balfour
    - Culham Brass
      - Dust
      - Chlores
    - Normanby Beauty
      - Unknown Pedigree
      - ____
  - Stella of Fyning
    - Astley Storm
      - Culham Coffee
      - Paddiford Duchess
    - Griff
      - Proud Ben
      - Red Queen
- **Stagden Cross Pamela**
  - Prior
    - Paxhill Brian
      - Crane Point
      - Inez
    - Culham Bronze
      - Culham Brass
      - Culham Rossa
  - Stagden Cross Honey
    - Ingestre Ben
      - Ingestre Bunty
      - Toptwig
    - Rossa
      - Klip
      - Ingestre Rubina

Pedigree 2

- **Ch. & F.T. Ch. Balcombe Boy**
  - Culham Tip
    - Culham Copper
      - Culham Brass
      - Culham Rossa
    - Beena
      - Ingestre Scamp
      - Ingestre Tyne
  - Culham Amber II
    - ____
    - ____
- **Balcombe Bunty**
  - Ottershaw Brilliant
    - Ottershaw Sovereign
      - Ch. Noranby Campfire
      - Ballingdon Floss
    - Ottershaw Blush
  - Syrup
    - Culham Tip
      - Culham Copper
      - Beena
    - Honey
      - ____

Pedigree 3

Binks of Kentford	Ch. Noranby Campfire	Culham Copper	Culham Brass
			Culham Rossa
		Normanby Beauty	Unknown Pedigree
			___
	Noranby Dandelion	Ingestre Dred	Ingestre Scamp
			Ingestre Tyne
		Ingestre Luna	Ingestre Scamp
			Ingestre Tyne
Balvaig	Rust	Rust Boy	Normanby Balfour
			Scotter Prim
		Glanduff Wanda	Normanby Balfour
			Betty
	Dinah	Normanby Sandy	Sandy of Wavertree
			Yellow Nell
		Bess Brass	___

Pedigree 4

Rory of Bentley	Normanby Balfour	Culham Brass	Dust
			Chlores
		Normanby Beauty	Unknown Pedigree
			___
	Columbine	___	
		Primrose Nell	Sandy of Wavertree
			Yellow Nell
Aurora	Triumph	Paxhill Brian	Crane Point
			Inez
		Columbine	
			Primrose Nell
	Amber	Ottershaw Sovereign	Ch. Noranby Campfire
			Ballingdon Floss
		Ottershaw Eclipse	___

Culham Rossa (Harold × Nellie). Ingestre Scamp (Sailor × Duchess).
Ingestre Tyne (Wavertree Sam × Corrie II). Yellow Nell (Ingestre Scamp × Ingestre Tyne).

tinued his interest in the breed to the end of his life, and was always prepared to give his help generously to the newcomer to the breed, and would always pass on a helpful 'tip'. He judged several Championship shows during the post-war period, and successfully exhibited his lovely Sprig of Yelme (sister to Ch. Lakol of Yelme).

Another kennel of the 1920s to have a wonderful run of success in the show ring was the Woolley kennel belonging to Mrs Cottingham, who owned ten Champions and one *Show Champion*. Her first success was with Ch. Cubbington Diver (sire of five Champions) who won at least fifteen c. c. s. Her next Champions were the brother and sister Vic and Banner of Woolley (bred by Mrs Charlesworth). Ch. Vic, when mated to Ch. Cubbington Diver, produced Ch. Diver of Woolley, a Crufts Gold Cup winner (this Cup was awarded to the best dog or bitch at Crufts which had also won an award at trials). The other Woolley Champions were Reine of Woolley (bought from Mrs M.B. Edwards – Mountclogg – about 1925), a consistent Field Trial winner, also Ch. Vesta, Ch. Marine, Ch. Mary Rose, Ch. Mist and Ch. Bachelor.

Mrs Charlesworth's Noranbys played a notable part in popularising Goldens in the show ring and as gundogs, and as well as many other winners she bred eight Champions during this same period, the first being Ch. Noranby Campfire. Others, spread over several generations, were Ch. Noranby Daydawn, a daughter of Dual Ch. Balcombe Boy, then the above-mentioned brother and sister, Champions Vic and Banner of Woolley (both out of Noranby Judith, who was also the dam of Ch. Noranby Jeptha). Next came Ch. Noranby Diana, herself the dam of the two Champions, Noranby Dutiful and Noranby Deirdre. Mrs Charlesworth's great interest in the breed continued right to the end of her life, from about 1906 until the 1950s. She made up the post-war Dual Champion Noranby Destiny, and she was to judge and to show and trial her own dogs until just before she died.

Mr and Mrs L. Evers-Swindell acquired their first Golden for work in 1921. This dog became the famous Ch. Cornelius, whose blood-line is still carried by many present-day dogs. Ch. Cornelius's success in trials led the Evers-Swindells to breed Goldens, and by using this dog as their foundation sire they produced Ch. Speedwell Beryl. They later bred Miss Mottram's Ch. Kelso of Aldgrove, their own Ch. Speedwell Molly, Ch. Speedwell Brandy, Mr J. Fox-Lowe's Ch. Joseph of Housesteads, Speedwell Emerald (*Sh. Ch.*) and the first American Champion Speedwell Pluto (who also became a Canadian Champion).

The year 1926 saw the beginning of the famous Yelme kennel of Major H. Wentworth Smith, carried on after his death eminently successfully by his wife, Mrs M.K. Wentworth Smith. His first bitch was Culnoran Bess, grand-dam of the famous matron and Field Trial winner Quick of Yelme, who, when mated to Gilder in the 1930s, produced many trial and show winners, including Ch. Chief of Yelme – a Crufts Gold Cup winner – and Ch. Kandyd of Skroy (Skroy being Mrs Wentworth Smith's prefix for a time). Another of Quick of Yelme's sons was the post-war Ch. Dernar of Yelme. Other title-holders from this kennel pre-war were Ch. Cubstone Bess and her daughter Ch. Gaiety Girl of Yelme, Ch. Davie of Yelme (who gained his title in Mr Jenner's ownership) and Ch. Bingo of Yelme, who later became an American Champion.

One of the earliest of Golden enthusiasts, the Hon. Mrs Grigg, owned Binks of Kentford (referred to earlier as being behind the pedigrees of many of today's Goldens), a son of Ch. Noranby Campfire and Noranby Dandelion. Binks was to sire Ch. and Indian Dual Ch. Flight of Kentford, who was also a good Field Trial winner in this country. Mrs Grigg also had the distinction of making up the breed's first bitch Champion – Bess of Kentford. Other Kentford Champions were Ch. Kib and his two sons Mischief and Rip – most of them were also Field Trial winners.

Lieutenant-Colonel the Hon. D. Carnegie's dual-purpose Heydown kennel was founded on Glory of Fyning, who, mated to Stagden Cross Pamela, produced Ch. Heydown Gunner, Heydown Gurth and Ch. Heydown Grip (all famous dual-purpose sires). Grip was also an outstanding Field Trial winner, and when mated to Heydown Bertha sired the other three Heydown Champions: Guider (a Crufts Gold Cup winner), Gillyflower and Goody-Two-Shoes. The Heydown kennel was carried on in 1936 by the Hon. Mrs Carnegie after her husband's death.

During this period Mr and Mrs Eccles' Haulstones had

many successes on the show bench as well as in the field, and they had an excellent dual-purpose dog in Ch. Haulstone Dan, with many Field Trial awards to his credit. Next came Ch. Haulstone Sprig, then Mr Jenner's Ch. Haulstone Marker and Mr Kirk's Ch. Haulstone Dusty. This kennel also produced the first Golden ever to win the Retriever Championship, which was F.T. Ch. Haulstone Larry.

Mr R.L. Kirk's purchase of the great Ch. Michael of Moreton as a young dog in the mid-twenties from Mr Jenner was a most enterprising stroke, for this dog, as well as winning more Challenge Certificates than any other pre-war dog, was a successful trial dog, a Crufts Gold Cup winner, and became a most influential dual-purpose sire, as mentioned earlier. Mr Kirk (Moreton) also owned Ch. Mary of Moreton and Ch. Abbots Winkle and his wife owned Ch. Abbots Trust.

Mr and Mrs H. Venables Kyrke started their Anningsley kennel about the year 1923 with a bitch from Mr Hunt called Anningsley Amber. This bitch was the dam of Anningsley Sunlight, a very famous trial dog, who has left his mark on the breed, and who sired Ch. Anningsley Beatrice – later exported to America. When mated to F.T. Ch. Anningsley Crakers, Ch. Beatrice produced Anningsley Ann, the dam of the breed's second Dual Champion, Anningsley Stingo, and Ch. Anningsley Fox, also a trial winner.

At about the same time, the Rev. E. Needham-Davies (chairman of the Golden Retriever Club from 1950 to 1964) was active in the breed and his Sundawn prefix became well known. His first two Goldens were from Mr Hunt's kennel about 1920, but his two most notable purchases were a bitch from Mrs Eccles called Sundawn Susie, and a dog from Major Metcalfe who became Ch. Sundawn Dancer. Dancer, when mated to Susie's daughter, Sundawn Dainty, produced the pale cream-coloured dog, Gilder, who as mentioned earlier, was to become such a famous dual-purpose sire.

Another kennel to start at about the same time was that of Mrs Vernon Wentworth, and amongst the dual-purpose dogs produced in the Donkelve kennel was Ch. Donkelve Jester, winner of fourteen Challenge Certificates (grandsire of Ch. Donkelve Rusty, and great-grandsire of the post-war Ch. Dorcas Glorious of Slat).

Mrs I. Parsons started her famous line of 'Torrdales' in the early 1930s with a wonderful 'buy' when she purchased from Mr Jenner the bitch puppy who was to become Ch. Dukeries Dancing Lady. She is the ancestress of a number of present-day title-holders, through Torrdale Tinker (sire of the post-war Torrdale Kim of Stenbury (*Sh. Ch.*) and Ch. Alexander of Elsiville) and Torrdale Laddie (grandsire of the first post-war Champion, Torrdale Happy Lad). In the show ring, however, it was Ch. Torrdale Betty who was the most outstanding, for her fourteen Challenge Certificates became a record for a bitch pre-war. The other title-holders owned by Mrs Parsons during the pre-war period were Ch. Donkelve Rusty and Torrdale Judy (*Sh. Ch.*).

The most famous dog from the Aldgrove kennel of Dr T. Wilshaw and Miss Mottram was the one purchased from Mr and Mrs Evers-Swindell about the year 1930. He later became Ch. Kelso of Aldgrove and was also a trial winner. Their next Champion was from Mr Jenner, Ch. Goldgleam of Aldgrove, then came Ch. Kelso's daughter, Ch. Golddawn of Aldgrove.

One of the largest kennels of the 1930s was that of Mrs A. Nairn of the Stubbings prefix. She started with Stubbings Lorelei, who, proving a great matron, produced Ch. Stubbings Golden Gloria in her first litter and later Stubbings Golden Gem (dam of Stubbings Golden Jacobite from whom many post-war Champions are descended) and Stubbings Golden Kraken, great-grandsire of the first post-war Dual Champion, Stubblesdown Golden Lass. Kraken was also great-great-grandsire of Ch. Alresford Advertiser. Another notable dog who was purchased in 1933 was Ch. Birling James of Somersby, who proved an ideal dual-purpose sire, himself winning first in trials. Many other winners in Mrs Nairn's ownership appeared both at shows and trials. The Stubbings kennel was carried on after the Second World War, when her mother died, by Miss S. Nairn, until her marriage to Mr S. Winston.

Mrs Elma Stonex, who had acquired her first Golden in 1931 from the Stubbings kennel, in the following year bought her famous foundation bitch Sally of Perrott. Sally won one Challenge Certificate, and established a place in the annals of the breed (through her mating to Ch. Davie of Yelme) by producing the great stud force Dorcas Bruin (winner of a reserve c.c. and the first gundog of any breed, except Cockers, to win a

Junior Warrant, just prior to the outbreak of war). But for this interruption of his successful career Bruin would almost certainly have become a Champion. His fame as a sire will be dealt with in Chapter 3. Sally of Perrott also had several daughters whose names appear in the pedigree of many post-war Goldens. Bruin's sister, Dorcas Betsinda, was great-great-grand-dam of Ch. Colin of Rosecott and Ch. Katrina of Kuldana. When mated to Gilder, Sally produced Dorcas December, dam of Dorcas Felicia– from whom are descended many Champions – and Dorcas Daffodil, grand-dam of Ch. Scaurend Susannah.

Mrs L. Pilkington (Alresford) also started her kennel in the same year and brought out several good winners, notably Alresford Superphine, who took a reserve c.c. in 1939, and Alresford Tessa (grand-dam of Dual Ch. Stubblesdown Golden Lass). This kennel, too, went from strength to strength right up to the 1970s, producing amongst other Champions, Ch. Alresford Advertiser, a winner at trials, whose thirty-five c.c.s was to remain a record for a long time.

Mrs C. Walker (Hazelfax) owned an outstanding Field Trial dog of the mid-'thirties, Ch. Hazelgilt. Although not used extensively at stud, he was the grandsire of Ch. Susan of Westley and Ch. Culzean Sulia, and was also the great-grandsire of Ch. Colin of Rosecott and my own foundation bitch, Golden Camrose Tess.

There were, of course, many other successful breeders during these years, but space does not permit mentioning all. Some others who successfully started their kennels during this period and continued after the war were: Mr and Mrs Clarke (Heatherdell); Mrs F.J. Cousins (Timberscombe); Mrs E.G. Cuffe-Adams (Honeyat, formerly Windward); Mr and Mrs P. Fraser (Westhyde); Mrs R. Harrison (Boltby); Mrs H.J. Morgan (Weyland) and Miss U. Quant (Biltor).

SOME SUCCESSFUL KENNELS AND DOGS IN FIELD TRIALS

After the First World War the first recorded trial win of a Golden (in the 1921 Kennel Club Stud Book) is that of Mr R. Herman's Balcombe Boy. This brilliant dog, bred by Lord Harcourt from Culham Tip and Culham Amber II, was later to take both his bench and Field Trial titles, and thus became the breed's first Dual Champion. It will be seen from Pedigree 1 (given earlier) that through his mating to Balcombe Bunty this dog has had a lasting influence on the breed.

The following year, 1922, Mrs Charlesworth took several awards in trials with Ch. Noranby Campfire – a Certificate of Merit in the International Gundog League's Stake, third in the Golden Retriever Club's Open and a second in the Club's Maiden Trial. During the same year Mr Meade's Noranby Crash won the Golden Retriever Club's Maiden, and took second place in the Open. Ottershaw Brilliant was also a winner in both these trials. Captain Hardy's Broadward Jane took a certificate of Merit in the Kennel Club's All-Aged Stake, and Lady Harris' Ochre was third in the Golden Retriever Club's Maiden Stake.

The 1923 Stud Book shows nine Goldens winning awards in Field Trials, and from this time on many more were successful in various trials. Thus the breed was successfully established in this important sphere. Another dog of the 1920s to do well in trials was Ch. Flight of Kentford – later exported to India, where he became an Indian Dual Champion.

One other notable contestant in trials at this time was Captain Hardy's F.T. Ch. John of Auchencheyne, a grandson of his trialler Vixie. Incidentally, giving his views of the Golden Retriever as a working dog, in an article in the Golden Retriever Club Year Book of 1925, Captain Hardy wrote: 'If bred right, I have found them excellent shooting companions, facing the most punishing covert and revelling in water.'

The Hon. Mrs Grigg's famous F.T. Ch. Eredine Rufus was a consistently successful performer in trials. His wins included first in the International Gundog League's Nomination Stake and a reserve in the Retriever Championship, and he won the F.T. Ch. title twice over. Rufus of Kentford, who sired the Champions Bess, Rip and Mischief of Kentford (all of which won at trials), was also bred by Mrs Grigg.

Ch. Noranby Jeptha, another of Mrs Charlesworth's dogs, had a noteworthy career in trials, taking a first and second in Any Variety Open Stakes and a Diploma in the Retriever Championship. She was also the dam of several trial winners. Amongst other Noranby Goldens to win at trials were Noranby Curfew, Noranby Jane, Noranby Jumbo and Ch. Noranby Diana.

The Ottershaws, bred by Mr W.S. Hunt, were also well to the fore in this particular sphere. Ottershaw Brilliant, Ottershaw Sunclad, Ottershaw Bronze, Ottershaw Bonzor, Ottershaw Buzzard and Ottershaw Brian all scoring notable successes.

Lieutenant-Colonel the Hon. Carnegie's Glory of Fyning produced several famous dual-purpose dogs in Heydown Gurth, Ch. Heydown Gunner and Ch. Heydown Grip – the latter only narrowly missing his Field Trial title. Mated to Heydown Bertha, Grip produced Ch. Heydown Guider and many other trial winners, whilst F.T. Ch. Haulstone Larry (winner of the Retriever Championship) was his grandson. Another excellent Field Trial winner from this kennel was Miss Murray Baillie's Haulstone Garm.

In the early 1920s Mr and Mrs Eccles had their first trialler, Haulstone Rufus, a full-brother to Ch. Cornelius. He was followed by Haulstone Simon, an Open Stake winner, and Ch. Haulstone Dan (who also won the Crufts Gold Cup). During this decade Mr and Mrs Eccles crossed one of their bitches with a Yellow Labrador (F.T. Ch. Haylers Defender) and a bitch from the resulting litter was put back to the Golden Retriever, Call Boy of Woolley. Certainly this inter-breeding seems to have achieved its object, which was to improve speed and drive, for the resulting interbred progeny won well at trials – F.T. Ch. Haulstone Bob and Haulstone Lizzie being outstanding products of this first cross. F.T. Ch. Haulstone Bob was mated with a sister of Dual Ch. Anningsley Stingo, which mating produced F.T. Ch. Haulstone Brock. Later, in 1937, one of Haulstone Lizzie's grandsons, F.T. Ch. Haulstone Larry (who was eligible to be registered as a pure-bred Golden Retriever, being the third generation from the first interbred litter), became the first Golden ever to win the Retriever Championship Stake.

Mr and Mrs Evers-Swindell's outstanding dog Ch. Cornelius, ran in his first trial in 1923. This was the Golden Retriever Club's Open Stake in which he was placed third. This dog was the sire of numerous winners in both the field and on the show bench. Mated to Ballingdon Betty, he sired the famous F.T. Ch. Anningsley Crakers, and was the grand-sire of F.T. Ch. Wilderness Melody.

The Rev. Needham-Davies' most famous dog was Ch. Sundawn Dancer, but it was his son Gilder, also bred by the

Rev. Needham-Davies, who was to prove the great sire, producing, amongst many others, five first-prize winners in trials
and eight Champions. Gilder was sold to Mr A.H. Gill
(Gillenches), who successfully trained him and won with him
at trials.

Mr R.L. Kirk's Ch. Michael of Moreton was another real
dual-purpose dog, for he had many awards in trials, and also
sired countless trial winners. In addition to Ch. Michael, Mr
Kirk also had another very good trial dog in Timothy of
Moreton.

Mr Jenner, to whom goes the credit of breeding the above-
mentioned Ch. Michael of Moreton, owned the good trial
winner Ch. Haulstone Marker, who appears in the extended
pedigrees of many Goldens of today through his grandson
Dorcas Bruin.

Mrs Cottingham, whose kennel has already been mentioned, also had many successes in trials. Her Ch. Diver of
Woolley, as well as being a trial winner, won the Crufts Gold
Cup. Diver was the son of Ch. Vic of Woolley (who was herself
the dam of Call Boy of Woolley). Another great trialler from
this kennel was Ch. Reine of Woolley. From 1925 until 1939
many other consistent trial winners were produced by this
kennel.

Mr and Mrs H. Venables Kyrke started their Field Trial
activities with Anningsley Sunlight, a very famous trial dog of
his time. Later Mr Venables Kyrke took the Field Trial title
with Anningsley Crakers, who was a most consistent winner
and took Diplomas in the Retriever Championship on two
occasions. F.T. Ch. Anningsley Crakers, in addition to being
the sire of Mrs Hextall's F.T. Ch. Avishays Lulu (bred and
handled in trials by Mr Venables Kyrke) and grandsire of F.T.
Ch. Avishays Brush (reserve in the Retriever Championship in
1938, and also handled by Mr Kyrke), also sired the trial
winners Anningsley Henry and Anningsley Ann (dam of the
famous trial winners Dual Ch. Anningsley Stingo and Ch.
Anningsley Fox).

Major H. Wentworth Smith's first famous Field Trial winner
was the wonderful matron, Quick of Yelme, who, amongst her
many awards, won a Diploma in the Championship. This
bitch produced many trial winners, including Ch. Chief of

Yelme, Ch. Kandyd of Skroy, Veritas, Grasper, Brisk, and Shifter, all 'of Yelme'. Other trial winners from this kennel during the pre-1939 period were Ch. Bingo of Yelme, Beppo of Yelme and Hornet of Yelme.

In the mid-1920s two other owners to produce trial winners were Mrs F.W. Vernon Wentworth, with Donkelve Toni, Donkelve Bess and Donkelve Roger, and Lieutenant-Commander Willoughby, with Wherstead Giltedge (a c.c. winner) and Haughton Noble.

In the early 1930s Dr T. Wilshaw and Miss Mottram had trial successes with several of their Aldgroves, including Ch. Kelso of Aldgrove and Sprite of Aldgrove (winner of two c.c.s).

Mrs Nairn of the Stubbings kennel had several Field Trial winning dogs, notably Ch. Birling James of Somersby, the brilliant Stubbings Golden Jerkin, who took a Diploma in the Championship, Stubbings Golden Ripple and Stubbings Golden Yorick.

Another outstanding trial dog was Mrs Cyril Walker's Ch. Hazelgilt (referred to earlier). His trial career was unfortunately cut short by the war, and but for this he must almost certainly have taken his dual title, for at only five years he had won fifteen awards in trials, including fourth in the Championship, and a first in an A.V. Stake. Mrs Walker also ran Gem of Hazelfax successfully.

To these and many others who during this period maintained the true dual-purpose qualities in the Golden Retriever we of the present day owe a great debt of gratitude. The feeling of most enthusiasts of the breed may be expressed in the words of Mrs J. Cottingham, written in 1925: 'The influence of shows upon the sporting dog has been most beneficial, for surely a working dog is all the better for having sound feet and legs, with good muscular quarters, combining good looks – yet still able to perform satisfactorily his legitimate work in the field.'

CHAPTER 3

THE BREED POST-WAR

There was little activity in any sphere of the dog fancy during the Second World War. There were no Championship shows and no Field Trials, consequently no title-holders were created during those years. Shortage of food, time spent in war work, and the sudden fall in the demand for stock, were responsible for numbers having to be drastically cut down and in some kennels, indeed, activities entirely ceased, and they were disbanded. Fortunately, as during the First World War, some well-established breeders, with an eye to the future, retained a nucleus of breeding stock from which the best of today's dogs have stemmed.

The Golden Retriever Club resumed its activities immediately following the cessation of hostilities, and its first post-war Championship show was held in 1946. During this same year the Northern Golden Retriever Association and the Golden Retriever Club of Scotland were formed, since when they have gone from strength to strength, both running annual Field Trials, and both holding their own Championship shows.

Unfortunately, with the lack of Championship shows throughout the whole of the Second World War period, there was no criterion for the new breeders who were to show in 1946. It is not, therefore, surprising that a rather 'mixed bag' began to appear in the show ring at this time. Understandably, too, there was a great demand for pet puppies, for which the highest prices were readily obtainable. These two factors – no suitable standard to judge by, and ready sales – were largely responsible for the market being flooded with rather inferior puppies, bred as a result of mating a bitch to the nearest available dog, without regard to suitability of pedigree, type or temperament. Consequently, many which appeared in the first few years after the war were quite useless as show dogs or gundogs, and their temperaments deviated considerably from that characteristic of the breed.

I recall my visits to shows in 1946 and, with a picture in my mind's eye of the beautiful Golden owned by an aunt of mine before the war, I could not believe that those I saw were all of the same breed, so varied were they in size and type. Some were large and light-boned, rather leggy with 'collie-like' heads, while others were very short on the leg, with extremely heavy bone, 'cloddy', and had massive Pyrenean-type heads. This diversity in type was, however, soon to be remedied, for during the next few years, when dogs became exhibited at Championship shows in all parts of the country, as was to be expected, the correct type of Golden consistently won. This soon discouraged those with untypical ones, who were thus compelled to improve their stock, but it was several years before the full effect of this was felt, and the general standard of exhibits raised.

During the next decade the breed became exceedingly popular, both for shows and trials. The entries became increasingly numerous and the Kennel Club registrations crept up and up. Indeed, the entries at Championship shows began regularly to be about sixth to eighth highest of all breeds, and classes of ten or more were in no way unusual. Type became almost universally good, and it was not unusual to find the quality so high, particularly in bitches, that judges had to 'split hairs' in the placing of the first six or seven competitors in the class. At the present time, when Championship show entries of Goldens often exceed thirty in a class and are, moreover, sometimes the highest in the show, a judge's task is made the more difficult, as will readily be seen.

During this post-war period there has been a great increase in the number of Goldens used as gundogs, and there have been many dual-purpose dogs who have won well both at trials and in the show ring. The breed's outstanding achievements in Field Trials of recent years have led many with shooting interests to turn to the Golden, for his natural working ability, trainability, desire to please, excellent nose and love of water, are qualities which all go towards the making of the ideal shooting dog. These natural qualities have been fostered to such an extent that each year sees more and more Goldens appearing successfully in trials, and many new owners joining those interested in working their dogs.

If this important aspect of a Retriever's inheritance were to be neglected it would be regarded by many as disastrous for the breed, and there were mixed feelings amongst breeders when the Kennel Club introduced the Show Champion title in November 1958 (see Chapter 9). It was feared that the division between the showing and working side would become even more marked, and lead to a situation where many more show dogs would never have a shot fired over them. Whether this proves to be so, of course, remains to be seen, but in spite of the fact that there are today many Show Champions in the breed, the present trend seems to be towards still more people training their dogs under the aegis of the societies who run gun-training classes. As long as there are these classes existing to afford help to the novice, there should be no likelihood of working instincts being lost, and in a later chapter I draw attention to the fact that many successful show dogs have become trial winners via these classes.

SOME INFLUENTIAL SIRES

One of the dogs who must be regarded as having a great influence on the breed is Mrs Stonex's Dorcas Bruin. Himself a Reserve Challenge Certificate and Junior Warrant winner in 1939, his blood is carried by most of our today's Champions, as well as by many F.T. Chs, and many other good show and trial winners. His name is perpetuated principally through his two sons, Ch. Dorcas Glorious of Slat and Dorcas Timber-scombe Topper (both referred to later), and through his daughters, Ch. Braconlea Gaiety (a Championship Show Best in Show winner), Dorcas Felicia (referred to under 'Influential Matrons') and Timberscombe Tansy (dam of Ch. Camrose Tantara who will also be mentioned later).

Many are the show- and trial-winning descendants of Mrs Stonex's Ch. Dorcas Glorious of Slat (winner of the Stud Dog Progeny Cup three times – a cup awarded annually to the dog whose progeny wins most points at shows and trials during the year). He sired four title-holding progeny, the most notable of

which was Miss Lucy Ross's English Ch. and F.T. Ch. and
Irish Ch. and F.T. Ch. David of Westley, bred by Miss J. Gill –
the only dog in the breed ever to win these titles – who in his
turn sired many good show and trial winners. Glorious's other
F.T. Ch. son was Mr W. Hickmott's Stubblesdown Larry
(whose dam was the famous Dual Ch. Stubblesdown Golden
Lass). As well as these, Glorious also produced Champions in
Mrs R. Thompson's Field Trial winner, Pennard Golden
Primrose, and Mrs G. Barron's Briar of Arbrook, who founded
a line of title-holders.

Mrs Stonex's other son of Dorcas Bruin to prove most
influential on the breed was Dorcas Timberscombe Topper
(winner of two c.c.s), and the product of an inbred mating
of father to daughter. He won the Stud Dog Cup on two
occasions, and was the sire of five Champions, and from him
are descended many others. He sired the litter sisters Ch.
Kolahoi Willow of Westley and Ch. Sally of Westley, and his
son Ch. Camrose Fantango also proved a great stud force.

Another dog which won Junior Warrant just prior to the war
and who was to leave his mark on the breed was Mrs I. Parson's Torrdale Tinker. The influence that this dog exerted
over the breed is shown through Torrdale Kim of Stenbury
(*Sh Ch*), owned by Mrs E. Minter. He played a great part in
helping to found Mrs Minter's famous line of 'Stenbury' bitch
title-holders, which amongst other successes has produced
two Championship Show Best in Show winners.

Mrs R. Harrison's kennel also owed some of its success to
Torrdale Kim of Stenbury (*Sh Ch*), for her Ch. Boltby Skylon
and Ch. Boltby Moonraker were his grandsons.

Another famous son of Torrdale Tinker whose name still
appears in many pedigrees was Ch. Alexander of Elsiville who
sired Ch. Alresford Advertiser (sire and grandsire of several
Champions).

Stemming from the same strain is another very influential
sire, the first post-war Champion, Mrs Parson's Ch. Torrdale
Happy Lad. He too has left behind him many Champion
descendants, for he not only sired two Champions and one
Show Champion himself namely Ch. Beauchasse Dominie,
Ch. Torrdale Faithful and Sonnet (*Sh Ch*), but his children in
their turn also produced several title-holders.

Ch. Colin of Rosecott (grandson of Dual Ch. Anningsley Stingo and Dorcas Clorinda), owned by Miss R. Clark, must also be regarded as one of the outstanding sires of the early post-war period, for he produced six Champions and several other c.c. winners, and he has numerous Champion and Field Trial-winning descendants through Ch. Charming of Ulvin (an outstanding bitch of her time), Ch. Bramble of Essendene and Ch. Nickodemus of Cleavers (both Field Trial winners), and the dual c.c. winning Camrose Antony.

Soon after the war Mrs R. Thompson (Pennard) bought from Mrs S. Winston (née Nairn) Stubbings Golden Nicholas, who was to win the Stud Dog Cup three times. Many winning descendants have been left by him for this kennel, and also through his daughter, Mrs Stonex's Ch. Dorcas Gardenia. Mrs Winston's own Stubbings Golden Dandylyon was another dog of the same period whose name appears in the pedigrees of many Champions. He was sire of Mrs Medhurst's Ch. Katrina of Kuldana, grandsire of the Anria foundation bitch Ch. Briar of Arbrook, and my 'Camrose' foundation bitch Golden Camrose Tess.

Boltby Kymba, owned by Mrs R. Harrison, and bred by Mr W.D. Barwise, was being shown in the late 1940s. He was a lovely dog, who won two c.c.s and produced two outstanding sons, Ch. Boltby Skylon and Ch. Boltby Moonraker, and his name lives on through them and their Champion descendants.

The number of the great Ch. Boltby Skylon's winning descendants must equal that of any post-war Golden, for his blood is carried in many strains. He sired one Champion and four Show Champions, amongst them being Waterwitch of Stenbury (Sh. Ch.), a Championship Show Best in Show winner, who when mated back to her sire produced Sh. Ch. Waterwitchery of Stenbury (herself the dam of two Show Champions). Amongst others Ch. Boltby Skylon also sired the multiple c.c. winner Sh. Ch. Boltby Sugar Bush.

Mrs Harrison's other great sire was Ch. Boltby Moonraker, who also produced five title-holders (three Champions and two Show Champions). The most notable of these were Ch. Boltby Annabel, who became an American Champion, and Sh. Ch. Watersprite of Stenbury who emulated her dam,

The Hon. Mary Marjoribanks on Sunflower with Cowslip or Primrose. (Painted by Gourlay Steel 1871)

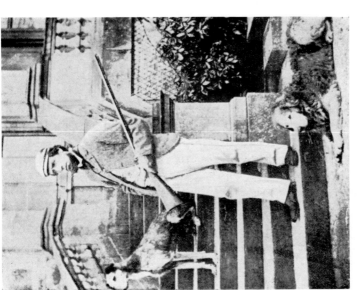

Nous (whelped 1864) with Simon Munro (keeper), at Guisachan

The Hon. Archie Marjoribanks' Lady, Ottawa, 1894

The first Viscount Harcourt's Culham Brass retrieving to a
keeper at Nuneham Park

Ch. Michael of Morton

Ch. Davie of Yelme

Ch. Torrdale Betty

Dorcas Bruin

Waterwitch, by winning Best in Show at a Championship show.

The influence of the afore-mentioned Dorcas Bruin is still very strong through my own Ch. Camrose Fantango, who carried three lines to this dog in his first three generations. As well as producing five Champions, one Show Champion and seven other c.c. winners, Ch. Camrose Fantango's greatest claim to fame is through his son, Ch. Camrose Tallyrand of Anbria (sire of seven Champions and a Show Champion) whose dam was Ch. Jane of Anbria, and his grandson, Ch. Camrose Cabus Christopher, owned by me and bred by Mrs Z. Morgan (formerly Moriarty), who won forty-one c.c.s, was twice Best in Show at All-breed Championship shows, and produced twenty-five title-holders in the United Kingdom and many overseas. This dog has had a great influence on the breed, having many titled descendants, and indeed many newer kennels owe their success to his progeny or his grandchildren. Another great sire who was a Ch. Camrose Fantango grandson was Ch. Camrose Nicolas of Westley (bred by me and owned by Miss J. Gill). He was by Ch. William of Westley and out of Ch. Camrose Jessica, who also has many titled descendants.

Ch. William of Westley was a descendant of the famous Gilder and Quick of Yelme mating through his sire Spar of Yelme. William sired three Champions and one Show Champion, of which Ch. Camrose Nicolas of Westley was one and Ch. Jane of Anbria (dam of two Champions) was another, and through them, and other winners, his name appears in many pedigrees.

One of the great Field Trial dogs post-war, was Mrs J. Atkinson's F.T. Ch. Mazurka of Wynford, who proved an excellent sire, and his descendants have done much to keep Goldens to the fore in trials. He was a son of the brilliant but ill-fated F.T. Ch. Westhyde Stubblesdown Major, who died at the height of his career. Mazurka had two Field Trial Champion progeny, namely Holway Zest and Holway Flush of Yeo, and he has countless Field Trial winning descendants.

Another good sire of Field Trial winners was Mr W. Hickmott's F.T. Ch. Stubblesdown Larry (a product of the famous Ch. Dorcas Glorious of Slat × Dual Ch. Stubblesdown Golden

Lass mating), for he too has left many descendants who are
trial dogs of today. Larry's most famous son was F.T. Ch.
Holway Lancer, another brilliant dog, who undoubtedly
would have had a wonderful career had he not met with a fatal
accident early in life.

Other influential sires whose names still appear in many
pedigrees of top winners are Mrs Z. Morgan's (formerly
Moriarty) Int. Ch. Cabus Cadet and Int. Ch. Cabus Boltby
Combine, both of whom produced numerous title-holders,
Cadet being the grandsire of Ch. Camrose Cabus Christopher.

In the 1980s the greatest stud force has been Mr and Mrs R.
Bradbury's Ch. Nortonwood Faunus (Ch. Camrose Cabus
Christopher × Nortonwood Fantasy of Milo), as he has produced many outstanding progeny, with fourteen title-holders
already and probably more yet to come. He is sire of the
breed's record-holding c.c. winner in Ch. Styal Scott of
Glengilde, bred by Mrs H. Hinks and owned by Mr and Mrs
R. Scholes, whose dam has produced two other title-holders
to the same dog. The greatest mating of all times must be that
of Ch. Nortonwood Faunus to Ch. Westley Victoria, for this
has resulted in six title-holders and other c.c. winners. The
next most influential sire of this era is Ch. Camrose Fabius
Tarquin, another Ch. Camrose Cabus Christopher son, bred
by myself and Miss Wilcock, and owned by me. He has produced several title-holders and very many Championship
show winners.

SOME INFLUENTIAL BROOD BITCHES

One of the earliest of post-war bitches whose dual-purpose
descendants have contributed much to the breed is Stubbings
Golden Olympia, owned by Mr F. Jessamy. Mated first to
Stubbings Golden Garry, she produced the first Dual Champion bitch, Stubblesdown Golden Lass. Lass herself produced
two Field Trial Champion sons and two c.c. winners – the first
of her F.T. Ch. sons being Westhyde Stubblesdown Major,
owned by Mr Peter Fraser, the other being the c.c. winning
F.T. Ch. Stubblesdown Larry. So from Lass is descended a line
of top-class Field Trial winners.

Another early post-war bitch to leave outstanding descendants right through to the present day was Mrs E. Minter's

Laughter of Stenbury, for when closely in-bred to, she produced Ch. Charming of Stenbury and Ch. Gaiety Girl of Stenbury. This bitch-line has continued to produce title-holders, amongst them being the previously mentioned Waterwitch of Stenbury (*Sh. Ch.*) and her daughter Sh. Ch. Watersprite of Stenbury.

Dorcas Leola, in Mr W.D. Barwise's ownership, has very many winning descendants. She was the dam of Ch. Beauchasse Gaiety, Beauchasse Bergamot (*Sh. Ch.*) and Boltby Kymba, all of whom have produced notable offspring, amongst them being Ch. Fordvale Gay Moonlynne, Ch. Beauchasse Dominie, Ch. Boltby Skylon and Ch. Boltby Moonraker.

From this period also came Miss Joan Gill's Ch. Susan of Westley (a Crufts Gold Cup winner), whose name appears in many pedigrees through her two sons, Int. Dual Ch. David of Westley and Ch. William of Westley (both referred to earlier in this chapter). Another of Miss Gill's bitches whose name will live in the annals of the breed is Westley Frolic of Yelme who was dam of three Champions, namely the Field Trial winning Ch. Simon of Westley, and her litter sister Ch. Sally of Westley and Ch. Kolahoi Willow of Westley (owned by Miss V. Wood). Later, Miss Gill took Mrs Philpott into partnership with her and, in Mr Philpott's ownership, the greatest brood bitch of all time, Ch. Westley Victoria (Ch. Sansue Camrose Phoenix × Ch. Westley Jacquetta) has had the greatest distinction of producing eight title-holders – six of them by Ch. Norton-wood Faunus and the other two by Ch. Camrose Cabus Christopher.

My own foundation bitch, Golden Camrose Tess (whose dam was a litter sister to Ch. Dorcas Glorious of Slat), was herself a c.c. winner, and has many Champion and Field Trial winning descendants. She was the dam of Ch. Camrose Anthea, Ch. Camrose Fantango, and Camrose Antony, two c.c.s (sire of Ch. Camrose Tantara). The outstanding brood bitches from my kennel were Ch. Camrose Tantara (bred by Mrs D. Wyn), dam of three Champions, and Camrose Wistansy, dam of two Champions and a Show Champion.

Mrs Dawson's Sh. Ch. Whamstead Emerald has succeeded in establishing her owner's Milo kennel, by producing three Show Champions and champion grandchildren.

Mrs Moriarty (now Morgan) also had a brood bitch to produce three champion off-spring, namely Cabus Boltby Charmer. She was the dam of the breed's top sire, Ch. Camrose Cabus Christopher, also Ch. Hughenden Cabus Columba and Ch. Cabus Caruso.

Mrs H. Hinks kennel has produced a great brood bitch in her Ch. Styal Susila. She is the dam of the great show dog Ch. Styal Scott of Glengilde, also of Sh. Ch. Styal Shakespeare and Sh. Ch. Styal Shelly of Maundale (all by Ch. Nortonwood Faunus), and Sh. Ch. Styal Symetrya (by Sh. Ch. Westley Munro of Nortonwood).

Another matron to produce three title-holders was Mrs Timson's Styal Sonnet of Gyrima. These were Ch. Gyrima Pipparanda, Ch. Gyrima Pippalina and Sh. Ch. Gyrima Pipparetta, who were from her only litter.

Another that must be mentioned for the part she has played as a brood bitch is Mrs J. Atkinson's F.T. Ch. Musicmaker of Yeo, for as the dam of F.T. Ch. Mazurka of Wynford and Melodymaker of Wynford she has left many outstanding trial-winning descendants. Mazurka's record as a sire has been given, and that of his sister as a dam is equally notable, for she produced the two Field Trial Champions, Holway Lancer and Holway Bonnie, both of whom, although they were to die whilst still young, left several good trial-winners behind them.

SOME OUTSTANDING POST-WAR DOGS AND BITCHES

Since the war there have been three Dual Champions (Champions both in the show ring and in trials). The first was Mr W. Hickmott's famous bitch Dual Ch. Stubblesdown Golden Lass. Mrs W.M. Charlesworth's Dual Ch. Noranby Destiny came next and was the first post-war bitch to become a Champion and took her Field Trial title in 1950. Then came Miss L. Ross's International Dual Ch. David of Westley, who was trained and handled throughout his trial career by Mr Jim Cranston, and won twenty-four Field Trial awards, which included a Diploma in the Retriever Championship.

The 1950s saw the advent of four great show dogs. The first of these was Mrs L. Pilkington's Ch. Alresford Advertiser, a 'personality' dog, who took his first Challenge Certificate at an early age, and went on to win thirty-five c.c.s, as well as awards at trials, and the Crufts Gold Trophy. The second was Mrs R. Harrison's Ch. Boltby Skylon, who was another wonderful showman. He won twenty-nine c.c.s and was Best of Breed twice at Crufts. The third was Miss J. Gill's Ch. Simon of Westley, another dog with an exceptional personality, who won twenty-one c.c.s, all under different judges, had a first and other awards in trials, and won the Crufts Gold Trophy five times. Also in Miss Gill's ownership, but bred by me, was Ch. Camrose Nicolas of Westley, who won twenty c.c.s, all under different judges, had several field trial awards, was a Best in Show winner at an All-Breed Championship show, and won the Crufts Gold Trophy.

An outstanding show dog of the 1960s was my Ch. Camrose Tallyrand of Anbria who won sixteen c.c.s. The 1970s brought forth the leading sire of all time, who was also an outstanding show dog, namely my Ch. Camrose Cabus Christopher, who won forty-one c.c.s, and is the only Golden to win two Best in Shows at All-Breed Championship shows, and sired twenty-six title-holders in this country, and many more overseas.

During this time Mrs Robertson's Ch. Stolford Happy Lad won nineteen c.c.s, and Mrs Price-Harding's Ch. Deremar Rosemary was best dual–purpose Golden for several years.

The top winning bitch of all times comes from this era and is my own and Miss R. Wilcock's Ch. Styal Stefanie of Camrose with twenty-seven c.c.s. Formerly, Miss J. Gill's Ch. Pippa of Westley had this honour with seventeen c.c.s. Since then Mrs Beck's Sh. Ch. Davern Josephine has won eighteen c.c.s. She was sired by Ch. Davern Figaro × Davern Gabriella. Now Mr Philpott's Ch. Westley Mabella (from the famous Ch. Faunus × Ch. Westley Victoria mating) has won nineteen c.c.s. In the early 1980s the top c.c. winning dogs were my own Ch. Camrose Fabius Tarquin who won twenty c.c.s and Mrs M. Wood's Ch. Brensham Audacity with nineteen. But in the mid–1980s another outstanding show dog came to light in Ch. Styal Scott of Glengilde – a double grandson of Ch. Camrose Cabus Christopher – and he became the top c.c. winner of all times, overtaking his grandsire's record by 1 c.c., with a total of 42.

In the Field Trial world perhaps the most illustrious dogs are the two which have won the Retriever Championship Stake. First, in 1952, was Mrs J. Lumsden's owner-bred, trained and handled F.T. Ch. Treunair Cala, who won his title in five days. The second, in 1954, was Mrs J. Atkinson's F.T. Ch. Mazurka of Wynford, also owner-bred, trained and handled, who merited the further distinction of a second place in the Championship the following year. Other dogs to win second in the Championship are Mrs Atkinson's F.T. Ch. Holway Zest and Mr E. Baldwin's F.T. Ch. Holway Teal of Westley (bred by Miss Gill) who by the end of 1966 had won his F.T. Ch. title twice over. 1971 saw Mrs J. Atkinson's brilliant F.T. Ch. Holway Gaiety add to her owner's laurels by being a F.T. Ch. twice over. Mrs Atkinson's son Mr R. Atkinson had the great distinction of winning the 1982 Retriever Championship with his F.T. Ch. Little Marston Chorus of Holway, who was bred by Mr M. Dare and sired by F.T. Ch. Holway Chanter × Belway Dove.

PROMINENT KENNELS

For reasons of space this survey cannot possibly include all the kennels which have had some measure of success during this period. It will, however, make mention of those which will go down in breed history for the part they have played in producing several outstanding Goldens in one or other sphere over the post-war years. This first section, therefore, lists in alphabetical order those who have bred or owned several influential title-holders:

Mr and Mrs M. Atkinson's Holway kennel, which has produced several generations of Field Trial Champions, started with the bitch F.T. Ch. Musicmaker of Yeo, and from this first bitch a wonderful line of outstanding trial dogs has been built up. The accomplishments of F.T. Ch. Mazurka of Wynford and F.T. Ch. Holway Zest have already been mentioned. Other outstanding triallers from this kennel have been F.T. Ch. Holway Bonnie (winner of five Open Stakes), F.T. Ch. Holway Lancer and F.T. Ch. Holway Flush of Yeo. There have also been several other F.T. Chs.

Mrs G. Barron's Anbria kennel, which had great success

over the years, has produced a wonderful line of title-holders, as well as several Field Trial winners. The first dog to be campaigned was Anbria Andrew of Arbrook (*Sh. Ch.*), who was followed by Ch. Briar of Arbrook (both bred by Mrs M. Wills), and from this bitch have stemmed several generations of Champions via Ch. Jane of Anbria (her daughter), through Ch. Miranda of Anbria (a Crufts Best of Breed winner) and Irish F.T. Ch. Moonbeam of Anbria to Ch. Melody of Anbria (best Dual-Purpose bitch of 1964). This kennel also produced Ch. Camrose Tallyrand of Anbria, Ch. Anbria Joriemour Marigold and two Show Champions.

Mr and Mrs D. Balaam's Pinecrest kennel has been successful both for themselves and for others, for their most influential dog Ch. Pinecrest Salvador (Ch. Davern Figaro × Pinecrest Patricia) was extensively used at stud and produced many winners.

Mr W. D. Barwise (Beauchasse), who was honorary secretary of the Northern Golden Retriever Association until 1964, produced several who have attained their titles, all descended from his successful foundation bitch Dorcas Leola, mentioned earlier. These are Ch. Beauchasse Dominie, Ch. Beauchasse Gaiety (owned by Mrs J. Burnett, *née* Brison), Beauchasse Bergamot (*Sh. Ch.*) and Sh. Ch. Beauchasse Nous.

Mrs V. Birkin's Sansue kennel's real success started with her stud dog, Ch. Sansue Camrose Phoenix (bred by me from Int. Ch. Cabus Cadet × Camrose Wistansy) who won fourteen c.c.s and was the sire of several Champions, and appears in the pedigrees of many of the later Westley's and Nortonwood's through Ch. Westley Victoria and Ch. Nortonwood Faunus. Later Mrs Birkin bred Ch. Sansue Tobias who was a Group winner at a Championship Show. He was by Ch. Camrose Tallyrand of Anbria × Camrose Justeresa. Since then she has owned Ch. Westley Topic of Sansue (Ch. Camrose Cabus Christopher × Ch. Westley Victoria) and Ch. Gaineda Consolidator of Sansue (Glennessa Escapade × Sh. Ch. Rachenco Charnez of Gaineda), who produced several title-holders for his owner and others. This kennel has produced double figures of title-holders, and has founded a very strong strain.

Mrs E. Borrow (Deerflite) had her foundation bitch Dorcas Aurora from Mrs Stonex. She was the dam of Sonnet (*Sh. Ch.*), who, though not used extensively at stud, produced both Ch. Deerflite Delilah and Ch. Avondale Brandy, and was the grandsire of Ch. Deerflite Headline. This kennel has also produced other Show Champions.

Mr and Mrs R. Bradbury's Nortonwoods were put on the map with their Ch. Nortonwood Faunus, winner of thirteen c.c.s and a Gundog Group. As already mentioned he was another of Ch. Camrose Cabus Christopher's sons, whose influence must be nearly as great as that of his sire, as he was a very dominant sire and seemed to 'click' with bitches from most strains. Other good sires from this kennel have been Sh. Ch. Nortonwood Checkmate and Sh. Ch. Westley Munro of Nortonwood.

Mrs J. Burnett (Rossbourne) had title-holders before her marriage with the affix 'Fordvale'. Since then she has produced others under the present affix. Her studs, Sh. Ch. Rossbourne Timothy (Rossbourne Osprey × Rossbourne Ripple) and Sh. Ch. Rossbourne Harvest Gold (Timothy × Kingsburgh Bryony-Ann) have both produced many winners.

Mrs S. Cochrane (Rachenco) has produced some title-holders whose influence has been great, most notable of which was Mrs E. Anderson's Sh. Ch. Rachenco Charnez of Gaineda (ten c.c.s, and a Group winner). She produced a good line of winners to whatever dog she was mated. Mrs Cochrane's own Sh. Ch. Rachenco Boomerang (full brother to Charnez) distinguished himself by taking his title at nearly ten years old, and has produced many winners. He and Charnez were sired by Ch. Christopher× Alexia of Tillwood Rachenco.

Mrs E. L. Ford's Elsiville kennel had many successes during the short time her dogs were being shown after the war. She produced two Champions and four *Show Champions*, the most notable of which was Ch. Alexander of Elsiville (ten c.c.s), who is further renowned as the sire of Ch. Alresford Advertiser. Another multiple c.c. winner was Ophelia of Elsiville (*Sh. Ch.*). Other title-holders from this kennel were Ch. Nickolai of Elsiville, Nyda of Elsiville (*Sh. Ch.*), Major of Elsiville (*Sh. Ch.*), owned by Mrs I. Broomhall, and Sonja of Elsiville (*Sh. Ch.*), owned by Mrs J. Turvey, *née* Allwood.

Miss Joan Gill had her first Golden in 1936. This was Simon of Brookshill, grandsire of Ch. Simon of Westley, referred to earlier. It was not, however, until after the war that she took out her Westley prefix, since when she has produced many title-holders, and several good Field Trial winners. Miss Gill has the distinction of breeding the only International Dual Champion in the breed, namely Miss L. Ross's David of Westley. This dog was a son of the first Westley Champion, Susan of Westley, who won an award at a trial and was a Crufts Gold Cup winner. Susan was also the dam of Ch. William of Westley (mentioned earlier under 'Influential Sires'). Next came the three Champion progeny of Westley Frolic of Yelme, Sally of Westley (nine c.c.s), Miss V. Wood's Ch. Kolahoi Willow of Westley and Ch. Simon of Westley (twenty-one c.c.s). Of her other Champions the most notable are Camrose Nicolas of Westley (twenty c.c.s) and Pippa of Westley (seventeen c.c.s.).

Miss Gill, on taking Mrs D. Philpott into partnership, succeeded in producing many more title-holders. Later Mr M. Philpott joined the partnership, who owned Ch. Westley Victoria. He also owns the breed's second highest bitch c.c. winner in Ch. Westley Mabella. There are now seven generations of more than twenty Champions, mostly descended from Ch. Susan of Westley and carrying the Westley affix. Miss Gill and Mrs Philpott later took out the affix of Standerwick, and have produced many Field Trial winners carrying this name.

Mrs D. Gostyn (Whamstead) has had considerable success, for her kennel produced Champion Whamstead Diana, who won ten c.c.s. and at the same time as she was campaigning this bitch, Mrs Gostyn had many wins with Ch. Flax of Wham, whose decendants have won awards in Field Trials. The Show Champions bred in this kennel are Whamstead Cavalier and Whamstead Emerald (owned by Mrs D. Dawson).

The late Mrs R. Harrison's kennel was founded before the war, but it is in the post-war period that her 'Boltbys' came to the fore in the show ring. Mrs Harrison produced six Champions and two Show Champions, as well as other c.c. winners. The most notable dog from this kennel was Ch. Boltby Skylon, whose record as a sire and as an outstanding dog is given earlier in this chapter. The others were Ch. Boltby Moonraker, Ch., and U.S.A. Ch. Boltby Annabel, Ch. Boltby Mystral, the two litter brothers and sisters, Show Champions Boltby Syrian and Boltby Sugar Bush, and Int. Ch. Cabus Boltby Combine and Ch. Boltby Felicity of Brierford.

Another Mrs Harrison to have a kennel operating for many years owned the 'Janville' affix and she too produced several title-holders. Her most influential bitch was Sh. Ch. Janville Renown, who was a multiple c.c. winner and was the dam of Ch. Cabus Janville Defender, so her name still appears in many pedigrees, through Defender's grandson, Ch. Camrose Fabius Tarquin. The Janville lines have been instrumental in ensuring the success of many breeders over the years.

Mr W. Hickmott (Stubblesdown), who had Goldens for many years before the war, did not start showing or trialling them until after the war. The most influential of this kennel's products was Dual Ch. Stubblesdown Golden Lass, mentioned earlier. The other Champion was Lass's half-sister Ch. Braconlea Gaiety (both of whom were bred by Mr F. Jessamy), who won nine c.c.s and was an All-Breed Championship Show Best in Show winner, as well as being a trial winner. These two, and Lass's son, the c.c. winning F.T. Ch. Stubblesdown Larry, were to win the Crufts Gold Cup outright for their owner. In addition, Lass was dam of Mr P. Fraser's F.T. Ch. Westhyde Stubblesdown Major (winner of a Diploma and a fourth place in the Retriever Championship). There have been many other show and trial winners from this kennel.

Mrs H. Hinks' greatest claim to fame for her Styal kennel is that she has bred both the breed's record holding c.c. winning dog and bitch in Mr and Mrs R. Scholes' Ch. Styal Scott of Glengilde (forty-two c.c.s) and his aunt, mine and Miss Wilcock's Ch. Styal Stefanie of Camrose (twenty-seven c.c.s). It is interesting to note that Ch. Scott is a double grandson of Ch. Camrose Cabus Christopher, and Ch. Stefanie is a Ch. Christopher daugher. Stefanie's litter sister Ch. Styal Susila has been a great brood bitch, as she not only is the dam of Scott, but has produced another three title-holders.

Wing Commander and Mrs Iles' 'Glennessa' kennel has produced many title-holders, some home-bred and some stemming from the Stenbury kennel, and several well-known kennels have been founded on their stock.

Mr and Mrs C. Lowe's Davern kennel's successes started with the foundation bitches Camrose Flavella and Ch. Camrose Pruella of Davern, both out of Camrose Wistansy, Flavella being sired by Ch. Camrose Nicolas of Westley, and Pruella by Int. Ch. Cabus Cadet. Pruella when mated to Ch. Camrose Tallyrand of Anbria produced Ch. Davern Figaro, who sired several title-holders and has been extensively line-bred to in several European countries. Figaro sired one of the breed's top winning bitches in Mrs A. Beck's Sh. Ch. Davern Josephine, who won eighteen c.c.s. The kennel has had several other title-holders.

Mrs J. Lumsden's great Field Trial winning line of Treunairs has been instrumental in starting several well-known kennels, as well as producing Field Trial Champions for herself, including the first Golden post-war to win the Retriever Championship in F.T. Ch. Treunair Cala.

Mrs E. Minter (Stenbury) had Goldens before the war, but her line of title-holders was founded on the post-war Laughter of Stenbury. The first of the title-holders to be made up was Torrdale Kim of Stenbury (*Sh. Ch.*), bred by Mrs I. Parsons, then followed Ch. Charming of Stenbury and Mr D. Hamilton's Ch. Gaiety Girl of Stenbury. The Show Champions bred by Mrs Minter are Waterwitch of Stenbury and her daughter, Watersprite of Stenbury (both Best in Show winners at Championship events). Waterwitch's other titled daughter, Sh. Ch. Waterwitchery of Stenbury, herself produced outstanding progeny in Wing-Commander J. Iles' Sh. Ch. Glennessa Waterwisp of Stenbury (Best of Breed at Crufts, 1964), Sh. Ch. Watersonnet of Stenbury (Reserve Best in Show at a Championship show) and Waterlaughter of Stenbury (a Gundog Group winner at a Championship show). The Stenbury Kennel has also produced other title-holders.

Mrs Z. Morgan (formerly Moriarty) produced three dogs to prove very influential to the breed, namely Int. Ch. Cabus Cadet and his son Int. Ch. Cabus Boltby Combine (out of Sh. Ch. Boltby Sugar Bush) who were both the sires of several title-holders, and whose names are in the pedigrees of most of the top winning kennels. Mrs Morgan also bred Ch. Camrose Cabus Christopher, who was the breed's record-holding dog for over ten years.

Miss J. Murray (Maidafield) was another to start soon after

the war with a Torrdale, and her kennel produced two Champions and two Show Champions. Torrdale Maida (*Sh. Ch.*) was the dam of Ch. Fiona of Maidafield, who in her turn produced the litter brother and sister Ch. Simon of Fionafield (owned by Mr J. Carney) and Pandown Poppet of Yeo (*Sh. Ch.*), owned by Mrs L. Sawtell.

Mrs I. Parsons (Torrdale) continued with her pre-war winning line for several years after the war, during which time there were two Champions and two *Show Champions* produced. Her Ch. Torrdale Happy Lad became the first post-war Champion, as well as winning Best in Show at a Championship show. The other Champion was Mrs J. Woods' Torrdale Faithful, who also left Champion descendants. Both the Show Champions have been mentioned earlier – they are Torrdale Kim of Stenbury (*Sh. Ch.*) and Torrdale Maida (*Sh. Ch.*).

Mrs L. Pilkington's Alresfords continued their winning way during the post-war years, and produced several title-holders. The first to take her title was Ch. Alresford Mall (bred by Mrs E. Cuffe-Adams), and was the dam of Ch. Alresford Advertiser (thirty-five c.c.s). Advertiser sired Ch. Alresford Atom and Sh. Ch. Alresford Harringay (later to become an American Champion) for this kennel, which also produced Sh. Ch. Alresford Purgold Tartan, and many Champions are descended from them.

Mrs P. Robertson's Stolfords have had an influence on the breed not only in this country but in many other countries, and she has produced several generations of title-holders, the most influential of which was Ch. Stolford Happy Lad (Stolford Playboy × Prystina of Wymondham). He won nineteen c.c.s and produced a number of title-holders for several different kennels, and is in the pedigrees of many top winners.

Mrs W.H. Sawtell's Yeo kennel is one to have produced both Champions and Field Trial Champions, as well as other c.c. and Field Trial winners. The first Champion was Masterpiece of Yeo (grandson of Dual Ch. Anningsley Stingo), who was the sire of F.T. Ch. Musicmaker of Yeo (owned by Mrs J. Atkinson), so from Masterpiece are descended all the Holway Field Trial Champions. The other Field Trial Champion bred

here is Holway Flush of Yeo. Pandown Poppet of Yeo (*Sh. Ch.*),
bred by Miss J. Murray, has Champions descended from her,
namely English and American Ch. Figaro of Yeo and Ch.
Toddytavern Kummel of Yeo, and a Show Champion. Int. Ch.
Mandingo Buidhe Column (jointly owned with Mrs Harkness)
took his title for Mrs Sawtell as did others.

Mrs M. Timson's successful Gyrima kennel was founded on
two different bitches, both of which produced Sh. Chs. The
first was Sh. Ch. Romside Raffeena of Gyrima who had a Sh.
Ch. daughter and a Sh. Ch. grandson in Sh. Ch. Gyrima
Oliver and a titled grand-daughter. The other foundation
bitch was Styal Sonnet of Gyrima (Ch. Camrose Nicolas of
Westley × Camrose Gilda), from whom are descended three
generations of title-holders carrying the Gyrima affix. Sonnet
herself was the dam of three title-holders.

My own kennel started with Golden Camrose Tess (one
c.c.), dam of Ch. Camrose Anthea and Ch. Camrose Fantango
and from Tess are descended many Champions and Field
Trial winners. Tess's grand-daughter, Ch. Camrose Tantara
bred by Mrs D. Wyn) produced Ch. Camrose Jessica (dam of
Ch. Camrose Nicolas of Westley), Ch. Camrose Loretta and
Ch. Camrose Lucius (eleven c.c.s). Tantara's grand-daughter
also produced three title-holders in the litter brother and
sisters, Ch. Sansue Camrose Phoenix, Ch. Camrose Pruella of
Davern and Sh. Ch. Camrose Psyche of Vementry. My kennel
has produced many other Champions and two Show Champions all descended from Ch. Camrose Fantango, including
Ch. Camrose Tallyrand of Anbria (sixteen c.c.s) and his son,
Ch. Camrose Cabus Christopher (forty-one c.c.s), and
grandson, Ch. Camrose Fabius Tarquin (twenty c.c.s). The
Camrose Kennel has now produced eight generations of title-
holders, of which there have been twenty-five.

Mr J. Tiranti and his first wife, Mrs P. Holmes started the
'Teecon' kennel with Sh. Ch. Gamebird Debonair of Teecon
and Sh. Ch. Peetling Stella of Teecon. When mated together
they produced title-holders, and from their progeny many
newer kennels have been founded and been successful.

Mr F. Tripptree and his wife started their kennel in the late
1940s, and from their foundation bitch they produced Ch.
Miss Rebecca. From her they have produced many gener-

ations of winners throughout the years, including several to attain their Champion status, and they have started several breeders' kennels abroad with their stock.

Mr and Mrs M. Twist's Bryanstown kennel was founded in Ireland, where they produced several Irish Champions, including those from the Pennard and Ulvin lines, as well as one from Westhyde. Their present line was started with Irish Ch. Bryanstown Shannon of Yeo and Irish Ch. Camrose Gail, both of whom won well in Field Trials there. When mated together they produced Irish and English Ch. Bryanstown Gale Warning, and since then they have produced other Champions and Field Trial winners with this dog in their pedigrees.

Mrs M. K. Wentworth Smith (Yelme) continued the kennel started by her husband before the war. She produced several Champions and other c.c. winners and Field Trial winners. The kennel's first title-holder after the war was Ch. Dernar of Yelme (bred by Miss E. Todd), who was the sire of Ch. Ulvin Vintage of Yelme (bred by Mrs L. Ulyatt). Vintage was a Crufts Best of Breed winner and was twice Best in Show at the Golden Retriever Club Championship show. The other Champions were Ch. Filip of Yelme (bred by Hon. J. Nelson) and Mr G. Search's Ch. Lakol of Yelme.

Other kennels to have success over the years by producing title-holders and to have started others with successful lines are: Mrs E. Anderson (Gaineda); Mrs L. Anderson (Linchael); Mr and Mrs D. Andrews (Catcombe), successful in both shows and trials; Mr E. Baldwin (Palgrave) who produced Field Trial Champions both for himself and others; Mr and Mrs J. Crosbie (Garbank); Mrs V. Jones (Ninell); Mrs H. Lambshead (Muskan); Mrs G. Medhurst (Kuldana); Mrs E. Melville (Crouchers) who has had such successes in trials as well as shows; Mrs Metcalfe (Gainspa); Mr D. Price-Harding (Deremar) winning well at trials as well as shows; Mr and Mrs R. Scholes (Glengilde, owners of the breed's record holder, Ch. Styal Scott of Glengilde; and Mr and Mrs J. Simister (Lacons).

CHAPTER 4

CONFORMATION AND TEMPERAMENT

The Kennel Club Standard for the breed is given in full below, and is a guide to breeders in their attempts to produce the ideal dual-purpose dog. One which conforms as nearly as possible to this Standard is made correctly for show and to carry out the many tasks required of a gundog. Alas, the perfect dog is yet to be born, for even the best-known winners have their faults! This striving for perfection is surely what makes dog breeding so fascinating, for one always cherishes the hope that the really faultless specimen will appear in the next litter!

KENNEL CLUB STANDARD OF THE BREED

General Appearance. Symmetrical, balanced, active, powerful, level mover, sound with kindly expression.

Characteristics. Biddable, intelligent and possessing natural working ability.

Temperament. Kindly, friendly and confident.

Head and Skull. Balanced and well-chiselled, skull broad without coarseness, well set on neck, muzzle powerful, wide and deep. Length of foreface approximately equals length from well-defined stop to occiput. Nose black.

Eyes. Dark brown, well set apart, dark rims.

Ears. Moderate size, set on approximately level with eyes.

Mouth. Jaws strong, with a perfect, regular and complete scissor bite, i.e. upper teeth closely overlapping lower teeth and set square to the jaws.

Neck. Good length, clean and muscular.

Forequarters. Forelegs straight with good bone, shoulders

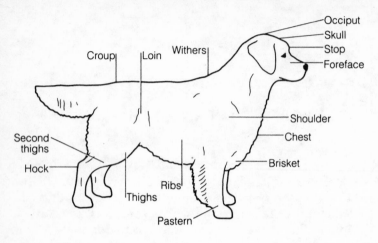

well laid back, long in blade with upper arm of equal length placing legs well under body. Elbows close fitting.

Body. Balanced, short coupled, deep through heart. Ribs deep, well sprung. Level topline.

Hindquarters. Loin and legs strong and muscular, good second thighs, well bent stifles. Hocks well let down, straight when viewed from rear, neither turning in nor out. Cowhocks highly undesirable.

Feet. Round and cat-like.

Tail. Set on and carried level with back, reaching to hocks, without curl at tip.

Gait/Movement. Powerful with good drive. Straight and true in front and rear. Stride long and free with no sign of hackney action in front.

Coat. Flat or wavy with good feathering, dense water-resisting undercoat.

Colour. Any shade of gold or cream, neither red nor mahogany. A few white hairs on chest only, permissible.

Size. Height at withers: Dogs 56–61 cm. (22–24 in.); Bitches 51–56 cm. (20–22 in.).

Faults. Any departure from the foregoing points should be considered a fault and the seriousness with which the fault should be regarded should be in exact proportion to its degree.

Note. Male animals should have two apparently normal testicles fully descended into the scrotum.

GENERAL APPEARANCE

As the description in the Standard says, the whole dog should present a symmetrical or 'balanced' appearance – that is, one in which each part of the anatomy is in proportion; in which the head, neck, length of body and hindquarters are all balanced one with the other, and these must also balance with the length of leg. A dog with a long neck and short body is not balanced, neither is one whose head and body are in proportion but which is too long or too short in the leg, for these do not present a symmetrical outline.

A Golden is specifically a gundog, so, of course, he must be active and powerful in order to perform the work for which he was bred. He may, for instance, have to carry hares over long distances and be required to jump obstacles with them. One which is 'weedy' in type would not conform to the Standard any more than would one which is too clumsily built or 'cloddy'. The ideal is one which has 'quality' – that indefinable element which gives the look of the thoroughbred – together with plenty of substance without any trace of coarseness, is alert, free-striding and active, and has the correct conformation throughout. This, as well as ensuring a well-built dog, should give soundness, provided that there has been no fault in his upbringing.

HEAD AND SKULL

The Standard lays down certain basic points but gives very little detail, and this probably accounts for the wide variation in head shapes.

The skull should be broad, but without any sign of coarseness, and should be slightly rounded but not domed or apple-headed. A head which is too flat and coarse gives a foxy, wedge-shaped look, quite alien to the breed, and such a head often has the ears set on too high. The stop should be well defined but the frontal bones above the eyes should not be too prominent.

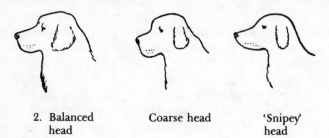

2. Balanced   Coarse head   'Snipey'
    head   head

The muzzle should be straight, with no sign of 'dishface' (as in the Pointer) or Roman nose. It should be approximately the same length from nose to stop as the skull is from stop to occiput, and should be broad and deep, and the lips should not be pendulous. A weak or 'snipey' muzzle is undesirable. The head should appear well chiselled and be without any sign of wrinkle or 'frown' and should be completely balanced.

EYES

The eyes should be dark brown, but any shade of brown is permissible, provided it is not lighter than the colour of the coat. A yellow eye should be avoided, as this gives a very hard, uncharacteristic expression. The eyes should be neither too small, nor too large and prominent, nor should they be set too close together. Obliquely-set or almond-shaped eyes equally detract from the correct expression, which should always be sweet and kindly, and show alertness and intelligence.

EARS

The ears are of correct size when their tips, if pulled forward, do not extend much further than the inner edge of the eye. Ears which are too long are inclined to give a 'houndy' look and to hang incorrectly both in repose and in the alert position. The set of the ear is rather difficult to define, but it is correct when the inner edge of the top of the ear is level with the dog's eye. If set on too high this gives an undesirable 'terrier' expression. The 'leathers' or flaps should be fairly thin, and not be too heavy or coarse to the touch.

MOUTH

The correct bite is a scissor one, with the front top teeth meeting and just overlapping the bottom ones. Occasionally there is the odd misplaced tooth, but this should not be confused with an undershot or overshot jaw. With a young puppy I like to see the jaws fitting less closely than in an adult, for the bottom jaw continues to grow after the top one, and a bite which fits too closely in early life may later become undershot.

NOSE

Should be black, but a brown one should not be penalised unless it detracts from the expression. The colour of the nose sometimes changes with the time of the year, the one which is black may take on a brownish hue in winter. Pigmentation is also affected when a bitch is about to come into season, and at this time her nose may lose some of its blackness, but it will always turn jet black again when she is nursing her puppies. Dogs which have really good pigmentation keep the blackest of noses all the year round and these usually are the ones which have a very dark skin.

NECK AND FOREQUARTERS

These two parts of the anatomy must be considered together, for they are interdependent.

The Standard says the neck should be 'clean and muscular'. This means that there should be no sign of dew-lap (or 'throatiness'), which is very ugly. Fortunately it is not seen much these days, but it was prevalent in some strains just after the war. Naturally, a dog to be able to carry heavy weights should have a strong and muscular neck. The Standard does not mention length of neck, but as a long, sloping shoulder is required, it necessarily follows that a good length of neck is desirable, as the two are complementary, just as are straight shoulders and a short neck.

Faulty shoulders are terribly difficult to breed out. They reappear generation after generation and therefore should be avoided like the plague! R. H. Smythe in his *The Anatomy of Dog Breeding* says: It would be almost impossible to think of any feature transmitted by dog or bitch to their progeny with greater certainty than faulty necks and shoulders.'

The shoulders should be well laid back, and have a long, sloping scapula (shoulder blade), with the humerus (upper arm) also fairly long and set at such an angle as to place the forelegs well under the body – not in a straight line with the chest, as in the Terrier breeds. Though our English Standard does not give the angulation of these bones, the American and Canadian ones give the desired angle between the scapula and humerus as approximately 90 degrees, and I think that most people with any knowledge of conformation would agree with this – though such an angle is all too rarely seen in this breed. If these two bones are set at too wide an angle the shoulder is straight, thus impeding length of stride, and possibly causing a prancing or 'hackney' action, which, of course, is incorrect in a gundog.

1. Scapula

2. Humerus

3. Upper arm

3. Correct shoulder   Straight shoulder
placement

The blades should be neither too wide apart nor too close together at the withers. If they are too wide apart upright shoulders and short shoulder blades are generally evident. This results in 'bossy' or overloaded shoulders – those with too much muscular formation on them. This excessive muscle on the shoulders can be formed by constant galloping, particularly on rough or hilly ground, whereas this does not happen with good steady road work. If the shoulder blades are too close together the chest becomes narrow and this gives a 'racy' appearance – they must be wide enough apart to allow of their convergence when the dog lowers its head.

Looked at from the front, the forelegs should be straight from elbow to foot, without any sign of turning outwards of pasterns or elbows. Some puppies tend to a slight weakness of pasterns, but this failing is sometimes improved through later muscular development. The elbows should be well set under the dog, giving no sign of looseness. The bone should be strong and solid but not excessively so, for coarse bone is not desirable in a working dog from whom speed and endurance are required.

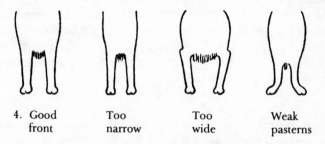

| 4. Good front | Too narrow | Too wide | Weak pasterns |

Viewed also from the side, the legs should be straight, with no sign of the dog being down on its pasterns, causing him to stand and walk with the weight on the back pad, rather than the weight being evenly distributed between all the pads. This is another sure sign of lack of exercise, which can soon be remedied. The forelegs should be well set back under the brisket.

5. Side view of   Weak pasterns
   good front

BODY

The general over-all balance of the dog has already been dealt with. The body itself to be well balanced must, of course, have length, depth and breadth, all in the correct proportions.

A short-coupled dog is one which has a short loin (i.e. the space between the last rib and the pelvis) and a reasonably long rib cage, to allow for adequate expansion of the lungs. The ribs will thus be carried well back, and the dog described as 'well ribbed up'. Though shortness of loin is desirable, the back should not be ultra-short or 'cobby', for excessive shortness of back goes with upright shoulders, a short neck and too short a croup.

The dog should have deep, well-sprung ribs, thus giving an appearance of substance. 'Well-sprung' ribs are those which are nicely rounded though without being excessively barrel-shaped – for a barrel shape does not allow sufficient depth of body for an ideal Golden. Flat sides too should be avoided, even though accompanied by a very deep body. Some judges spend a considerable amount of time looking at a dog in profile; if, therefore, the dog is deep-bodied, he scores heavily, even though he may be slab-sided. More thorough judges, however, will spend as much time examining the dog by looking down on it from behind, for this gives a complete picture of the rib shape, as well as the muscular development of shoulders, loins and thighs. It is useless trying to disguise flat sides with layers of flesh, for the discerning judge soon discovers this. Layers of fat do nothing to improve the dog, they merely make it 'roll' in movement. The ribs should be well covered but not excessively so.

If the dog is too shallow in body it presents a 'shelly' look, and appears too long in leg. Goldens, are, however, a slow-maturing breed, and full depth of body is not generally attained until about three years old. Those which fully develop too early in life are not usually good lasters, and may in consequence have to be retired from the show ring much earlier than the later-developing ones.

| 6. Correct level topline | Sloping from shoulder | Dipping in back |

The back should be perfectly level from the withers to the set-on of the tail. A top-line which slopes from the withers, giving a 'settery' look, is not typical, neither is one which has a roach, nor one which dips in the middle. Many Goldens have a sloping croup, which also is incorrect, as this gives a low set-on of tail.

HINDQUARTERS
The loin should be short and broad, and covered with the hard muscle necessary to add strength to the back. The same applies to the loin as to the ribs, the breadth must not be the result of superfluous flesh. Though the loin should be short, I would not penalise too heavily a slightly longer one if it were in balance with the rest of the dog. Provided the loin is broad and strong, a little added length increases the elasticity of the spine, and is of no detriment to a dog bred for work.

The dog should stand four-square, with hocks straight, neither turning in nor out. One with hocks turning inwards while standing or moving is 'cow-hocked', a weakness which can be inherited, or it can be due to faulty feeding or environment. Standing constantly on its hindlegs, for example, peering over a stable door, is very bad for the growing puppy required to be a show specimen, as this can cause cow-hocks.

7. Correct   Cow hocks
hind view

For a long, free stride it is very important that the dog should have well-bent stifles and good angulation of the hindquarters. This as well as looking more attractive, affords the added impetus when in motion that is so essential for a dog which spends much of its time working with nose to the ground.

This correct hindquarter is present when the pelvis and the femur are set at a somewhat similar angle to that of the shoulder and upper arm, and when the angle formed by the femur and tibia (referred to as the stifle joint) is not too great. A good 'bend' is then assured. The tibia should be of good length to allow the hock to be low-set (or well let down).

Straight stifles and hocks make the hindlegs swing rather like a pendulum, resulting in a lack of drive behind. Of course, one does not want such angulation as is found in a German Shepherd, for this would be too exaggerated for a Golden, and, aesthetically as well as practically, should only accompany the longer body.

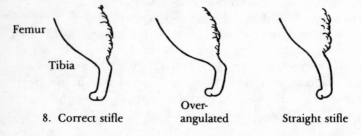

Femur

Tibia

8. Correct stifle   Over-angulated   Straight stifle

The croup, as has been mentioned earlier, should not fall away or slope towards the tail. It should continue level with the rest of the back right to the set-on of the tail. A sloping quarter is often accompanied by somewhat straight stifles and hocks, and an attempt is often made to disguise this fault in the show ring by making the dog stand in a slightly crouching position.

9. Correct croup   Sloping croup
                          with low set tail

Excellent bone structure is of little consequence unless it is well covered by good muscle, for well-shaped hindquarters lacking muscular development give the impression of weakness. They are, in fact, usually only the outward and visible sign of a lazy owner! Plenty of regular trotting exercise on a hard surface is the quickest way to form the good firm muscle so essential on thighs and second thighs.

FEET
These should be round and 'cat-like', well knuckled and not too large. Open or splay feet can sometimes be improved by exercise on hard ground, which will also keep the claws well worn down, but the really good foot is bred, not made! Another fault is that of 'hare-foot', one which is too long and too flat.

10. Good feet   Bad feet

TAIL
The tail should be carried level with the back when the dog is moving. This true tail-carriage adds to the general balance of the dog. It may not seem a very important part of the anatomy, but a tail which is carried over the back, or tucked between the legs, is not characteristic of the breed. It should be set-on level with the rest of the back, and be of moderate length, reaching to, or just below, the hocks. The underside should be profusely feathered and this should be trimmed to about 4 in. at the longest part, tapering gradually to the tip if the dog is to be shown.

COAT
This can be either straight or wavy, but it should lie flat without much upward curl. Some coats which tend to be wavy will curl at the ends if allowed to dry rough, but if they are combed into place while still damp will resume the flat waves which are attractive. The true thorn- and water-resisting coat will have a dense undercoat. This is the shorter more fluffy

hair seen underneath the longer top-coat when this is rubbed up the wrong way. It will help to protect the dog against the hazards of the weather and is most advantageous to a working gundog. The texture varies with the individual, and to be ideal should not be too soft and silky, or too hard and coarse, to the touch. An 'out-of-coat' dog is naturally at a great disadvantage in the show ring, and it is best for him not to be shown until the new coat has fully grown – which will take two or three months from the commencement of the moult. Dogs generally moult once a year, whereas bitches tend to moult after each time they have been in season.

One of the features of the breed is the long feathering on the front legs, the hindlegs from tail to hock (the 'trousers'), and on the underside of the body and tail. This plumage, of course, adds so much to the attractiveness of the dog.

Colour

This can be any shade of gold or cream, but it must not be red or mahogany (Irish Setter colour). The variation in colouring adds to the delights of the breed, for in one litter the whole range of colours is sometimes displayed – cream, pale, mid and dark golden. Very little notice can be taken of the puppy colour, as the coat goes on darkening with successive moults until about three years old – sometimes even later. The colour of the ears is the safest guide to the final colour. Provided the dog does not come within the red or mahogany range, colour should play little part in a judge's decision in the show ring, as all the varying shades are correct. Actual personal preference should not be taken into account.

The feathering on the underside of the body, tail and on the 'trousers' looks most attractive if it is several shades lighter than the rest of the coat – in fact the paler it is, the better.

Weight And Size

The Standard which was amended in 1986 omits to give any guide as to weight, though earlier standards did. I consider a dog in good show condition of about 23 in. should weigh about 70–75 lb. and a bitch of 21 in. about 60–65 lb. However weight will vary according to the amount of bone the dog has and his muscular condition. My yardstick for this is that when

Ch. Camrose Fantango, who was exactly 23 in. at the withers, was going through a very thin period he weighed 68 lb. and certainly was not then carrying nearly enough condition to be able to win in top competition. Here let me say that I do not like to see Goldens being shown in fat, soft condition, for this detracts from their general appearance and activity, and when judging I penalise heavily one which has layers of fat covering its ribs and loins, as this makes the body appear straight from shoulder to hindquarter if viewed from above. The correct shape should show the spring of rib, not cover it up, as I have pointed out earlier in this chapter.

Size can be most deceptive, for a dog which is very compact will seem smaller than a long-bodied one of the same height, and I have often seen and heard a dog criticised for being too small when it was really well within the Standard size. A classic example was Ch. Sally of Westley, who was very neat and compact and beautifully put together – she was often called small, though she was actually mid-way in the standard height (21 in.). There are far more oversized bitches than undersized ones, and in fact many that do well in the show ring would find it very difficult to come under the measure at even 22½ in. On the other hand, very few oversized dogs win, and I doubt if any present-day Champion goes much over 23½ in. if correctly measured.

MOVEMENT

To complete the overall picture, your Golden must be a level mover, that is, one whose legs and feet move in a straight line forwards and backwards, neither turning inwards nor outwards, and who keeps his elbows well into the body. The lateral view of the Golden in action should present a good length of stride both in front and behind, with no unnecessary lifting up of the front legs and consequent wastage of energy, as would be incurred in a 'hackney' action. The hindlegs should flex well from the stifles and hocks, thus thrusting the dog forward.

A common fault, which very often accompanies heavily loaded, straight shoulders, is for the toes to turn inwards in front or 'pin-toe'. Another faulty movement is that of being 'out at elbows'. This is when the elbows are loose and not tucked well into the body, so that the dog throws them out when moving. Yet another incorrect front action is to 'plait' or cross the front legs, which is generally associated with a dog who is narrow in front.

The most common fault of hind action is that of moving 'close' behind. This is when the hindlegs, viewed from behind, move rather close together from the hock downwards. A very much worse fault is that of cow-hocked movement – hocks turning inwards and actually touching or crossing when in motion – and this constitutes real unsoundness. A puppy may sometimes turn its hocks in a little, but as this may be due to looseness, plenty of road exercise will strengthen the muscles, and may correct, or at least improve, this failure.

The remaining bad hind movement is that of turning the hocks outwards, giving a bow-legged appearance. In this movement, instead of the hocks flexing and pushing forwards, they swing sidewards, and this is termed 'sickle-hocked'.

Goldens, if not checked, are prone to adopt a 'pacing' movement at slow speed. It should be checked by jerking the leash sharply and quickening the pace. 'Pacing' is not an attractive action, for it causes a rolling gait, in which the dog moves both legs on the same side of the body one after the other, then those on the opposite side, instead of the conventional trotting movement, in which the legs move diagonally in turn, i.e. left front, right hind, right front, left hind.

TEMPERAMENT

A Golden is by nature gentle, friendly and trustworthy at all times. He is also courageous, intelligent, easy to train and has a great desire to please his owner. It is a combination of these attributes which makes him the ideal family companion or shooting dog. One of the great attractions of the breed is their love of children. Their well-known gentleness, with even the youngest member of the family, makes them such wonderful companions.

Although he should be a good house-dog, i.e. give warning of the approach of strangers, he should not be resentful of them, and when told all is well by his owner, should immediately offer a friendly welcome. He should certainly not have a guarding instinct so highly developed as to make him hostile, for a Golden's rôle in life is not primarily that of a guard-dog.

Goldens are not generally fighters, and should mix with all and sundry without any sign of aggressiveness, and indeed will go out of their way to avoid trouble. This is most essential in a gundog, who must be prepared to be on good terms with all his canine shooting companions. He should not be nervous or timid. One which slinks away when approached is no more typical than one which is aggressive.

A Golden which shows any sign of having too highly developed a guarding instinct, any tendency to bite, aggressiveness or nervousness, has not the true Golden temperament. These differing faulty temperaments are hereditary and dogs possessing them should never be bred from. Admittedly, such failings can be intensified by a bad environment and incorrect treatment, but I maintain that there must be some inherent tendency towards them in the dog for them to be displayed.

However well a dog may be constructed, and however good a showman or worker he may be, unless his temperament is sound he should not be bred from. Once bad temperament is introduced into a strain it is difficult to eradicate, for it reappears generation after generation.

A good nature, alertness, obedience, kindliness and intelligence – these are some of the qualities which go towards the make-up of Golden character, and are probably even more important than physical perfection. A dog may have a fault of construction yet be typical. An unsound temperament is certainly not typical, and it should never be tolerated.

Goldens are a most affectionate breed, and love human companionship, and it is this probably more than anything else which gives them the desire to please their owners, and there is no doubt that, given the opportunity, they can learn to do almost any type of work. Many are trained as Guide Dogs for the Blind, others do extremely well in competitive obedience work, and their capability as gundogs is universally acknowledged. They could not be expected to perform these varying rôles if their character deviated very much from the ideal.

CHAPTER 5

YOUR GOLDEN'S FIRST YEAR

Before you decide from which kennel to purchase your Golden Retriever it is advisable to consider well the purpose for which he is required. Of course, all Goldens make ideal companions, but if you are buying one with a view to running it in trials and showing it, approach a breeder who has consistently produced trial and show winners – not just one winner but several. It must be born in mind that the occasional dog which is good in both spheres may be produced, but the test of a kennel's success is not in reaching the top but in keeping there with successive generations, for working instincts, points of conformation and temperament are all inherited factors.

Should you require your puppy solely as a show prospect it is advisable to approach a kennel known to have produced several really top-class winners – preferably Champions or Challenge Certificate winners. Again, a good one is sometimes produced from a chance mating, but its like may never again be seen in the kennel.

For the puppy required solely for trials, contact one of the leading breeders of trial-winners. You should then get one which, given the correct training and handling, will have 'biddability', style and speed, all of which are so essential.

Having considered these factors, consult the various kennels, and be prepared to wait, if necessary, until the puppy with the desired qualities is available ensuring that both parents are free from eye defects and hip dysplasia.

CHOOSING THE PUPPY
This is a very difficult thing to do when a family of eight-week-old Goldens comes rushing up to greet you, with happy little faces and wagging tails! But one must be firm and think ahead,

and not be tempted to take the most appealing puppy. Even at this age temperament is most important, so look for the puppy which is alert, friendly, playful and bold, for all things being equal, this is the one most likely to have the correct Golden temperament. Do not choose one which prefers to slink off to its bed rather than come up to you when you approach, for it may later turn out to be nervous of strangers; also avoid one which bullies its litter-mates, for this may indicate an aggressive tendency.

A healthy puppy should be plump, but it should not have a distended stomach, for this may indicate the presence of worms – nearly all young puppies have worms, but by eight weeks these should have been dealt with by the breeder. Its eyes and nose should be clear of any discharge, the ears clean and free from odour, skin free from fleas and lice, and there should be no trace of eczema. The puppy should look generally bright and lively, and have a clean, wholesome 'puppy' smell.

Make sure that the teeth are properly placed, i.e. with a scissor bite, and be wary of the one whose teeth just meet at the front. At this age I like to see the front top teeth completely overlapping the bottom ones, almost giving the appearance of a slightly overshot bite.

Naturally you will not choose one with too much white on it. A very small blaze on top of the head nearly always goes, as do small pieces of white on the tips of the toes, but white higher up on the foot very seldom disappears entirely. My experience is that if any part of the pad does not turn black there is a likelihood of the white on the foot remaining. Puppies occasionally have a white tail-tip, but as the hair on the tail lengthens this usually leaves only a few white hairs visible. I have also occasionally seen small patches of black hair on a puppy's side, head or legs, but these never disappear. Your puppy should also have a black nose, eye-rims and lips, and this good pigmentation is usually accompanied by a dark roof to the mouth and a dark-coloured tummy.

Picking the puppy which will finish the best is certainly no easy task even for the expert. Some breeders rashly say of the young puppy 'this one is a future Champion', but this can only be wishful thinking, for so many incalculable factors are involved in the making of a Champion. A fairer assessment would be to say: 'Given the correct feeding, exercise and good luck, this one is a potential winner!' Undoubtedly one learns to know what to look for in one's own strain, and the novice would be well advised, therefore, to accept the experienced person's opinion rather than to rely on his own hunch. The following will serve as an illustration of this. Someone who purchased a puppy from me had the choice of several bitches in a litter. The one I considered the best was rejected as rather 'doggy' in head, and a more feminine one was chosen. This 'masculine' bitch later turned out to be a Champion and was a very beautiful and truly feminine bitch! This is in no way to claim infallibility but to show that one learns to know one's own strain by experience.

Future conformation is very difficult to predict, therefore I advise you first to observe the puppy's general balance, then to 'set it up' on a table and study its head, which should have a broad, deep muzzle, good stop and kindly expression – breadth of skull is not so essential in one so young. Ensure that the shoulder placement is good, that the blades are not too wide apart and that there is a good length of neck. It is import-ant that the bone be strong, the front legs straight as possible, stifles well bent, and the back level and short-coupled. Goldens nearly always finish several shades darker than the colour of the puppy coat. Do not think that a cream puppy will necessarily remain this colour, for more often than not they go on darkening until about three years of age, and, as has been said earlier, the colour of a puppy's ear is the safest guide to its final colour.

INOCULATIONS

The puppy should be inoculated against Hard Pad, Distemper, Hepatitis, Leptospiral Canicola, Leptospiral Icterohae-morragiae (commonly known as rat jaundice) and Parvovirus before he is allowed to come into contact with other dogs, or indeed before he is allowed out of his garden. There is an effective inoculation which can be given as young as eight weeks, with 'boosters' at twelve weeks, and for Parvo again at sixteen and twenty weeks. The dog must be kept at home until about ten days after the final inoculations have been given.

Int. Dual Ch. David of Westley   *C. M. Cooke*

Dual Ch. Stubblesdown Golden Lass

Golden Camrose Tess (with Ch. Camrose Anthea and
Camrose Annette)   *E. Cummant*

F.T.Ch. Mazurka of Wynford and Melodymaker of
Wynford   *Leslie D. Frisby*

F.T.Ch. Treunair Cala   *C. M. Cooke*

Ch. Boltby Skylon

Ch. Alresford Advertiser (35 C.C.s)

Sh.Ch. Watersprite and Sh.Ch. Waterwitch of Stenbury

HOUSING

Any reasonable size of box will be suitable for the puppy to sleep in. A tea-chest put on its side is ideal, for then the puppy is out of all draughts and keeps so much warmer in the small, enclosed space. It is a good idea to fit a wire door to the box, so that he can be shut in for short periods during the day as desired. I do not advise kennelling one dog on its own – in fact, if anyone comes to me for a puppy and tells me that it is to live alone in a kennel I discourage them from buying one. Several dogs kennelled together are happy, but one Golden without human or doggy companionship is something I cannot bear to contemplate.

When the puppy grows out of his early box there are various kinds of dog beds obtainable with metal frames and canvas coverings, which, with a rug spread over them, are excellent, and they are easily cleaned and moved around.

FEEDING

The breeder will supply you with feeding instructions and it is advisable to follow these closely at first in order to avoid upsetting the digestion, for any change of diet can easily cause diarrhoea and sickness, and sometimes even a rise in temperature. As the puppy grows, so it needs an increasing supply of protein (found in meat, fish, etc.) and carbohydrates (biscuit meal, brown bread, etc.) and milk, to give a balanced diet. Cows' milk is not concentrated enough for young puppies, who should be given some form of full-cream dried milk. Most essential additions to the growing puppy's diet are calcium – to help form good bone and strong teeth – and Vitamin D, without which an adequate supply of calcium is not absorbed. Other necessary vitamins are A, B and E, while phosphorous and other minerals are also needed. These can all be found in the correct proportions in powdered form in Vivomin, made by Crookes. Alternatively, the use of three of Phillips' products (Stress, Kenadex and Vetzyme) will also supply these supplements in the correct quantities.

A specimen feeding chart for a puppy of eight weeks onwards is given here, and shows roughly the amounts which should be given – but here I stress again follow the breeder's instructions exactly, and only change these gradually if you

wish. These quantities cater for the average puppy and may be
varied slightly according to the needs of the individual. (Those
who require feeding instructions for younger puppies should
refer to Chapter 7, 'Rearing of Puppies'.)

8 weeks	8– 9 a.m.	6 oz. fresh or tinned meat + 1 oz. biscuit meal or 1 Weetabix mixed with warm water
	12– 1 p.m.	½ pint milk mixed exactly as breeder's instructions + 1 Weetabix
	4– 5 p.m.	6 oz. fresh or tinned meat + 1 oz. biscuit meal or 1 Weetabix mixed with warm water
	9–10 p.m.	½ pint milk + 1 Weetabix
9 weeks	8– 9 a.m.	7 oz. meat + 1½ oz. biscuit meal or 1½ Weetabix mixed with warm water
	12– 1 p.m.	½ pint milk + 1½ Weetabix
	4– 5 p.m.	7 oz. meat + 1½ oz. biscuit meal or 1½ Weetabix
	9–10 p.m.	½ pint milk with 1½ Weetabix
10 weeks	8– 9 a.m.	8 oz. meat + 2 oz. biscuit meal or 2 Weetabix mixed with warm water
	12– 1 p.m.	½ pint milk + 2 Weetabix
	4– 5 p.m.	8 oz. meat + 2 oz. biscuit meal or 2 Weetabix
	9–10 p.m.	½ pint milk + 2 Weetabix

Continue feeding in this way, gradually increasing all food
as required until about 1½ lb. meat (or 1½ large tins of puppy
meat) is being given and increasing the biscuit meal as the
puppy will take more. I prefer using tinned puppy meat rather
than fresh meat, as this is perfectly balanced with the correct
amount of supplements added, so there is no chance of giving
too little or too much in the way of vitamins – an imbalance or
over-vitaminising can cause much damage to the puppy's
health. Some people are afraid of overfeeding their puppies – I
do not believe that this is possible, within reason, for they
need all the nourishment they can take, as their growth is very

rapid. Of course, some will eat until they look like barrels, but generally Goldens can be relied on to take only what they need. A voracious appetite is often the sign of worms that are still present, and even if these symptoms are not present, it is advisable to administer a reliable worming medicine containing piperazine citrate – see Chapter 7, 'Rearing of Puppies' – at about ten and twelve weeks of age. The puppy will, of course, have been wormed earlier by the breeder.

At three months meals can be cut down to three a day, quantities being increased as before. As the meat ration is increased, so the intake of milk can be decreased, and at this stage cows' milk can be substituted for powdered milk. Give the puppy at least a pint of milk a day until it is six months old if it will take it, though some take a dislike to milk before this.

At six months old only two meals a day are required, and this can be reduced to one at nine months if so desired. Up to this age the daily quantity of food eaten may well be much more than that of an adult, for nearly all growing Goldens need these larger amounts to keep them looking really solid. At about nine months of age the main part of their growth has been completed and it may be necessary to curtail somewhat the carbohydrate intake, otherwise too much weight may be put on, which would be detrimental to bone structure, for at this age bones are still soft, and superfluous weight may tend to make the dog go 'out at elbow' or become 'cow-hocked'.

The average total quantity of food required to keep an adult Golden in show condition is about 2–2½ lb. of food a day for a dog, somewhat less for a bitch. This should consist of roughly 1 lb. of meat and about 1–1½ lb. biscuit meal. Some young dogs are difficult to get weight on so they can take considerably more food than one which is inclined to become obese. There are those dogs who lie around all day and are loath to take much exercise, consequently the need less starchy food than the quantities mentioned above. Some owners tend to grossly overfeed their dogs, which then become fat and sluggish at an early age. A fat dog is not a happy dog, so those which tend to put on weight rapidly should be strictly dieted, and, if necessary, all starch cut out of the diet for a time.

The foregoing should be the basis for feeding throughout the dog's life – good meat is as essential to the adult as to the growing dog. Tinned dog meat, which has a very high nutritional value, is becoming increasingly popular as fresh meat becomes more expensive and more difficult to get. Other good foods are paunches (sheep or ox), herrings and liver. Any one of these several foods should provide the daily diet with the addition of good wholemeal biscuit or brown bread soaked in gravy, milk or water, and the dog should keep in excellent condition. Eggs given occasionally are also beneficial, for they are full of protein. I remember the late Mr Jenner (of Abbots fame), whose pre-war kennel produced more title-holders than any other, telling me that judges used to compliment him on the beautiful coats and condition of his dogs, and this he put down to the fact that their diet included plenty of eggs.

The only bones which can safely be allowed are marrow bones, which, as well as giving much pleasure to the dog, help to keep the teeth free from tartar, and the gnawing process helps to stimulate the gastric juices. Never let him have any other bones – those from poultry or game and chop bones splinter easily and may puncture the intestines, and they nearly always cause digestive troubles. A young puppy almost always tends to guard its first bone, and he may growl if you try to take it away. At the very first sign of this he must immediately be tapped on the nose and severely scolded. If the bone is held and the puppy allowed to chew on it, confidence will be established, and you will seldom find that there is any recurrence of this behaviour. In the same way get the puppy used to having his dish held occasionally whilst feeding, for this too will prevent any possessiveness over his food developing. I stress that correction must come on the first occasion on which the puppy shows this possessive tendency, for once he has been allowed to guard something, the situation subsequently can be very difficult to deal with.

Grown dogs need only one meal a day, and I have rarely found it necessary to give more. Some people, however, prefer to give two meals daily. I think this to be a good idea for 'bad-doers', for it means that they probably eat more than they would if given only the one meal, from which they invariably pick out the meat and leave the rest! Those who feed twice daily usually give biscuits and meat separately – one late in the morning and the other early evening. This practice is advocated by those who have adopted the Natural Rearing Method. This method entails the use of many types of herbs, strict fasting one day a week, and it discourages the use of all drugs and inoculations. I have never reared any of my dogs by this method, for the risk of infection incurred at shows and from the various other sources is so considerable that to be deprived of the protection of modern inoculations would, for me, be too great a source of anxiety.

HOUSE-TRAINING

Begin house-training immediately, for it is made much simpler if it commences before any bad habits have developed. Avoid 'incidents' in the house by taking the puppy outside immediately it wakes up from a sleep, after each meal, and at very frequent intervals during the day. Each time that you see it preparing to 'squat' in the house, pick it up and rush it outside before it has a chance to do anything. Stay out with it until your object is achieved, then give plenty of praise and allow it to return indoors. Do not scold it for performing indoors unless it is actually caught in the act, for this will only cause confusion in its mind – the fault, after all, has been yours in not anticipating trouble!

Goldens learn to be clean in the house very quickly, but, of course, you cannot expect a puppy to contain himself throughout the night until he is about four months old, so put some newspapers as near to the door as possible, and he will soon learn what these are for.

LEASH TRAINING

Before introducing the puppy to the leash accustom it to wearing a collar – it will probably scratch frantically at first, but it soon gets used to the feeling of wearing something round its neck. Then attach the leash to the collar, and, with several tit-bits in your pocket, walk a few paces away, holding the leash and calling his name. As soon as the puppy makes a move towards you give it a titbit and praise it. Take a few more steps away, again calling its name and holding the titbit just in front of its nose (donkey-and-carrot fashion!). Soon the puppy will begin to follow the tempting piece of food and when you have got him walking a few paces – encouraging him continuously – let him feel the leash pull slightly. He will probably leap frantically about, so attract his attention again with the food, while patting him encouragingly. This method soon works, for his eagerness for the titbit generally overcomes his worry over the restraint of the leash. This early leash training must, of course, be done at home and the puppy should not be introduced to the outside world until it is completely unperturbed by the leash.

CAR TRAINING

It is advisable to get the puppy used to the car as early in life as possible, though before it is ever taken for rides it is a good idea for him to sit in the car for short periods while this is stationary. As soon as the puppy is able to go off the premises – i.e. when all inoculations are complete – take him for a very short ride, and allow a romp on the grass at the end of it. If you have suitable exercising ground only a few minutes away from home this is ideal, for the puppy has not then had time to feel ill through the vibration of the car. If this is repeated frequently the puppy soon begins to associate car rides with the delightful experience of a walk, and you can then extend the distance. Should it be sick on these journeys, give a travel-sickness tablet about half an hour before each journey, but it should not be necessary to continue this for long. Most Goldens adore car travelling and there is usually a mad rush to get in as soon as possible in case they are left behind! I find they so love the car that if ever the door is inadvertently left open whilst some of them are around, in they leap, and when the time comes for a roll-call the missing dogs will be found happily ensconced in the car! They appear to regard this as an extra kennel – but a very special one which takes them to exciting places – and when away from home they would much rather sleep there than in a strange kennel. Presumably they think of it as part of home, and they seem to know that they cannot be left behind if they are in it.

Car travelling is also a good method of getting the youngster used to seeing traffic, and to the noise of passing cars, whilst in the security of a familiar enclosed space.

EXERCISE

Puppies need plenty of free exercise from eight weeks onwards if they are to grow into sound, free-moving dogs. Mine start going for short romps in the paddock from ten weeks old. At about three to four months, when they are being leash-trained, they are given walks on the leash, still in the paddock. At five months short daily road walks should commence, of about fifteen minutes a day, on a quiet road with, if possible, a footpath and a wide grass verge, so that the cars do not pass too closely. This should be increased gradually to about forty minutes daily, and as the puppy becomes accustomed to traffic, it should be taken on busier roads, and when quite unmoved by these conditions, take it into a shopping place to get it used to the bustle of crowds, prams, other dogs, etc. When such a walk can be faced without the puppy being unnerved, then it is not likely to be afraid of any strange places or circumstances.

From about six months all Goldens should have at least forty minutes of regular roadwork, and this, with the addition of about thirty minutes' free running on grass each day, should suffice to keep them in good muscular condition. It is no use, however, turning the dog out into garden or field hoping that he will exercise himself – he won't. It is much more likely that he will stand waiting for you to join him, or go off and dig for mice or moles! So to ensure that he is properly exercised you should exert yourself as often as possible and go with him, for Goldens need human companionship, and you owe it to them to spare them a little of your time.

TEETHING

At about four months the first teeth will start to come out and they will gradually be replaced by the second and permanent ones. Throughout this process it is most essential that there should be an adequate quantity of calcium absorbed into the system to enable good strong teeth to be formed. A daily inspection should be made to ascertain that none of the first teeth remain as the second ones come through, or these may be pushed out of alignment. Be extremely careful in your handling of the mouth. If you are at all rough and frighten the puppy it may always be suspicious of having its mouth examined, and thus cause trouble if it is to appear in the show ring. When the new teeth are coming through you may get the impression that a correct scissor bite will never develop. Sometimes there is quite a gap between the two jaws, and the bite looks slightly overshot, but this will usually right itself as the teeth grow to their full size. In a puppy this bite is preferable to one in which the teeth just meet, for this may often finish by being undershot, as has been explained earlier.

GROOMING AND BATHING

It is important to accustom the puppy to being groomed, and this should be done very early in life. A fairly soft brush should be used to begin with and a metal comb. The puppy will probably enjoy this daily grooming and think that this is the time for a wonderful game of chewing the brush! You must teach it to stand still whilst the grooming is in progress or it will always prove an exhausting task, which will usually then only be half done. As the dog gets older a stiffer brush can be used, or a wire hound glove which puts a beautiful gloss on the coat. Dogs generally love this, and mine usually queue up for their turn when it appears.

Whilst doing this daily routine it is well to check that the dog is free from livestock of any kind. No matter how carefully it is looked after, it is possible for the occasional flea to appear. If the presence of livestock is suspected it is a simple matter to deal with by dusting the whole coat with Alugan powder, or some other similar preparation, and this should be repeated after about five days to make quite sure that no more have appeared.

Goldens do not need bathing very often, provided they get their regular grooming. But sometimes a wonderful roll in mud is indulged in, and a bath becomes essential. Make quite sure that the water is not too hot or the dog will be afraid of baths for the rest of his life. Thoroughly wet the coat, then use a good Lanolin shampoo, rub well in and rinse. (Bathing is dealt with in more detail in the chapter dealing with show preparation.)

DRYING

One of the best ways of drying a dog is with a good chamois leather first squeezed out in warm water. This gets all the moisture out of the coat in an incredibly short time and is much preferable to using towels. If the dog is to be kennelled another good method of drying is to rub handfuls of sawdust into the coat. Newspaper, being absorbent, is a suitable substitute for a leather or sawdust if neither of these is available. Take care that if the dog is to be shown soon afterwards his coat is not left to dry rough but is combed into place while still damp. (This drying process will also be dealt with in detail in the chapter on show preparation.)

EARLY LESSONS

The physical well-being of your young dog is now assured if the foregoing suggestions have been closely followed, for he is well fed, has all the protection which modern inoculations afford against the deadly virus diseases, and is given sufficient exercise to ensure that he is sound and healthy. It now remains for you to see that he grows up to be a socially acceptable creature; that he is a credit to his breed, and to you, in his general behaviour. Here I must stress how essential it is that he should have plenty of human contact, for there is no doubt that Goldens develop so much more character and intelligence if given individual attention and training from early puppyhood. He will be much more responsive to later training for trials, shows, obedience, etc., and more satisfactory as a companion, if certain basic lessons have been learnt.

In the early stages of training, bribery with the aid of titbits is very helpful, but this should not be continued when the puppy has advanced sufficiently for him to realise what is required of him – praise is then an adequate reward.

A most important lesson which should be given as early as possible is that of learning to come to you immediately he is called. Nothing is more annoying than a dog which does not respond when called, but it is fatal to lose one's temper and scold him when he finally does so. It is too late then for punishment, for he has done what you asked by coming back to you. An essential thing to remember is that a puppy should always associate coming to you as a pleasant experience, and be confident that you will always greet him in a friendly manner. Never scold or punish the dog unless he is actually caught in the act of wrong-doing, for he cannot be expected to understand his mistake when he comes happily up to you and is reprimanded for something which is already forgotten. He will assume that he erred in coming to you, and will probably avoid this in future.

Another early lesson of equal importance is for him to learn to respond to the word 'No' – but when you say 'No' the puppy must realise that you really mean this. Insist, therefore, that you get complete obedience right from the start, for it is useless to give commands if you do not see that they are carried out immediately. For example, do not give the command 'No' unless you are sure that you can effectively stop him in what he is doing. Always be consistent and do not forbid something at one time and allow it the next, for this only causes confusion in his mind.

Goldens are usually very sensitive and it is seldom necessary to do more than scold them to bring home to them that they have displeased you. If, however, the misdemeanour is repeated a good shaking is the best method of correction.

It is a good idea to accustom him to various noises whilst feeding – clapping hands, banging dishes, etc. – so that extraneous noises are not likely to be regarded as frightening. For the puppy that is later to be gun-trained (see Chapter 10), bursting paper bags whilst he is eating is an excellent way of preparing him for the louder sound of gun-fire, for he is generally so interested in his food that he hardly notices the bang. When you find that he is impervious to this, wait till he has finished eating, then attract his attention, burst the bag, and give it to him to play with.

FIRST STEPS IN RETRIEVING

The retrieving instinct is shown very early in this breed, and they frequently develop a penchant for carrying shoes and gloves, so in the interest of the rest of the household it is advisable to give them their own 'toys'. A very hard rubber ring, which is too large to be swallowed, and an old shoe are ideal, so that when he appears with someone's favourite slipper you can gently take if from him and give him his own toy in exchange. Never discourage this retrieving instinct – irritating though it may be at times – for it is the work for which he was bred and it is up to you to adapt it to the real thing later on. A puppy which has been scolded for bringing unwanted objects to you is going to be difficult to teach to deliver to hand in the future, so always encourage him to bring his toys to you, for this is one step towards his future training.

To teach the puppy to retrieve while fairly young, use a small 'dummy' made from a stuffed sock. Throw this a short distance from his bed. He will rush to the dummy, pick it up and start to return. You can then intercept him near the bed and get hold of the dummy so that he learns to bring it back to hand. Do not take it away from him immediately, but let him hold it for a minute whilst you praise him for bringing it. Repeat this several times and soon he will realise that this is a good game, and will enthusiastically bring it back to have it thrown again. This is just the initial lesson, and later retrieving will be dealt with in Chapter 10 ('Gun-training').

Heel Lessons

It is not necessary to commence heel-training until the puppy is about eight months old, though it may be started earlier if desired. Put a slip-leash on the puppy, and, with him on your left side, start walking away and at the same time give the leash a jerk and say 'Heel'. Should the puppy get ahead of you, jerk the leash backwards, repeating 'Heel'. This applies also should he lag behind – give the leash a forward tug and the command 'Heel'. Try to keep him concentrating on you by saying 'Good dog', and encouraging him by patting your knee. Some people advocate a reprimanding tap on the nose if the dog pulls forward, but with this breed it should not be necessary. If he has been allowed to become a persistent puller, then, of course, your job is much harder. The command 'Heel' will quickly be associated with the action of being pulled into the correct position, and he will then soon respond without any pressure from the leash.

Should he persistently walk wide of you, or pull sideways, take him close to a fence or wall, so that he has to keep well in to heel. Never try to walk the dog at heel off the leash until you are quite confident that he will remain in the correct position. It is better to spend a further few days perfecting his response before going on to 'heel off the leash' than to risk your earlier lessons having to be repeated.

It is unwise to make the training sessions too long. Ten

minutes daily should suffice, then you will almost certainly have a dog keenly interested in his work. Longer sessions would probably mean a bored dog, who would remember his boredom each time lessons were resumed.

Training To Sit And Stay

Once again, for the first lessons have him on a slip-leash, so that you are in complete control and he cannot bolt. To make the puppy sit, give the command 'Sit', and at the same time push his hindquarters down, thus causing him to adopt a sitting position. Hold him like this for a while, and if he attempts to move, say 'No, sit', and increase the pressure on his rear. Let him get up again and praise him. Repeat the process until he remains in the sitting position when you take your hands off him.

Soon he will learn to sit on command, and when he will remain so until allowed to get up, you can take a few paces backwards, holding up your hand and saying 'Stay'. This holding up of the hand is very useful in later training, for the dog soon associates it with the order to sit and wait for a further command. If a move is made towards you immediately say 'No, stay' and push him back into place. Considerable time and patience may be needed to reach the stage where you are able to walk away without the dog following. If any undue difficulty is experienced with this lesson have him on a long slip-leash, passed round a stake in the ground behind him, and the other end held by you. The rope should be slack when you walk away, but if he gets up say 'No, stay' and pull the leash taut with a jerk. This will pull him back into position, and cause him to realise that you still have control of him even though you are not close to him (see diagram).

In the early stages of this lesson always return to the dog rather than calling him up to you, which would most likely cause him to anticipate the recall command, and to follow when you move away. Later you can make him sit and stay off the leash, then, when you are able to move a good distance away without his making any attempt to follow, you can vary the exercise by calling him to you.

These basic lessons learned, you now have a dog which is a pleasure to take anywhere and which is well mannered in

11. 'Sit, stay'

everyday life. Goldens are so easy to train, and when well trained such delightful companions, that a few minutes daily spent in teaching them this good behaviour is so very well worth while. It is a tragedy to see a beautiful Golden completely uncontrolled, straining at the leash, unruly and disobedient, which no one would wish to have brought into their home. One which will sit quietly in a corner when told to stay is, however, a joy to behold, and always a welcome visitor.

CHAPTER 6

ESTABLISHING A KENNEL OR STRAIN

If the intention is to breed Goldens seriously – i.e. to try to produce winning stock generation after generation whether in shows or in trials – there must be no haphazard selection of either the founders of the kennel or their future mates. This chapter, it is hoped, will show the various ways in which success on these lines may be sought.

CHOOSING THE CORRECT BREEDING STOCK

First-class foundation stock is, of course, essential for a successful kennel. A start can be made with one or two bitches from a good strain, which have the correct conformation and temperament. It is not necessary, in the early years, to have your own stud dog, for the best dogs in the breed are available at public stud, but are rarely likely to be for sale. For preference, the foundation stock should come from a strain which has bred true to type for some time.

If one intends to concentrate on a show kennel it is advisable, before purchasing your first Golden, to visit as many Championship shows as possible, to see the winning dogs and, if possible, to study their pedigrees, so that you may form some idea of the strains to which you are most attracted.

Should you intend your Golden to be a future trial participant, as well as being up to show standard, your foundation stock should come from a kennel which has consistently produced winners in both spheres over the years. Those interested solely in trials have the choice also of kennels specialising in producing trial winners.

Rarely in this breed is it found that breeders will sell first-class adult stock, but if or when this is available you must be prepared to pay a good price. It is much more likely that you will find a promising puppy from a well-bred litter. Be prepared to wait until you are able to get just the right one, as so much depends on your first choice, for if the puppy does not turn out well, much time can be wasted, and you may have to start all over again, or try to breed something better in the next generation.

The study of pedigrees should include finding out all you can about the faults and the attributes of the parents, grandparents, etc., of your proposed foundation stock, and the general quality of their progeny. Your puppy's potential is largely governed by the genes it carries, so, although environment plays a certain part in shaping the individual, no matter how well reared he may be, the finished product is only as good, both physically and temperamentally, as its genetic make-up allows. Naturally, it follows that, to build up a winning kennel or strain, you require these forbears to be as near the ideal as possible, for without this prerequisite you cannot hope for top-class animals, themselves likely to produce outstanding stock.

The first essential is breed type, consequently the dog to look for should conform as nearly as possible to the breed Standard as set out in Chapter 4. This Standard was drawn up to indicate a typical Golden Retriever which is capable of doing the natural work of a gundog, and, in addition, has the correct head, bone formation, muscular development, etc., without which the dog is not truly representative of its breed. Some faults can be overlooked, but an untypical specimen should on no account be bred from, for its lack of breed type would be perpetuated. If mated to a typical Golden some of the offspring may possibly be improved, but in their turn they will carry the undesired genes and transmit them to their progeny.

Other essentials in your foundation stock are soundness of temperament and physical soundness. The dog's temperament should be typical of the breed, i.e. kindly and trustworthy in all circumstances, with no sign of nervousness or aggressiveness, and these qualities should be combined with the desire to please that is so vital in a gundog. The physical soundness which should be sought must include the freedom from hereditary veterinary defects, such as Entropion (inverted eyelids), Cryptorchidism, Hereditary Cataract and Hip Dysplasia (all referred to in Chapter 12). In passing, it must be stated that the perfect show dog has yet to be produced, and as they all have their faults, a discerning judge weighs a dog's good points of construction and deportment, etc., against his failings. The outstanding dog with one or two faults invariably wins over the well-made but mediocre dog, lacking in quality.

BREEDING METHODS TO ESTABLISH A STRAIN
The term 'strain' as applied to dog breeding denotes those animals from one family with varying relationships. Of course, it must be born in mind that all dogs carrying one pre-fix will not necessarily be of the same 'strain'. Some, having been bought in by a breeder and his prefix added to their names, may be completely unrelated to the rest of the kennel.

The three methods given here apply equally to dogs required for shows or trials, but in the latter case one must look for outstanding trial records in the forbears.

a. MATING UNRELATED DOGS. It would be extremely difficult to produce consistently good stock generation after generation by constantly mating unrelated dogs. Though this method may produce satisfactory results in the first generation (if the animals bred from are outstanding), it is extremely unlikely that they will breed true to type unless mated back to their close relations. Thus, if the offspring of this unrelated mating are of the desired type and quality, and have the desired tem-perament, the only method of fixing these outstanding qualities in future generations is by mating them in their turn to their relations, who are likely to carry similar genes.

b. LINE-BREEDING. This term generally refers to the mating of individuals related, in varying degrees, to one particular outstanding dog – the aim being to keep the relationship as near as possible to that dog, and to perpetuate his or her qualities. Naturally the best results are obtained when the related dog and bitch to be bred from are themselves good specimens and closely resemble their famous ancestor. It should be stressed that it is useless to line-breed to a mediocre animal, for the whole object of line-breeding is to reproduce greatness, and breeding from animals with poor backgrounds is unlikely to produce satisfactory results.

Typical examples of the relationships which can be described as line-breeding are the mating of uncle to niece, or cousin to cousin.

Example of Line-breeding

Ch. Camrose Fantango

Dorcas Timberscombe Topper	*Dorcas Bruin* Timberscombe Trefoil	{ *D. Bruin*
Golden Camrose Tess	Sunshine of Slat	{ *D. Bruin*

(This example shows line-breeding in which the mating is that of half-uncle and niece, and also of half-cousins – Dorcas Bruin being the common ancestor.)

In order to line-breed successfully it is essential to recognise faults likely to be encountered, and possibly transmitted, equally with the good points which it is hoped to stamp-in, so that these faults may be judiciously eradicated by the careful selection of the individuals to be bred from.

c. IN-BREEDING. This can be the quickest way to 'fix' type, for it is the mating together of very closely related animals (such as father to daughter, brother to sister, etc.), who should conform as nearly as possible to the breed Standard. The resulting progeny may then be expected to carry in duplicate the genes for the outstanding characteristics of the parents.

This method is not advocated for the novice, for in order to create a successful strain in this way it is most necessary to have a full and intimate knowledge of the forbears. As with line-breeding, so in-breeding can fix virtues and also stamp-in faults. It cannot introduce anything new into a strain, it merely brings out what is latent, both good and bad. Because of this, animals used for in-breeding must themselves be outstanding in type and temperament, and have no physical defects or weaknesses. Troubles which may emerge should not be blamed on the system of in-breeding, they are inevitably the

Examples of In-breeding

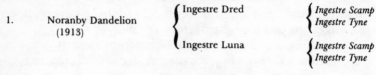

1.   Noranby Dandelion   Ingestre Dred   Ingestre Scamp
         (1913)   Ingestre Tyne

                                Ingestre Luna   Ingestre Scamp
                                                     Ingestre Tyne

(Mating of full-brother and sister)

2.   Dorcas Timberscombe   Dorcas Bruin
         Topper (sire of
         five Champions)   Timberscombe Trefoil Dorcas Bruin

(Mating of father to daughter)

result of faulty judgement concerning the animals used. It is absolutely necessary to be resolute if one wishes to in-breed, refusing any dog a place in the breeding programme who does not closely resemble the ideal, and who is not completely sound in every way.

Planning Future Matings

Much time and thought should be given to planning future matings, and pedigrees should be worked out, putting those of various dogs together with that of your bitch to see how they 'tie up', and bearing in mind, at the same time, how the individual animals are likely to suit one another both physically and genetically. It is advisable to form a 'plan of campaign' from the beginning, with several unborn generations worked out on paper. One must, however, be prepared to alter this plan if the need arises, for the results from some particular mating may not turn out as hoped, and it may be necessary to delete some particular animal from the original breeding plan if its progeny should not come up to the desired standard.

Having decided which breeding plan to adopt, the remaining factor is the selection of the actual dogs to mate together. Through making a study of pedigrees prior to founding your kennel you will have learnt as much as possible about the animals derived from the strain of your choice, and therefore you will have some idea of the good points that you will try to perpetuate and the faults you must endeavour to eradicate. As stated earlier, the two animals to be mated together must both be of high quality, and the good points that it is desired to reproduce must be evident in both partners. It is unwise to mate together two animals carrying similar faults, thus, when a bitch shows a certain failing which you hope to eliminate, she must be mated to a dog who is well-nigh perfect in that particular point. It is useless, for example, mating a very weak-headed bitch to a coarse-headed dog hoping thereby to produce the happy mean. The chances are that you will have some puppies resembling one parent and some the other. The correct method would be to mate your weak-headed bitch to a dog with a head of the correct strength.

Naturally the stud dog to which your bitch is mated will be as nearly ideal as possible, but you would be wise also to make sure that he generally sires really good, typical puppies resembling himself to a large degree – in other words, that he is prepotent. Such a prepotent sire is invaluable when one is trying to establish a good strain, for several bitches can be mated to him and the resulting offspring line-bred back to him.

SELECTING PUPPIES
Your second generation must be selected with the same care as your first, for a mistake may incur much wastage of valuable time. It necessarily follows that if one is breeding with the object of producing some specific qualities, puppies excelling in those points will be retained, while if the object is to eradicate certain failings you will certainly not wish to keep those showing these faults, unless they are absolutely outstanding in other respects.

It is advisable to 'run-on' as many of the puppies as is possible until about six months of age. It is extremely difficult to assess the potential of a puppy younger than this, either regarding points of conformation or temperament, unless, of course, one has an intimate knowledge of the strain from which he comes – and, indeed, even then the expert can experience difficulty. It is a very rash person who will predict with any certainty just how good a two-month-old puppy will turn out when fully grown! If, however, it is essential to choose one at an early age, the way to pick the one with the best conformation, and which looks the most promising, is described in Chapter 5.

SUMMARY
1. To found a successful kennel, start with first-class, typical stock, sound both physically and temperamentally.
2. In order to acquire these attributes, make a thorough study of the individual dogs in the breed, their pedigrees, etc., and make sure your foundation stock is as near to your ideal as possible.
3. Decide which method of breeding is to be carried out, viz.: *a.* Mating unrelated animals of similar outstanding qualities –which may not prove to be successful for more than one generation. *b.* Line-breeding (the safest way to creating a strain). *c.* In-breeding, which should be carried out only by someone with an intimate knowledge of the breed, or under the guidance of such a person.
4. Carefully plan the future matings with a view to determining the most suitable mates for the varying dogs, both from the point of view of pedigree and conformation. Select the resulting puppies carefully, and be prepared to dispense with dogs or lines from your plan of campaign if they do not produce the desired results.

CHAPTER 7

BREEDING

The constant striving for perfection makes breeding the most fascinating of hobbies. It is a good thing, therefore, to set oneself an ideal and it is this which creates the incentive to continue trying to improve one's stock. Disappointments there are in all spheres, but 'hope springs eternal', and there is always the possibility that the ideal will appear in the next litter! The longer the association with the breed, the more of a perfectionist one becomes, and consequently the more difficult it seems to produce the dog which completely satisfies. However, perhaps this is a saving grace, for as long as the failings are recognised something can be done towards improvement.

Goldens are not the breed for anyone desiring to breed for profit, for the raising of Goldens cannot be regarded as a lucrative undertaking. With good management and good luck they can be made to pay their way, but I think very few breeders expect vast profits from their hobby. A word of warning may not come amiss at this point! Be firm and restrict yourself to manageable numbers, for Goldens are very 'taking' dogs and before long you may well find that you have quite a collection!

Some of the great delights of this occupation, apart from the actual process of breeding, are the outside interests which can be derived therefrom. Having reared your 'young hopeful', tried it out at shows and trained it, one may have many happy outings both in the show ring and on the shooting field if it comes up to standard.

THE STUD DOG

The question is often asked whether or not a dog kept as a pet should be used at stud occasionally. Some owners think that it is good for a dog to serve a bitch, but unless he is likely to be regularly used this may possibly store up trouble for the owner, for having had his instincts aroused, he may look for other attractive females, and if they do not come to him, may wander from home in pursuit of his pleasures (Goldens seldom display those objectionable signs of sexual activity common to many other breeds, and are usually gentlemanly in their behaviour).

If it is decided to place the dog at public stud it is the owner's duty to ensure that he is in good condition and virile, and that he is physically sound, and not actively afflicted with any hereditary veterinary defect. It is usually taken for granted that a dog placed at stud is a proved sire. One sometimes sees an advertisement 'free service to prove' applied to a young dog about to be placed at stud, but if a dog is good enough his services will be well sought after, and there is no special reason why his first mating should be a free one. In the unlikely event of his proving sterile, a later free service should be offered to another dog or the fee refunded.

It is advisable to start a young dog at stud fairly early in life and he should serve his first bitch at about a year old. After that he should be restricted to a few bitches for the ensuing year. If left too late before his first attempted service he can become very difficult to manage at a mating, and I have known several dogs who have actually refused to mate. Always make quite sure that his first engagement is likely to be an easy one, and that the bitch does not snap or is otherwise troublesome, for a young dog can easily be put off and lose his confidence for a long time afterwards.

It is just as important for the stud dog to be well cared for and housed as it is for the brood bitch, and in order to safeguard his virility he should be kept in the pink of condition at all times. It can be very disconcerting to take a bitch to a well-known sire and find him untidy and unkempt, and looking as if a square meal were needed, or, alternatively, so fat that the effort of mating the bitch seems exhausting! To keep the dog in top condition it is important that he be given a good balanced diet containing an adequate supply of protein, carbohydrate and vitamins, and that he has plenty of exercise to keep his muscles in good tone.

Where both dogs and bitches are kept there should be adequate facilities for segregation, for it is not easy to keep a keen stud dog in good condition if he is constantly seeing, or encountering the smell of, an in-season bitch. The odour is exuded not only from the vaginal discharge but also from the urine, so no matter what precautions are taken, it is very unlikely that the dog is unaware that some of his kennel mates are interesting, but by keeping him well away he is not constantly sexually excited.

Golden stud dogs are generally not pugnacious, but it is safest not to kennel more than two together, for though they may live together perfectly amicably for years, there may come a time when there is a disagreement. If a quarrel starts between two dogs, invariably others will join in, so care should be exercised at all times. For this reason, it is most unwise to return a stud dog to his kennel-mate immediately he has mated a bitch.

The In-season Bitch

Goldens very seldom have their first season before nine months of age. Usually it occurs from nine to twelve months, and occasionally as late as fifteen months. After this first season it may recur every six months, but it is quite common for there to be an interval of nine months or more.

It is certainly not advisable to mate the bitch until she is fifteen to eighteen months old, nor is it a good thing to wait much longer before mating her, for it is my belief that she produces her first litter more easily when her muscular tone has just reached its peak. If she is to be mated it is wise to take the precation of worming her before she comes into season, and for this use one of the preparations containing piperazine citrate, such as Bob Martin's Dextrox Minor, given according to the instructions. Of course the bitch must not be mated too often, and she should certainly not be expected to rear more than one litter a year.

The season (or oestrus) is generally preceded by the enlarging of the vulva, a slight mucous discharge, frequent urination and constant licking of the vulva. These preliminary indications may last for several days or longer, or may indeed be hardly noticeable at all before the season really starts, which is when the blood-stained discharge commences. This discharge may be slight for the first day or two, but it increases as the season progresses. The vulva becomes swollen and hard during the first week, and the bitch is not ready to be mated until this has softened, which is usually about ten days from the onset, at which time the coloured discharge decreases.

It is a fallacy to suppose that one should wait until the coloured discharge has entirely ceased before mating, for it sometimes continues for the whole three weeks of the season. A far safer guide to the right time is the bitch's own behaviour. If kennelled with other bitches she usually displays this readiness for mating by standing with the hindlegs rigid and the tail turned to one side if they are attentive to her, and she will also encourage them to mount her. If she is kept alone her reactions can be tested by rubbing the hand round her thighs or 'trousers', or by touching the vulva, when, if the time is ripe, she will twitch her tail to one side. There can be no hard-and-fast rule as to the correct time for mating, but Goldens will usually stand for a dog from about the tenth to the fifteenth day of their season, and I have had fruitful matings on all these days – the correct time, of course, varies with the individual. Occasionally some may be ready earlier and others later, but the twelth or thirteenth day is the one on which most bitches are mated.

During the third week of the season the genital organs begin to subside and the season is usually over by about the twenty-first day.

Naturally, the in-season bitch must not be allowed her freedom or she may seek out her own mate. This can happen even within the first few days, so exercise great care in ensuring her security, for ten minutes away from home is quite long enough for the local roué to get to work! Should such a misalliance occur it can upset all your breeding plans for that particular season. In the event of this happening, contact your vet within twenty-four hours and he will administer an injection of stilboestrol, which brings the bitch fully into season again, and usually avoids the unwanted litter. Do not however, allow this to be a regular procedure, for the frequent use of this injection may cause womb trouble later in the bitch's life.

It is also essential to keep her away from all other dogs after she has been mated, for it is well known that dual conception can take place, and even though she has been mated with one of her own breed, if, later in the same season, she has a union with another dog, there is no way of knowing whether or not all the puppies are the progeny of the first dog.

The theory of Telegony (when a bitch had conceived to a mongrel and future litters were thought to be tainted with his blood) has been scientifically proved to be impossible, so a misalliance at one season cannot have any detrimental effect on subsequent litters.

There are various preparations on the market for deterring unwanted suitors, though my experience with these is that the really troublesome dog soon associates these strong-smelling substances with in-season bitches. They may well be very useful in deterring the inexperienced dog, who would probably not be a nuisance in any case, but I have watched an 'old campaigner' wind the smell of oil of eucalyptus or citronella, and track my bitch right round the perimeter of a very large field! Dosing with Amplex and swabbing the hindquarters with Amplexol, however, helps to remove the odour, and seems to be quite effective.

If the bitch is to be taken out for exercise it is wisest to take her away from home in the car, there will not then be the nuisance of followers tracking her home. Naturally she must not be let off the leash if there is any likelihood of her running off, or if there are any other dogs in the vicinity.

MATING

The stud dog owner should be approached well before the bitch is due to come into season so that he may plan his dog's commitments. He should then be notified immediately the coloured discharge commences, so that the day for the mating can be determined. It is advisable to keep a strict watch to make sure that the prearranged day is going to be acceptable to the bitch, for a mating too early or too late may not prove fruitful.

It is, of course, the accepted practice for the bitch to be taken to the dog (life would be very hectic for the owner of a popular sire were he to consent to visit bitches all over the country!). It is usual for the dog to stand at stud at a specified fee, payable at the time of service, and any variation in terms should be agreed beforehand. It must be stressed that the fee is payable for the actual service, not for results, for if a bitch 'misses' it is unlikely to be the fault of the proven stud dog. Owners of stud dogs will generally offer a free service at the bitch's next season should the previous mating prove fruitless, but this should not be regarded as a right, rather as a courtesy.

Only in the most exceptional circumstances should the bitch not be accompanied by her owner for the mating. In this event, and should she have to travel by train, she should be sent in a travelling box which has adequate ventilation and sufficient room for her both to stand up and to turn round. A good plan is to have an inner half-door made, so that the person meeting her at the other end can attach a leash to her collar before taking her out of the box, thus making quite sure that she cannot escape.

Accustom her to sleeping in the box at various times before she undertakes the journey, to lessen her anxiety *en route*. Make sure that the stud dog owner knows the full travelling arrangements, and particularly the arrival time, and do not send her until she is ready for mating. Ask that she be kept overnight after the mating, and returned the next day.

On arrival at the stud dog's home, the bitch should be allowed to relieve herself. The dog and bitch should be introduced in a run or other confined space, both being kept on the leash. If the bitch appears flirtatious, and shows no sign of snapping, the dog can be released, the bitch being kept on the leash all the time. She may at first resent the dog's advances, so time should be given for a preliminary courtship. Often ten minutes spent in allowing her to settle down and get used to the dog can save endless trouble, and will result in a relaxed animal, rather than one which might snap and try to pull away at the crucial moment.

The dog should then be encouraged to mount the bitch, whilst her collar is held by her owner, and she is supported under the flank by the dog's owner, to prevent her sitting down. If the dog will not co-operate whilst she is being held, allow him to mount her without interference, but as soon as he shows sign of having penetrated, she should be held steady. It is most essential to get the young dog used to having the bitch held for him in his early stud work, otherwise it is possible that he may resent help on later occasions, when this may be very necessary.

If, after giving the bitch sufficient time to settle down, she should still appear unwilling to allow the dog to mount her, hold her firmly, keeping her head forward, and should she attempt to snap it is advisable to tape her muzzle. Usually she becomes quite submissive when the dog mounts her, and most of this resistance is found with pet bitches who are not used to mixing with other dogs, and who actually have to be taught the facts of life! The experienced stud dog owner can usually tell whether a bitch is being difficult through fear or obstinacy, or if she is not ready for mating, through having been brought too early, or when the acceptance period is nearly over.

The dog sometimes has difficulty in penetrating, and this may be overcome if the vulva is well greased with vaseline. Should he still experience difficulty, it is well to make sure that there is no malformation of the bitch, such as a vaginal stricture or polypus. If organically all is well, perhaps there is some maladjustment of heights. Should the bitch be too tall for the dog, it is helpful to stand her on a slightly lower level, and should the opposite be the case, then obviously she should be raised for him. Some dogs seem incapable of getting themselves into the correct position, and the placing of two fingers around the bitch's vulva will help to guide him into position. Should things still prove unsuccessful, rest both animals for about half an hour, and often, when they are re-introduced, all goes well.

When the 'tie' is effected, i.e. when the dog becomes quiescent and the union is taking place, his front legs should be gently lowered from the bitch and he should be allowed to stand side by side with her. Some dogs will immediately get off the bitch and turn back to back with her, by throwing a hindleg over her back, but unless he appears uncomfortable, never insist on his doing this, for any interference can upset a young dog, and it is not necessary for him to adopt this position.

The tie may last from about ten to thirty minutes, or even

longer, during which time it is advisable to hold the bitch, as she may become restless and try to pull away or sit down, with disastrous consequences for them both. During the whole of the tie the two animals are locked together, and nothing should be done to separate them. When the union is completed the dog will come away naturally. The bitch should then be allowed to rest quietly for an hour or so before the homeward journey is undertaken.

It is quite possible for a bitch to conceive even though there has been no actual tie. If the dog penetrates and comes away fully extended, it is possible that he may have ejected sperms, so on no account should another dog be used. It is advisable, however, later to repeat the mating with the same dog to ensure success.

After the mating the dog should be rubbed down with a Dettol solution, to remove the odour of the bitch, then he too should be shut up on his own for a while. If this precaution is not taken he will probably receive unwelcome attention from his kennel-mate, who will sniff him all over. Should he smell the bitch, he may attempt to mount him, and not even the best-tempered stud dog cares for this attention, from another male.

THE IN-WHELP BITCH

The bitch will already have been wormed, but if there are still any doubts as to whether she is clear of these parasites it is advisable to re-worm her, using the same preparation as previously, as this has no toxic effects, about a week after mating and again one week later, to obviate the possibility of worms being transmitted to the puppies.

She should be allowed to lead a normal life for the first few weeks, and needs no special care up to four weeks after mating. She should be allowed plenty of exercise throughout her pregnancy to enable her to keep in muscular condition, thus making whelping much easier. Throughout the gestation period she should have a diet containing plenty of protein, and an adequate supply of calcium phosphate and Vitamin D added to her food. She will need at least one pound of meat a day for the first four weeks, which should be increased to one and a half pounds from then on, but her normal intake of carbo-hydrates should not be increased. No matter how appealingly she may look, do not be tempted to pander to her, hard though this may seem, for a bitch in whelp generally develops a large appetite, but she must not be allowed to put on superfluous flesh. Towards the end of her time her meals should be divided up into two or three a day, as large quantities of food only serve to distend the stomach and make the bitch uncomfortable. During the last two weeks she may be given milk, and the occasional egg is always beneficial.

One sometimes finds that a bitch becomes finicky over her food during early pregnancy, and even has occasional bouts of sickness. This generally lasts only for the first few weeks, and from then on all goes well, and no concern need be felt if she seems otherwise in good health and eats her full ration of meat.

It may be difficult to ascertain for several weeks whether or not she is in whelp. One of the early signs of conception having taken place is that the vulva remains somewhat enlarged during pregnancy, and it stays slightly swollen right through the gestation period. Sometimes the behaviour of the bitch changes. She becomes lethargic and takes care of herself, but this can be no real guide, for some matrons do this after every season whether they have been mated or not. Other signs of pregnancy are the enlargement and pinkness of the teats by about the fifth week, the filling out of the loins after this time and the desire to drink more water than usual. If she is carrying a large litter the bitch usually fills out considerably during the last two weeks and may become very heavy. During the last week before parturition the movement of the puppies is very obvious, particularly when the bitch is lying on her side.

She should not be allowed to play too exuberantly, for any undue roughness may injure her or her unborn puppies. Most probably she will refrain from violent exercise of her own volition. After the fifth week she should not be allowed to jump, and long car rides are inadvisable, and towards the end of the pregnancy they should be discontinued. Otherwise her life should continue along normal lines.

The full term of gestation is sixty-three days, but this varies, and some bitches will whelp earlier than this, others a few days

later. Provided the bitch is well and shows no undue
restlessness or loss of appetite, has no dark-coloured discharge
or rise in temperature, nature is best left to its own devices.
Should she, however, go three days over her time without any
sign of impending parturition it is advisable to consult
your vet.

WHELPING QUARTERS

The whelping quarters, which must be scrupulously clean and
disinfected, should be made ready well in advance, for a bitch
can easily surprise one by starting to produce her family early.
If she is to whelp out of doors she should be housed in a large,
light kennel, high enough for you to stand upright in, and it
must have plenty of room for the puppies to run about in
when they are old enough. I think the ideal whelping kennel is
about 6 ft. high, by 6 ft. wide and 10 ft. long.

The whelping box should be about 4 ft. × 4 ft., with the sides
and back being 2 ft. 6 in. high, for this keeps the box free from
draughts. The front should be in two or more sections, so that
it may be heightened as the puppies grow. Before whelping,
only one section should be inserted, so that the bitch has easy
access, but when the puppies are about ten days old it will be
necessary to add another section to prevent them climbing
out.

A rail round the inside of the box (at the back and on the two
sides) will prevent the bitch from crushing the puppies, and
this should be about 5 in. from the sides and 5 in. up
from the floor.

When the puppies are old enough to be allowed out of the
box there should be somewhere for the dam to get out of their
way, for she should not be constantly plagued by frolicsome
puppies. It is useful to have a lid which fixes over the top of the
whelping box, so that when the puppies are four weeks old
this may be put on and used for the bitch to lie on. Alternatively, have a bench fixed in some other part of the kennel high
enough to be out of the puppies' reach.

Regardless of the time of year, it is essential to have heating
and lighting in the kennel, as whelpings often take place during
the night. Even in summer the nights can be quite cold, and
newly born puppies need a temperature of at least 75°F.

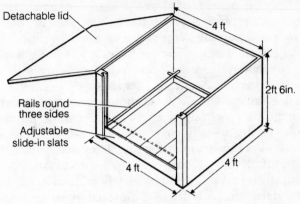

Detachable lid

4 ft

2ft 6in.

Rails round
three sides

Adjustable
slide-in slats

4 ft

4 ft

12. Whelping box

(24°C.) I find that infra-red lamps of the dull-emitter type are
ideal. They should be suspended about 3 ft. above the whelping box, but should be capable of being adjusted, and the
strictest of safety precautions should be taken. If the weather is
not too cold a 150–250 watt lamp is adequate, but if the litter
arrives during the worst of the winter, when the temperature is
very low, as much as 450 watts may be necessary. Even if the
litter is to be reared in the house it is advantageous to have an
infra-red lamp over the box, for no matter how warm the
room is, the puppies are much more restful if they have a
direct, gentle heat on them and they do not have to use up
energy trying to keep warm.

Of course, this heating is only used when the puppies are
very small, and it should be discontinued as soon as they are
able to move around, for they should be gradually hardened
off before they have access to the outside world. Puppies of
mine reared thus have come through some of the toughest of
winters, and have been able to play outside by the time they
were five to six weeks old without any adverse effect.

WHELPING

Have everything in readiness so that there is no last-minute
panic whilst you are keeping an eye on the bitch. The infra-red
lamp should be in place (as described in 'Whelping Quarters'),
and layers of newspapers should be spread in the whelping

box. Large quantities of clean, dry papers should be readily available to replace those in the box as they become soiled during the whelping. You will also need sterilised scissors, several towels, brandy for the bitch if required, a Thermos flask of warm milk, a bowl or bucket of Dettol solution and some soap for hand washing. I also have a Thermos flask of tea or coffee for myself, in case it should prove difficult to leave the bitch, for whelping is a very thirst-making process!

Goldens are usually easy whelpers and it is unusual for them to experience any difficulty. They also generally make wonderful mothers. Notify your vet well in advance as to when the puppies are due, so that he may note down the anticipated arrival date. I usually leave a message as soon as the bitch shows signs of the onset of parturition, so that he knows the position, and is available if required.

As mentioned earlier, the usual gestation period is regarded as sixty-three days, and most bitches whelp fairly well to time, but it is not uncommon for them to be a little early or a little late (I have experienced perfectly normal whelpings as much as seven days early, and also seven days late, but these are extremes and should not be regarded as usual). If there should be no sign of the onset of labour by the sixty-sixth day it is advisable to have your vet ascertain that all is well. The bitch's temperature always drops to approximately 99°F. (37°C.) some twenty-four hours or so before labour starts, and this temperature fall is one of the safest guides as to when this is about to happen.

The first stage of parturition is the gradual softening and dilating of the birth passages, and until this is completed the puppies cannot be born. It can last for an hour or two, or continue up to twenty-four hours, and it manifests itself in the restlessness of the bitch, who constantly digs holes and makes beds. There is violent panting, interspersed with periods of quiescence, and a 'far-away' or glazed look is noticeable in her eyes – this look is quite unmistakable in the bitch about to whelp. During this first stage there may be a loss of appetite, occasional vomiting and also a white mucous discharge from the vagina. She should be closely watched during this period so that the beginning of the second stage is not missed, and it is wise to keep her with you if you are not able to spare the time to stay in the kennel with her.

Ch. Camrose Tallyrand of Anbria

Int. Ch. Cabus Cadet

The author showing Ch. Camrose Lucius

Ch. Camrose Nicolas of Westley

Ch. Styal Stefanie of Camrose (top winning bitch of all time –
27 C.C.s)   *Dog World*

Ch. Nortonwood Faunus

Ch. Camrose Cabus Christopher (top winning sire of all time –
41 C.C.s)   *Diane Pearce*

Ch. Camrose Fabius Tarquin

The second stage is when a puppy enters the pelvis, and this becomes apparent by the bitch straining downwards. This straining is usually accompanied by a slight grunting noise, and is followed by persistent panting and possibly trembling. The time at which these first strains take place should be noted, for this is the commencement of actual labour.

At first these contractions may be few and not very strenuous, but later they become stronger and more frequent. The time taken for the first puppy to be born varies; some bitches give only two or three strains and a puppy appears, whereas others may take up to three hours. The experienced eye can generally tell, by the increasing regularity and strength of the strains, that all is progressing normally, but those in doubt should contact their vet if no puppy has been born within two hours of the strains beginning.

Some time before a puppy is born the water bag may be seen at the entrance to the vulva and this will then break. This is a sure sign that a puppy is on its way. Each puppy is born completely encased in a thin membranous bag, and has its own placenta or afterbirth attached to the umbilical cord. Occasionally this bag will be broken just before the puppy emerges and a clear fluid is released.

Normally, the puppy will appear head first, though it is not uncommon for them to arrive the wrong way round, with the hindfeet appearing first (breech birth). When the first part of the membranous sac containing the puppy appears, as a result of the downward straining of the bitch, it may be partially withdrawn, but it will reappear with the new strains, and subsequently will be produced in its entirety. When the bag is intact it is usually broken by the bitch immediately the puppy is delivered. After this she will eat the placenta (this is perfectly normal and should not be discouraged), cut through the umbilical cord with her teeth, near the puppy's naval, and proceed to clean the puppy.

Occasionally a bitch fails to take any interest in her first-born, and it is then up to the owner to do the vitally necessary removing of the membrane, which should be broken round the puppy's mouth, with finger and thumb, for until released the puppy is unable to breathe. The umbilical cord should then be severed at least 1 or 2 in. from the body to avoid the possibility of rupturing the puppy. This should be done by tearing it apart with your finger nails, pulling towards the puppy's body, to avoid any excessive bleeding. Rub the puppy well with a warm towel to dry it and to stimulate its breathing, then put it to the dam. She will usually take an interest in it when it starts to feed.

Should the 'envelope' be broken before birth – particularly if the puppy appears feet first – it is vital that its delivery be completed as soon as possible, as it is in some danger of suffocation, and may have become half drowned *en route*. Hold the puppy round its middle (never pull a puppy by its hindlegs) and gradually ease it from the vulva with each downward strain the bitch makes. Never pull hard, but gently, with a little downward pressure in rhythm with the bitch. When the puppy has been freed from its afterbirth hold it in a warm towel and shake it, head downwards, to get any fluid out of its lungs. Should it appear limp and lifeless when born, it is well to rub it vigorously with a towel down the whole length of its back, and with strong movements in both upward and downward directions, to stimulate the breathing. This usually revives the puppy, but should it still seem rather weak, it is beneficial to administer a drop or two of brandy, and, rather than putting it with the bitch, keep it separate for a while – either on a hot-water bottle or by a fire.

Occasionally, a puppy may be born completely devoid of membrane or afterbirth, but this need cause no alarm, for the retained afterbirth will usually come away later without any difficulty.

There is no regular interval between the birth of the puppies, the second may come only a few minutes after the first, or half an hour or so may elapse before it appears. Sometimes a bitch may have a long rest between the birth of her puppies and may have a sleep of up to two hours before straining recommences. This is quite normal and often happens after the birth of several puppies when there is a large litter on the way. If, however, she should keep straining constantly for two hours or more without a puppy being born, it is advisable to contact your vet, for there is a possibility that a puppy may be wrongly placed, and this constant straining over a long period will only exhaust her. Some bitches whelp quickly, and may produce a litter of eight puppies in two hours, others may take as long as eight hours to produce the same number.

Offer the mother a drink of warm milk and glucose occasionally, and should she appear at all tired, a teaspoonful of brandy will help to revive her. Stay with her throughout the whelping, for most Goldens seem much happier with their owners present. I have known several bitches who would not settle at all if I left them once labour had actually started, and many puppies would have been lost had I not been there during the whelping.

Some people advocate placing the puppies in a separate box away from the bitch until the whelping is over, but I think this causes her to fret unduly, and to become apprehensive when she hears them crying. I prefer to put each puppy round the 'milk bar' as soon as the bitch has cleaned it up, and encourage it to feed – although this is usually unnecessary, for they nearly always find their way there immediately! Consequently the bitch is contented and prepared to settle down to the job of producing the rest of her litter. When the arrival of another seems imminent it is advisable to move the puppies to one side, so that she may attend to matters without harming the earlier arrivals. After the birth of a puppy I remove as much of the soiled paper as possible and put down clean layers, and as soon as this is done the puppies should again be placed to her.

It is sometimes very difficult to be certain that all the puppies have been born, for if any afterbirths have been retained the bitch may continue to strain for some time after the birth of the last puppy. This is most confusing, for one is often unable to distinguish between the effort to expel the afterbirth and the strains for a puppy about to be born. I think it advisable, therefore, if there is any doubt, to call the vet, for if there is a puppy remaining, an injection of oxytocin usually produces it.

When the whelping is over, the bitch should be given a good drink of milk and glucose, and allowed to settle down to a well-earned sleep for several hours before getting her out and changing her bedding.

The usual size of a litter is from six to eight puppies, but Goldens, being prolific, often produce litters of ten or more. I am not one of those who would destroy a healthy puppy, and I unhesitatingly assert that all should have their chance of survival. It is necessary, for obvious humanitarian reasons, when there is malformation or chronic weakness for the puppy to be painlessly destroyed by an injection administered by a veterinary surgeon as soon as possible. Never attempt to dispose of a puppy yourself, for this will almost certainly cause unnecessary suffering.

There is no reason why a strong healthy Golden should not successfully rear eleven or twelve puppies as long as the breeder is prepared to spend the time to supplement food intake right from the start, nor is it necessary to contemplate a foster-mother, unless the bitch has very little milk, or is ill. It is very easy to teach puppies to take additional food from a syringe (with the needle removed, of course!), as will be described under 'Rearing of Puppies', and with this, together with a protein-full diet for the dam, neither she nor her puppies should be any the less robust than if there had been a normal-sized litter.

Care Of The Nursing Bitch

After whelping, the bitch may be reluctant to leave her puppies, but she should be made to go out periodically, if necessary taken out on a leash. During her absence her bedding can be changed and layers of clean newspapers put down on top of which you can add some of the modern acrylic, canvas-backed bedding, which aids the puppies to get a grip, and helps to keep them warm. I find this (or just newspapers) much the best bedding for the first three weeks, as straw can harbour livestock, wood-wool enables puppies to become wrapped up in it, and rugs or sacking can be pushed into a heap with the consequent risk of puppies suffocating.

For the first twenty-four hours after whelping the diet should be light, and the bitch should be encouraged to drink as much milk and water as she will to help increase her production of milk. The sooner she is put on to the normal nursing diet the better, and this should contain about three times her normal diet, so should consist of 3 lb. of meat (or three large tins of meat) and three times her normal ration of biscuit meal. An occasional egg is good and, of course, her calcium and vitamin supplements must be continued throughout the nursing and weaning periods (if this is not already provided in the food). Meals should be given three or four times a day, for she will have a large appetite, and therefore should be given as much food as she can reasonably take. Such foods as Complan, which is full of protein, and Lactagol, both of which stimulate the milk production, are excellent additions to the diet.

The normal vaginal discharge, which at first is dark green, later becomes red, and this may continue for two weeks or more, but any sign of a yellowish discharge, containing pus, should be regarded with suspicion. The motions for the first day or so after whelping will be loose and almost black, but they should become normal within a few days. The bitch's temperature should be closely checked for the first few days, and should it rise above 102.5°F. (39°C.), veterinary advice should be sought. There will always be a rise of a degree or so, but it should drop to the normal of 101.5°F. (38.6°C.) within four days of whelping. It is unusual for there to be any troublesome after-effects, but she should be watched for signs of undue restlessness, apprehension or loss of appetite.

During the first week make sure that the milk is being drawn from all the glands, for it is quite common for the bitch to lie in such a way as to stop the puppies sucking from some of the teats, and, in consequence, the glands become hard, and if prompt attention is not given, abscesses may form. At the first sign of hardening, some of the milk must be drawn off and the puppies encouraged to suck from that gland. If this attention is given periodically all should be well, but if it is left for any length of time it may become necessary to apply hot fomentations to soften the gland before drawing off some of the milk. If the condition is allowed to progress, mastitis may set in, and the milk may be affected, and there will be a rise in temperature. In this event it is advisable to call your vet, who will give the bitch injections of antibiotics, which will soon put matters right.

A regular watch should also be kept on the puppies to make sure that all are thriving equally. The surest sign of their contentment is that they lie peacefully with their dam, with full tummies, have chubby necks and fat little thighs, and are almost as broad as they are long! Do not be perturbed if you see the little creatures twitching in their sleep, for this is the normal thing for a healthy puppy. Any thin, elongated member of the family has probably been pushed out of the 'milk bar', so its attendance there must be supervised to ensure that it draws its full ration. If the puppies cry a lot, are always restlessly moving around, and are constantly giving protesting squeaks when sucking, it is probable that the bitch's milk is not flowing easily, or that she has not enough to satisfy their needs. In this case it may well be necessary to supplement their food with a feeding bottle, and to have your vet make sure that the bitch is not ill.

Because of their gentle natures, most Goldens, if their owners are present do not resent strangers visiting them and their litters. It is, however, advisable to restrict visitors to the minimum at first, so that the bitch remains undisturbed, for a restless bitch often means discontented puppies. Visit her only to feed her and let her out for exercise for the first week or so, and keep her shut in her kennel between times. She should not be allowed very much exercise until the puppies are being weaned.

The puppies' claws soon grow, become needle-sharp, and after a time lacerate the bitch, which may cause her to be reluctant to feed them. It is therefore advisable to cut the claws once a week until the puppies are able to wear them down by running about on a hard surface.

Should it be considered desirable to have the dew-claws taken off, this should be done by a veterinary surgeon within a few days of birth, but this is not essential for Golden Retrievers, and I have never considered it necessary to have it done.

For the normal-sized litter of up to eight or nine puppies there is little for the breeder to do for the first three weeks other than to care for the dam, change her bedding regularly and to see that all is well with her and her family, as she will keep her puppies warm and well fed, and their nest scrupulously clean.

When the weaning process begins, the bitch's intake of food should be gradually reduced, for as the puppies take less milk from her she will consequently require less food, and by the time the puppies are completely weaned she should be back on to her normal diet.

REARING OF PUPPIES

There is no reason, as was said earlier, why a bitch should not rear eleven or twelve puppies as long as the breeder is prepared to supplement their food from the start, and that the bitch is being very well fed and given a protein-full diet and additional calcium and vitamins. There is absolutely no reason why the puppies should be undernourished or smaller than if there had been only eight who had been given no additional food until three to four weeks old, nor will the bitch herself be pulled down. I have reared two litters, both consisting of eleven puppies, born within a week of each other, and with this supplementary bottle-feeding most of the puppies were, if anything, larger than average at eight weeks old. I admit that bottle-feeding twenty-two little mouths three or four times a day is certainly time-consuming, but anyone who intends to breed dogs must be prepared to devote time to it.

I have found that supplementary feeding three or four times a day is quite adequate, and for the first ten days I use a small syringe. I prefer this to trying to persuade the puppies to take the milk from a feeding bottle, as the milk can gradually be squeezed into their mouths and you can tell exactly how much each puppy has taken. Give each one as much milk as it will take at each feed – usually about 5 ml. to begin with, but this will increase rapidly as the puppy becomes accustomed to this method of feeding.

For this supplementary feeding (as for weaning and rearing the puppies later on) one of the proprietary full-cream dried-milk powders should be used, mixed strictly according to the instructions. Cows' milk is not sufficiently concentrated for puppies, and does not contain an adequate supply of fat, and should only be used if fortified with full-cream dried milk. A little sugar or glucose added to the mixture is also beneficial.

Newly born Goldens have pink noses and pads, but these gradually turn black within the first day or so. For the first ten days of their lives they do not see or hear, but at two weeks their eyes are completely open, though they do not focus properly, and by this time they are also able to hear. Until they are about three weeks old their activity is limited to crawling round the box, but gradually strength comes to their limbs, and at about this age they get up on their feet and begin to stagger around.

Unless the litter is exceptionally large, the bitch will feed all the puppies for the first three weeks of their lives, but after this the breeder must start taking over. At this age the puppies should be wormed for the first time, preferably with a preparation made from piperazine citrate, and given exactly according to the puppy's weight. Your veterinary surgeon will be able to supply you with this worming substance. Puppies do not need to be fasted, and the tablet is given just after feeding. Three weeks is also the time for the puppies to have their first meals. Start by putting a little meat on your hand and placing it in the puppy's mouth. He will soon realise that this is good, and avidly eat it, sniffing round for more. This hand-feeding at first helps to establish the human-puppy bond, for soon the human hand is associated with something pleasant. Do this twice a day for the first two or three days (giving a piece of meat about the size of a walnut), then the meat can be put on to a dish, and the quantity gradually increased. It is not necessary at this stage to give extra milk, as the puppies are getting plenty of this from their dam.

By now the puppies will be exploring every corner of their box, and their mother will be leaving them for several hours at a time, only returning to the box to clean and feed them. The bedding will be getting very wet now, so will need changing much more often.

At four weeks they will be very active, and the boards at the front of the box should be removed to allow the puppies free access around the kennel. At this stage I remove the acrylic bedding and newspapers, and replace them by shredded paper in the whelping box – this gives a warm, comfortable bed, and is easily replaceable when necessary. I also put sawdust on the floor of the kennel, as this helps to keep the puppies clean and sweet smelling. Now is the time to put the lid on the whelping box, if you have one, as this will allow the bitch to get away from the puppies. Alternatively, she should have a bed out of their reach, so that she can rest peacefully when she wishes. If the weather is good enough she should be given free access to the kennel, and be allowed into her run

when she so desires. At this stage a third meal, made of milk
and cereal, should be introduced into the puppies' diet – I use
Weetabix, but one of the prepared baby cereals can be
given if preferred.

There are many good puppy milks on the market, which
should be given according to the instructions. Alternatively,
goats' milk or tinned milk may be used, which must be somewhat diluted. Start giving the milk feed on a small saucer, and
put each puppy to it in turn. Should the puppy not attempt to
lap, then put its nose to the dish and let some of the milk go
into its mouth. It will soon decide that it tastes good and look
for more.

By the time the puppies are five weeks old they should have
been introduced to various types of food, for by now their
mother's supply of milk is decreasing. It is very important that
this weaning process be a very gradual one, so all additions
and increases to the diet should be made carefully, for if large
amounts of strange foods are suddenly given, stomachs may
easily become upset and the puppies may develop diarrhoea.
If this should happen a little gripe water is helpful, and one
level saltspoonful of kaolin powder given three times daily will
soon clear it up. At five weeks an additional milk meal should
be given, mixed with Weetabix or baby cereal. If fresh meat is
being consumed the puppies should now be given calcium
and vitamin supplements, but these should not be taken if the
puppies are on a diet of tinned meat as these are already
included. If the weather is good the puppies can be allowed
into the run for short periods, always being returned to their
kennel when they are ready for a sleep; they should never be
allowed to lie around on cold concrete or in the pouring rain.
At five weeks they should be given their second worming, and
this should be repeated every two weeks until the puppies are
three months old. This is a very important regime and one
which should never be neglected, for the sooner the puppies
are free from worms then the healthier they will be.

At six weeks the feeding should be in the following quantities for each puppy:

8.30 a.m.   4 oz. fresh or tinned meat with ½ Weetabix
              or other cereal mixed with warm water

1.00 p.m.	¼ pint warm milk with Weetabix
5.30 p.m.	4 oz. meat with ½ Weetabix or other cereal mixed with warm water
10.00 p.m.	¼ pint warm milk with ½ Weetabix

The dam should still have free access to the puppies whenever she wants, but she may prefer to be taken away from them at night. Most of my bitches stay with their puppies until they go to their new homes and do not want to be separated from them, and I consider it cruel to take a bitch from her puppies if she still wants to be with them. I find that this way the bitch's milk will dry up almost completely by the time the puppies go, leaving no problems. If you should find the bitch still full of milk when you are trying to get her away then it is advisable to draw a little milk off periodically – not too much as this will merely stimulate the milk production.

At seven weeks the feeding should be:

8.30 a.m.	5 oz. meat with 1 Weetabix or other cereal mixed with warm water
1.00 p.m.	⅓ pint milk with 1 Weetabix
5.30 p.m.	5 oz. meat with 1 Weetabix
10.00 p.m.	⅓ pint milk with 1 Weetabix

It is quite usual for the bitch to regurgitate some of her food for her offspring from the time the puppies are about six or seven weeks old. This can generally be prevented by holding her head up and keeping her mouth closed whilst she is feeding them, for this is the time when she most usually vomits back her food. It is also a good idea to keep her away from the puppies altogether for an hour or so after she has had a meal, for it is essential that she should retain the nourishment from her own food.

By the time the puppies are eight weeks old she will probably be reluctant to allow the puppies to feed from her very much, and she will certainly only permit this for short times. Now they are completely weaned and are ready to go to their new homes their feeding should continue as given in Chapter 5 under the heading 'Feeding'.

SELLING PUPPIES

It is advisable to insert the advertisements for your puppies when they are about four weeks of age, so that prospective buyers will see them at the time when they are most appealing. Prospective purchasers are not likely to appear unless the advertising has been done skilfully. If the puppies are to go either as pets or as show dogs the local papers and dog journals are excellent media. If they are to be sold principally as working dogs the advertisements should be inserted in the usual magazines read by shooting people. The age, breeding and potentialities should be clearly stated. Undoubtedly you will wish to find the best possible homes for your puppies, so it is never good to sell them cheaply or on 'hire purchase' terms. People who are unwilling or unable to pay a good price for a puppy are not usually able to offer the best homes. On the other hand, no one paying a good price is likely to neglect the puppy.

Try as far as possible to ensure that the right puppy goes to the right home. Some idea can be formed of the puppies' characters when they are still of quite tender age, so the really boisterous one is not for the house-proud who want a docile pet. Persuade these people to take one who seems gentle and quiet. Neither should the one which appears rather timid go to a family containing several noisy children.

Have the puppy's registration card, pedigree and transfer form all made out ready for the purchaser to take when he comes for the puppy. He should also be given a feeding chart, comprising all instructions for feeding the dog throughout puppyhood and adult life, instructions with regard to worming, particulars about inoculating him, etc. Impress upon the purchaser the importance of keeping the puppy at home until it has been inoculated against distemper, etc., and advise him to contact his vet regarding this as soon as he takes his puppy home. Most of the present-day inoculations can be done at eight weeks and the second injection given a few weeks later. The puppy should then be re-inoculated against Parvovirus at sixteen and twenty weeks. Also advise the new owner to worm the puppy again regularly until three months.

TRANSPORTATION

If the puppies are to be sent by train or air, travelling boxes made of strong plywood which are light and durable are the most suitable. They are easily obtainable, for many firms make them in various sizes, and, of course, they can be used over and over again. The type I recommend has a door at the front which is half plywood and half weldmesh or steel bars, thus giving plenty of ventilation. These also have holes at sides or back, which allow air to circulate throughout. The dimensions must allow sufficient room for the puppy to stand up, lie down and turn round. To determine these he must be measured from the root of his tail to the tip of his nose, and from the top of his head to the ground, plus about 2 in. over each actual measurement.

Whenever fully grown dogs have to be sent on a journey an inner half-door, made of weldmesh on a wooden frame, should be fixed to the kennel, inside the door proper. This enables the box to be opened and the dog to be fed or put on a leash without the possibility of its escaping, and it will also prevent the dog chewing its way out of the door.

If he is to be sent by train find out well in advance the time of trains and fully inform those meeting him at the other end. Make certain that the stations involved will handle livestock and routing of the puppy. If he has any change *en route* be certain that the officials at the station concerned are notified so that they can ensure his making his connection.

If he is to be sent by air the same things apply, but contact the airline concerned about a week before the dog is to travel, for there are considerable formalities to be completed in connection with his passage.

If the dog is to go abroad, by whatever means of transport, it will require a veterinary certificate of health, issued within a week of its departure. It also must have an export pedigree, issued by the Kennel Club. To obtain this for a male you must have a certificate from a vet stating that the dog is entire (i.e. that both testicles have descended into the scrotum). You must also enquire from the Ministry of Agriculture and Fisheries if the country of his destination has any special import restrictions.

Whenever possible I avoid sending dogs by sea, but if this has to be it is wise to engage one of the shipping agents to complete the arrangements for you, for they know the shortest routes and most suitable shipping lines.

CHAPTER 8

KENNELS AND RUNS

The subject-matter of this chapter is essentially for those intending to keep several Goldens, when kennelling is, of course, necessary. If, however, you only have two or three it is not essential to kennel them. Goldens are clean in their habits, easily trained and are ideally suited to being part of a household. I think all Goldens should spend a certain amount of time in the house, for it is essential to their well-being, and they thrive on human companionship. In view of this, numbers should be so restricted that all can receive individual attention and have a certain amount of home life.

KENNELS

Goldens are hardy dogs and do not need cosseting, but they must have draught-proof sleeping accommodation, with plenty of good, dry bedding in the winter. (Although puppies need artificial heating, this is not necessary or desirable for adult Goldens.) I consider it extremely practical to have separate daytime and night-time kennels, for no matter how wet the dogs and their kennels may become during the day, they then have clean, dry beds at night, without the inconvenience of sleeping places having to be re-cleaned at bedtime. If you have not sufficient separate kennels, then the existing kennels should be subdivided in order to provide an inner sleeping section, which can be entirely shut off during the day.

a. *STABLING.* Old stabling or other suitable brick-built buildings are easy to convert into kennels. By partitioning these to make several separate sections, excellent kennels with indoor runs attached are easily made. The primary consideration should be the type of sleeping accommodation to be provided. Each sleeping compartment should house two Goldens and should be about 4 ft. by 3 ft. or larger, and should preferably be almost completely enclosed. Old high-roofed buildings can become very cold indeed, and unless the sleeping kennel or box has a top on it all the warmth the dogs generate is dissipated, thus they use up much more energy in keeping warm and consequently are not likely to keep in such good condition. Small wooden kennels inside these stables are ideal, but if these are not available, large boxes, with sides at least 3 ft. high and with removable lids, can be suitably adapted. The removable lid makes cleaning-out much simpler, and its removal in summer allows the dogs to be cooler. These boxes are similar to the whelping boxes described in Chapter 7.

It must be borne in mind that the dogs tend to lie near doors in the daytime, not in their boxes; it is therefore essential that at least part of the floor should be of wood, for brick or concrete, even though liberally covered with sawdust, can strike very cold in the winter.

b. *WOODEN KENNELS*. The timber of these should be either tongued and grooved, or ship-lapped, both types being equally good. There are many types and makes of wooden kennels and garden sheds on the market, most of which are suitable, and it is generally only a matter of taste which you buy, though there are variations in cost, relating to quality and finish. There are, however, certain specifications which should be insisted on. First and foremost see that they are high enough inside for you to stand upright, for it is exceptionally tiring to have to bend nearly double whilst cleaning out, and it is also very aggravating if one keeps bumping one's head! Secondly, insist on a wooden floor to go with the building. Thirdly, ensure that there are adequate windows, each of which can be opened, for wooden sheds become stifling during very hot weather. It is necessary to have either bars or wire-mesh inside the glass to discourage any 'escapologist' Goldens which may be housed therein! It is also advisable to line the kennel at least half-way up the sides with hardboard, for, no matter how well built, it is surprising how much draught gets through the cracks.

A suitable size of kennel for two or three Goldens is about 5 ft. wide by about 8 ft. long, part of which can be partitioned for sleeping quarters. For convenience, the door should be on the front, and in order to facilitate subdivision should not be centrally placed. It is also helpful to have the door made in two sections, so that only the bottom half need be closed in hot weather.

c. KENNEL RANGES. If a number of dogs are to be housed together, ranges of corridor kennels have been found to be the easiest to manage. Again, these should have individual sections capable of comfortably housing two dogs, and the corridor should run the complete length of the range. It is essential with this type of kennelling to ensure adequate ventilation. The compartments should be about 4 ft. wide and at least 6 to 8 ft. long. The corridor need only be about 3 ft. wide, and in order to stop the dogs pushing out when the doors are opened it is advisable that these should open inwards.

d. WHELPING KENNELS. The whelping kennel must be large enough to contain the whelping box (about 4 ft. by 4 ft., as described in Chapter 7 under 'Whelping Quarters') and to give the puppies plenty of room in which to play about when they are out of the nest when the weather is too severe for them to be out of doors. Therefore this kennel should be about 6 ft. wide by 10 ft. long, and at least 6 ft. high. A slightly smaller one can be suitably adapted so that it is adequate, if these dimensions are not possible.

One of similar design to the ordinary wooden shed or kennel mentioned earlier is quite suitable, with the whelping box instead of the partition. It is imperative that the kennel be completely free from draughts.

There should be a supply of electricity to enable the kennel to be lighted and to have an infra-red lamp suspended over the whelping box, for I think it is a 'must' for newly born puppies to have this additional heating.

RUNS

These are usually constructed of heavy-gauge chain-link fencing, or iron railings. Whichever material is used, it must be at least 6 ft. high. Even this is not high enough to contain some Goldens, and for these high-jumpers it may be found necessary to have an 18 in. strip of chain-link on top of this, angled inwards. The fencing must be trenched into the ground for at least 6 in. to prevent the dogs with digging propensities burrowing out (persistent diggers may necessitate the wire being fastened into concrete for complete security).

The runs should be as large as space will allow, so that the dogs may have plenty of freedom. My runs are large (approx. 100 ft. by 50 ft.) and they can be divided into two as and when required. One half has a concrete surface, the other is rough grass. In runs of this size I keep several Goldens together. Runs as large as this are not, of course, essential, and where space is restricted a run of 14 ft. by 8 ft. should be adequate for two Goldens – but, where space is available, spacious runs are an asset, for then the young dogs tend to exercise themselves more.

The question of the surfacing of the runs is always a difficult one to decide, as there are many good materials available, such as concrete, brick, concrete slabs, gravel or clinker, but I think concrete the best, as it is easiest to keep clean and free from infection, and if the run is correctly sloped, presents no drainage problem. My dogs have the large grass run to play about in, and the concrete part keeps their feet tight, and their claws worn down.

It is also advisable to concrete the parts of the run which get most wear and tear i.e. round the kennel and gates, and to have a concrete or paving-stone path down the whole length of the run on the side or sides which get most use, to obviate unsightly muddy tracks in winter and bare earth in summer.

Whatever the type of surface decided upon, it is a very good idea to have wooden boards, about 3 ft. by 4 ft. raised some 4 or 5 in. from the ground, placed in strategic positions, such as outside the kennel door, near gates, and other favourite resting places, for the dogs greatly prefer lying on wood to the often damp or cold ground.

BEDDING

I think wood-wool or shredded paper is much the best form of bedding for the sleeping quarters. It is less likely to harbour livestock than hay or straw, is very warm and does not break up into small pieces as readily as other types of bedding. Do not, however, use wood-wool or straw for tiny puppies to sleep on, for there is the considerable danger of their becoming entangled in it and suffocating.

In summer, wood shavings may be substituted for wood-wool, for this form of bedding will enable the dogs to remain cooler during the warm nights.

The floor of the outer part of the kennel should be spread liberally with sawdust, for this readily absorbs the damp.

CLEANING

The kennels should, of course, be regularly cleaned out, and the bedding changed. If they are scrubbed out and disinfected be sure that they are quite dry before the new bedding is put in. It is a good idea to sprinkle the floor and the new bedding with a good insecticidal powder, to make sure that the dogs are housed in kennels which are quite free from fleas and lice.

CHAPTER 9

SHOWS AND SHOW PREPARATION

Before entering a dog at a show it must first be registered at the Kennel Club on the appropriate form, bearing the breeder's signature. Most breeders register their whole litters from the outset, and where this is done, the puppy must be formally transferred to the new owner, for no dog is eligible to compete at a show run under Kennel Club rules unless it is the registered property of the person entering it.

Visit as many shows as possible as a spectator before entering your dog, then you will be able to watch your breed being judged and will see just what is expected of both dog and exhibitor in the show ring. You will also see the condition of the dogs exhibited, and thus discover how much trimming your own dog requires. Having seen several Goldens in the ring together, you will be able to judge whether or not yours comes up to the desired standard – for it is only by this comparison that you will be able to assess his potential as a show dog. It is advantageous to attend one or two Championship shows, where the standard of the competitors is appreciably higher than at local shows, again to assess the possibilities of your 'young hopeful'. Many an owner sees his dog through rosy-hued spectacles, so this comparison helps to get things into their true perspective!

ENTERING THE DOG IN A SHOW
The first thing to do before launching your Golden on its show career is to ascertain which of your local societies schedule the breed. The weekly dog papers *Our Dogs* and *Dog World* contain advertisements for forthcoming shows, list the various breeds to be catered for and give the name and address of the secretary of the society to whom application should be made for a schedule of the show.

The next step is to send in your entries, together with the entry fees, by the appointed date. Assuming that he has been well reared and cared for, your dog will need little more conditioning than to see that the extra pound or two comes off him, or the little extra is put on, in the week or two before the show, together with the pre-show trimming and bathing as described later in this chapter.

TYPES OF SHOWS

1. EXEMPTION SHOWS. These are generally run in conjunction with some local fête or show, catering also for the showing of flowers, rabbits, cage birds, etc. Awards won at this type of show are not taken into account when entering the dog at a Kennel Club sanctioned or licensed show, and it is not necessary for the dog to be registered to compete – in fact these shows usually have classes in which even the mongrel can compete, e.g. those for 'the happiest dog' or 'the dog with the longest tail', etc.

2. SANCTION SHOWS. These are the smallest of the shows at which dogs are required to be registered with the Kennel Club, and they are restricted to members of the promoting society. They cater largely for 'Any Variety' classes, which means that dogs of all breeds are eligible to compete in them, and only a few classes for separate breeds are scheduled. Sanction shows are open only to dogs who are eligible for classes up to post-graduate, i.e. dogs which have not won five or more first prizes in post-graduate or higher classes. Sanction shows, of course, exclude all Challenge Certificate winners. Entry fees are lower for this type of show than for others, so is the prize money, if any.

3. LIMITED SHOWS. This type of show is similarly confined to members of the society, and to those dogs which have not won a Kennel Club Challenge Certificate. While some of these shows have their separate classes for several breeds, they also schedule 'Any Variety' classes, and though entry and prize money is more than for Sanction shows, it is less than for Open and Championship shows.

4. OPEN SHOWS. These are open to all exhibitors and all dogs, and may contain any number of classes. The smaller events are not 'benched', but the Kennel Club stipulates that the large Open shows must be benched – which means that the dog must be kept on the special bench provided for him for the duration of the show, except when he is taken off for exercise or is in the judging ring. This type of show is very popular, and often provides four or more classes for each separate breed scheduled, and again there are the usual Any Variety classes. Open shows encourage the owners of young dogs to enter, for the win of a first prize at Open Shows counts one point towards the Junior Warrant (referred to in this chapter under 'Kennel Club Titles and Awards').

5. CHAMPIONSHIP SHOWS. This is the most comprehensive type of show. These are the only ones at which Kennel Club Challenge Certificates are offered for competition. There are at present many All-Breed Championship shows, and several Specialist Club shows where Challenge Certificates for Goldens are offered. At each of these shows a Challenge Certificate is awarded to the best dog, and one to the best bitch. Three such awards under three different judges entitles the dog to be called a Show Champion (see later in this chapter). Goldens are usually allotted at least twelve different classes, and sometimes as many as twenty, divided according to sex, and graded according to age and previous wins.

6. OBEDIENCE CLASSES AT SHOWS. A great number of shows, as well as providing classes for 'beauty', put on classes for obedience work. These, again, are graded according to previous wins, and there is provision for the winning of Obedience Certificates at Championship shows.

There are many obedience societies under whose aegis the training of dogs for this work, of a highly specialised nature, is carried out. The training classes, which are generally held weekly, concentrate solely on training dogs for the set exercises used in competitive obedience tests. Many of these societies hold their own Obedience shows, at which Obedience Challenge Certificates are sometimes awarded.

KENNEL CLUB TITLES AND AWARDS

CHALLENGE CERTIFICATES. These are awarded to the best of each sex at Championship shows, if the judge is of the opinion that the exhibit is of such outstanding merit as to be worthy of the title of Champion.

SHOW CHAMPION. This, as previously mentioned, is the title given to a dog which has won three Challenge Certificates, under three different judges. It is a title solely for gundogs, for these do not become full Champions until they have gained a Show Gundog Working Certificate or have won an award at a recognised Field Trial.

CHAMPION. A Champion is a dog which has won three Challenge Certificates under three different judges, and has won at least a Certificate of Merit at a recognised Field Trial, or has been awarded a Show Gundog Working Certificate. This Qualifying Certificate can be obtained at a Field Trial for Retrievers at which there is an 'A' list judge. The dog is required to be tested in the line, show that he is not gun-shy, was off the leash during gun-fire and that he hunts and retrieves tenderly. No dog is eligible to run for a Qualifying Certificate until it has won at least one Challenge Certificate. A dog may not run for a Qualifying Certificate more than three times in all, and not more than twice in any one Field Trial season.

FIELD TRIAL CHAMPION. A Golden Retriever is given the title of Field Trial Champion if it wins:

1. The Retriever Championship
2. Two twenty-four-dog Open or All-Aged Stakes
3. One twenty-four-dog and one twelve-dog Open or All-Aged Stake
4. Three twelve-dog Open or All-Aged Stakes

In a twelve-dog Stake there must have been no fewer than eight runners, and in a twenty-four-dog Stake no fewer than sixteen runners. One of these wins must have been in a stake

SHOWS AND SHOW PREPARATION

open to all breeds of Retrievers. The Golden Retriever must also be proved to have sat quietly at a drive and have passed a water test.

DUAL CHAMPION. To become a Dual Champion a dog must be really outstanding both in the field and in the show ring. He must be a Field Trial Champion and also a Champion at shows, and to gain the coveted title of Dual Champion is the ultimate in gundog achievement.

OBEDIENCE CHAMPION. A dog is entitled to be called an Obedience Champion after winning three Obedience Challenge Certificates under three different judges, though the winning of the Obedience Certificate at Crufts automatically gives the dog its title. At this show the competition is of the highest order, for only dogs which have won Obedience Certificates during the previous year are eligible to compete. Obedience Certificates are not awarded if more than ten points are lost by the winning dog.

JUNIOR WARRANT. After winning twenty-five points in breed Classes at Open and Championship shows before reaching the age of eighteen months a dog is entitled to its Junior Warrant, application for which must be made to the Kennel Club. The points are given on the following scale:
>One for a first at an Open show.
>Three for a first at a Championship show.

CONDITIONING FOR SHOWS
Having become acquainted with show procedure, you probably now feel ready to engage in this engrossing hobby of showing. If you are successful on several occasions with your first exhibit you are likely to become fired with enthusiasm and join those exhibitors who make country-wide journeys from show to show, year in and year out!

Your Golden should be presented in good hard muscular condition, carrying neither too much nor too little weight. If he tends to put on flesh easily he should have the carbohydrates in his diet cut to a minimum, but if the tendency is towards leanness, then obviously his ration of biscuit meal and other starchy foods should be increased.

The dog's beauty is greatly enhanced when his coat is presented in a glossy, shining condition, and he should not, therefore, be shown when he is in the process of moulting – he is best left at home until the new coat has had time to grow. It is a great temptation to continue showing the dog even though out of coat 'because Mr X liked him last time he judged him'. No doubt he did when the dog was in good coat, but a Golden without his coat is at such a disadvantage, as there are always others equally good in full plumage – so Mr X is hardly likely to be nearly as impressed with your dog when he is lacking such an obvious breed essential as his coat!

The instructions and suggestions with regard to the upbringing of your dog, as given in Chapter 5, will, if carefully followed, enable you to present him in good show condition, for he will have been groomed, fed and housed correctly, and given his regular exercise.

TRAINING FOR SHOWS

Show training is generally not a difficult task with this breed. If the dog has been taught to walk on a leash without pulling he can soon be taught to adopt the stance which will show his good points in their most favourable light. This can be done during the early leash-training. Encourage the dog to stand looking at you as a titbit is produced from your pocket. Do this several times when you are out with him and you will find that he will almost certainly look at you expectantly each time your hand goes to your pocket. He can, if need be, be coaxed into the desired position by moving the titbit in front of his nose. Soon he will associate the rustle of paper in your pocket with his titbit, and later your hand moving to your pocket is all that is necessary to make him put his ears up and adopt an alert stance. Never overdo this part of the training or the dog will become bored long before he gets into the show ring. Keep it up for only a few minutes each day, and stop whilst the dog is still enthusiastic about it. A bored dog is unlikely to show off his good points to advantage, and is thus considerably handicapped in the ring.

This way of presentation in the ring – encouraging the dog

to stand naturally with tail wagging and ears forward – is so much more effective than that of placing each foot in the desired position then clamping head and tail into place with both hands! So, if he will stand naturally, encourage him to do so, but if he loses interest in your titbit, a hand placed under his chin and his tail held out level with his back will show his outline to advantage.

Assuming that he is now trained to stand, you must accustom him to having someone run their hands over him, and to having his mouth inspected. Do this yourself from time to time from puppyhood, so that he does not find it disturbing or strange when he first enters the show ring. It is a good plan also to get various visitors to do this occasionally.

He must next be accustomed to trotting up and down at a steady pace, without pulling sideways or leaping into the air (this moving up and down in the show ring is a routine followed in order that the judge may form an opinion of the dog's movement). Some dogs persistently 'pace', i.e. move both legs on the same side of the body one after the other. In order to break them of this somewhat ungainly 'rolling' gait, give the leash a fairly sharp tug and move a little faster.

An alert, free-striding dog with plenty of 'showmanship' is at a great advantage in the show ring, for he readily catches the judge's eye with his 'bounce', and if added to this he has personality, quality and good conformation, he will be a consistent winner. To stay at the top at show after show the 'personality' dog is certainly the one to have! The four outstanding post-war show dogs (Ch. Styal Scott of Glengilde Ch. Camrose Cabus Christopher, Ch. Alresford Advertiser and Ch. Boltby Skylon) all had this great personality and showmanship. They all moved with great style and each readily adopted the show stance which showed to advantage their good points.

TRIMMING

After training your dog to do what is required of him in the show ring you must learn to trim him in such a fashion as will enable him to show his outline to advantage. Fortunately, Goldens do not need a vast amount of trimming, but they must have their tail-feathering, ears, 'ruff', hocks and feet properly trimmed. The well-trimmed dog has a great advantage when it comes to a close decision, for his good points can be considerably enhanced by skilful trimming, and the judge sees the dog at his best.

A start should be made with the trimming some two or three weeks before the dog is to be shown. Begin with the tail – a well-trimmed tail can add so much to the appearance and general balance of the dog. It is advisable to trim from the tip first, leaving only about ½ in. of feathering beyond the end of the last vertibrae, then continue in a gentle arc up to the root, leaving about 4 in. of feathering at the longest part. The correct shape of the tail when trimmed can be seen in the diagram of the 'Outline of a Golden' in Chapter 4. Some people prefer a trimming knife for this operation, others use a razor blade, but most people, of whom I am one, find it much more practical to use scissors. Provided that the trimming is undertaken well before the day of the show, any uneven cutting effects are unlikely to show, and the finished article looks so much neater than when it is trimmed by the other methods.

My next item in the trimming programme is the 'shirt-front'. Goldens tend to grow a considerable amount of hair round their neck and on their shoulders, so this operation can be quite a lengthy one. Using thinning scissors with an upward movement, take out as much hair as is necessary to leave a smooth effect, constantly combing out the hair, in order to see how the trimming is progressing. A stripping knife or razor comb is sometimes necessary to shorten any remaining long hairs on the chest, and again, if the trimming is done well before the show, there will be no evidence of cut marks left by the time the show comes along. Tidy neck and shoulders can make a great difference to the outline, for those dogs which have vast quantities of long hair in these places may look quite short in neck, but when trimmed out, the true lines are exposed, and the whole outline of the neck and shoulders is shown to advantage.

The long hair on top, in front, and at the sides of the ears should be taken out, so that the ear shape is easily discernible and there are no untidy tufts around it. A stripping knife or thinning scissors is best for this – any dead hair being pulled out with finger and thumb.

Hocks should be freed from any long feathering, and the back of the leg from hock to foot looks neater if the superfluous hair is removed.

All that now remains is the trimming of the feet, the appearance of which can be greatly enhanced when all the long hair surrounding them has been removed. First, trim the outline of the foot with the scissors – as near to the top of the pads as possible – then, with the trimming knife, take out any hair which sticks up between the toes, so as to give the desired rounded cat-like shape. Even poorly shaped feet can be made to look passable if this trimming is skilfully carried out!

BATHING

All Goldens' coats are improved by bathing with the correct preparations, and nearly all look better on the day if it is done as near to the show date as possible. Here I must give a cautionary word. If your dog has one of the very wavy types of coat he should not be bathed the day before the show unless you are able to give plenty of time to the drying operation. Owners of straight-coated dogs have the advantage when it comes to show preparation, but the extra effort required to present the wavy-coated ones looking at their best is certainly well worth while.

It is important to use plenty of water when bathing the dog, and a good human or dog shampoo should be rubbed into the coat in the same way as one would for one's own hair. After this process the dog should be rinsed, preferably using a shower spray. To impart an immediate shine, the use of a human hair conditioner is very helpful. This is rubbed into the coat after the shampoo has been rinsed out, and it should be allowed to remain for a few minutes before rinsing.

An alternative to the shampoo and conditioning cream method is to use Quellada Veterinary Shampoo strictly according to the instructions. This preparation imparts the same sheen to the coat as does a conditioning cream, and, in addition to cleansing the coat, acts as an insecticide.

DRYING

Equally important with the bathing process is that of drying. As mentioned earlier, if the dog is straight-coated it is an easy matter to part-dry with a chamois leather and comb the hair into place and allow it to dry naturally – if you are fortunate enough to have a sunny day the task is made even easier. If, however, your dog is wavy-coated you must be prepared to devote plenty of time to getting the hair properly into place. Part-dry with a chamois leather or towel, then use a hair-dryer, combing the coat into place all the time throughout the drying process. On a very sunny day this can be done by keeping the dog outside, but the coat must be continuously combed into place until completely dry, and this can be very time-consuming. It generally takes from half to one hour to ensure the hair being sufficiently dry to keep in place. If you are un-able to spare this amount of time, then, having combed the hair, wrap the dog in a rug or towel until he is completely dry. This is not as effective as the first method, but it will ensure some measure of success. If these toilet operations are all satis-factorily completed on the day before the show the coat should be at its best, showing beautiful flat waves that are such an attractive feature.

When the coat is completely dry it is advantageous to give the dog a really good brushing with a wire hound glove, finish-ing off with the comb, and smoothing with the hand. This should get a wonderful bloom on to the coat – half a dozen strokes with brush and comb are quite ineffectual, and you must spend at least ten minutes giving this final 'spit and polish' so that your dog will be really sparkling.

THE SHOW DAY

For the show equipment you will require a travelling bag large enough to take a rug for the bench, chamois leather to dry the dog with if he gets wet, water bowl and a packet of titbits (liver or some other favourite food) as 'ring-bait'. The bag should also contain your grooming equipment (hound glove, comb and spirit cleaner). Other essentials are a bench chain and collar, and a show leash, which should be a type of 'slip', which will open out to enable the judge to see the dog's neck without hindrance. Never take the dog into the show ring on a collar and leash, for this completely spoils the lines of the neck.

Leave plenty of time to exercise the dog *en route*, or before taking him into the show, and have your exhibitor's pass in an accessible place, so that you are not held up at the entrance to the show. The dog should be taken to its bench, given a final cleaning with the spirit cleaner, and be groomed once more. This final attention is very necessary, for a long, cramped journey can play havoc with a dog's coat. Therefore, a quick rub over with the chamois moistened with the spirit lotion (or diluted toilet eau-de-Cologne) which will dry off quickly, then five minutes' good brushing with the hound glove and a quick application of the comb – particularly to all the feathering – and your dog is ready to take on all comers.

CHAPTER 10

GUN TRAINING AND FIELD TRIALS

This chapter will not be found to be a lengthy discourse for the experienced trainer, it is merely intended as a short guide for the beginner who aims at producing a reliable gundog. To go into all the aspects of training and the many problems which may be encountered would take up far more space than is available here. For those who want detailed help on more advanced training there are many books on the subject, two excellent examples being P. R. A. Moxon's *Gundogs: Training and Field Trials*, published by Popular Dogs, London, and R. Sharpe's *Gun Training by Amateurs*. There are also many societies in various parts of the country who provide excellent facilities for gun-training for their members' dogs by running regular training classes with experienced instructors. These are most helpful to both owner and dog, and the dog gets used to working in similar circumstances to those which he will encounter on a day's shooting or in a Field Trial. These societies also run competitive working tests, which help to assess the dog's possibilities for trials, and many good dogs have gone via these classes to become winners in trials.

I have already explained in Chapter 5 ('Your Golden's First Year') how the elementary lessons on walking to heel, sitting on command and simple retrieving, etc., should be dealt with, and it is essential that before any actual gun-training is commenced the puppy is capable of doing these exercises. He should also have been taught to come immediately he is called. These early lessons in obedience will render him more responsive to advanced training, which should not be commenced until he is at least eight months old.

The equipment you will require for the training lessons is a whistle, a slip-leash and several dummies. There are the so-called 'silent' whistles, which emit a high-pitched sound, or those made from bone or metal. Some trainers use two whistles differing in tone, one as a 'stop' whistle and the other as a 'calling-in' whistle. At least three dummies will be required, and should be fairly light at first. They can be made from canvas or old socks (stuffed with wood wool or some other soft substance), and as the puppy gets older they can be made from stuffed rabbit or hare skins, and as the training progresses they should be made gradually heavier. With a headstrong dog it may be necessary to use a check-cord to halt any sign of unsteadiness. This is made from a long piece of rope, with a slip knot at one end.

Before commencing this actual training it should be stressed that to get the best out of your dog you must have endless patience, and be prepared to be lavish in your praise when the dog has pleased you. As soon as you experience the least irritation it is better to put him away, as he must regard these training sessions as enjoyable outings and must have complete confidence in you. Only punish him when he is caught in the act of disobedience, and remember that you can get the best results from a Golden which is firmly, but kindly, handled.

WHISTLE TRAINING
Having taught the dog the first essentials of obedience, and made him sit to a hand signal, and to come as soon as he is called, it is now important to be able to get him to do these things to a whistle command. Use several short blasts on the whistle as a 'recall' command, and one long one as the signal to 'sit'. If these whistled commands immediately follow the spoken word he will soon begin to associate the two, and will respond when the whistle alone is used.

To teach him to come to you by means of the whistle, call his name, give the command 'come' and when he starts towards you blow the 'recall' whistle. When he has obeyed these commands praise him, then having realised that he has pleased you he will probably be even more ready to respond to your commands in future.

When he has successfully learnt to sit to both command and hand signal, as described in Chapter 5, follow these com-

mands immediately by one long blast on the whistle. If this
exercise is repeated several times it should result in his sitting
to the whistle and hand signal alone, without the need for the
spoken command. Later it will be possible to get him to stop in
his tracks and sit, when the 'stop' whistle is used on its own.
When he is sufficiently responsive to do this at close quarters
you may then try to 'drop' him at increasing distances from
you, until you can eventually make him sit in any desired
place.

These whistle-training lessons should be thoroughly instilled
as early as possible, and should be perfected before more
advanced training is undertaken. The whole of the dog's
usefulness as a gundog depends on the control you have over
him at any desired distance, it is therefore essential that you
are able to get him to come to you on command, and also to be
able to stop him immediately, in order to give further
directions.

SIMPLE RETRIEVES

Simple retrieving should commence early in his training on
the following lines: make him sit, and throw the dummy a
short distance, preferably into long grass to encourage him to
use his nose. Insist that he wait a few seconds before being sent
for it. Then say 'Get out' and wave your arm in the direction of
the dummy, when he will probably rush out and pick it up. As
soon as he does this, blow your whistle and call him back to
you. When he comes to you put your hand under his mouth
and hold it there for a moment or two before taking the
dummy from him. This is to ensure that he learns to deliver
properly to hand and does not drop the dummy at your feet.
Repeat this simple retrieve several times, throwing the
dummy further each time. Should he experience any difficulty
in finding it, go with him, and encourage him to hunt by saying 'Hie lost', and wave your arm in the desired direction.
When he eventually finds his dummy, praise him and call him
straight up to you.

Most Goldens are natural retrievers, and unless something
has happened in their early days to discourage them they
instinctively pick up anything thrown for them. If, however,
initial difficulty is experienced in getting the dog to pick the

Sh.Ch. Davern Josephine   *Dog World*

Sh.Ch. Zach of Dunblair

Ch. Westley Mabella *Sally Anne Thompson*

Ch. Styal Scott of Glengilde (42 C.C.s)

Canadian Dual Ch., American Field Ch., American
Amateur Field Ch. Rockhaven Raynard of
Fo-Go-Ta retrieving to Charles Bunker
Norm Pelkey

American, Canadian and Bermudan Ch. Cummings Goldrush
Charlie (top winning Golden in USA during the mid-1970s)

F.T.Ch. Westhyde Stubblesdown Major winning the Scottish Field Trial Association's Open Stake

dummy, put it in his mouth and, holding it there for a while, make a fuss of him. When he will hold it without assistance take a few steps backwards and call him to you, then gently take it from him and throw it a short distance, letting him go straight for it. This plan generally works, for he will usually pick the dummy up and return with it. Should it fail, the example of a trained dog bringing the dummy back to hand will often encourage the puppy to do likewise. Some dogs who refuse to pick a dummy at first may retrieve a favourite 'toy', such as an old shoe or a ball, and this may be used for the early lessons. Having become enthusiastic about hunting for and retrieving this object, he will usually take quite easily to others.

Another problem which may be encountered in early training is that of the dog who prefers to run off with the dummy or circles wildly round, inviting you to participate in an exciting 'chase me' game rather than coming back to hand. This is most annoying, but on no account should you display your annoyance, and never make the cardinal error of chasing after him. If he should go off with the dummy, call his name and whistle him back, at the same time run in the opposite direction yourself. This will often induce him to come, when he should be praised on his return. If this method does not quickly produce the desired results a further expedient is to contrive that the exercise take place in a narrow passage-way, fenced on both sides and at one end. Throw the dummy to the closed end, send the dog for it, and as soon as he picks it up, give the 'recall' whistle, then run away from him. He has no alternative but to come to you, and by repeating this routine several times he will soon learn that this game is just as much fun as the one he wants to play, and will consequently come back to hand.

Having ensured that he will sit and wait for the command to retrieve, and having established a good delivery, he should now be at the stage where you are able to 'drop' him, walk away, throw the dummy into cover, return to him and then send him for it. In this way he will get used to marking a fall – and a good marker is a great asset – and to using his nose. As soon as he will readily hunt for the dummies he has seen drop, vary the exercise by giving 'unseen' retrieves, the dummy being hidden on the usual training ground before the dog is brought out. He is then made to sit to the windward side of the dummy, but not too far from it. Show the general direction by waving your arm and send him for the dummy. If he experiences difficulty in his search gradually walk nearer to it and encourage him to hunt by giving the command 'Hie lost', and waving your arm again in its direction.

Another good retrieving exercise which will teach him to use his memory and to make him learn to 'get out' well, rather than always working at close range, is to walk him to heel, 'drop' him, throw the dummy into cover, then walk him at heel away from it for a short distance before sending him back for it. Having marked the fall of the dummy, he will almost certainly rush out and get it. The distance he is sent back for the dummy can gradually be increased until he will go back the whole length of a field.

These simple retrieves should be practised from varying types of cover, so that the dog learns to hunt in all types of country, and will face all kinds of undergrowth as well as working on open plough, stubble or in fields.

GUN-FIRE

It is advisable to accustom the dog to gun-fire at an early age, and the preparation for this is done in puppyhood by conditioning him to the noises of the bursting of paper bags and the banging of dishes, etc., when he is feeding. The next stage is to fire a starting pistol (not too closely at first) during mealtimes. Most puppies accept this noise quite happily, just looking up enquiringly, so that soon you can fire nearer to them.

When it is quite evident that the dog is not disturbed by the starting pistol at close range he can be introduced to the louder noise of gun-fire – again not too close at first, but gradually decreasing the distance until the gun can be fired with him at your side without his being worried. Gun-fire can now be introduced into the training lessons. Do not, however, always train to the accompaniment of gun-fire or he may think that there is only something to retrieve when a gun has been fired, and consequently may assume that it is useless to hunt without this, and, worse still, he may assume that each time a gun is fired there is something for him to retrieve, and this can lead to unsteadiness. This theory is supported by Mr P. R. A. Moxon in the book mentioned earlier, who says that many promising dogs are ruined by allowing the association of gun-fire with something to retrieve too early in life.

DIRECTION TRAINING

Having taught the dog to retrieve on command, it remains now to teach him to hunt in the required direction. The first stage in this directional training is to throw a dummy to each side of him as he sits in front of you. Make him wait a moment while you walk one or two paces towards the first-thrown dummy, then wave your arm in its direction and tell him to 'Get out'. Should he go straight out and pick up the dummy to which he has been directed, whistle him up and give him plenty of praise. If, however, he makes a move towards the wrong one – which is more than likely – blow the 'stop' whistle. His earlier lessons, if properly learnt, will ensure his stopping, so that he can be redirected. If he still persists in going for the wrong one, make him come back to you, then take him a little nearer the right dummy before sending him out again. This should lead him to understand what is required of him. Should he get to the wrong dummy before you can stop him, do not discourage him from bringing it back to you. A young dog is easily confused and any rebuff may spoil his 'pick up' in future.

Having successfully got him to retrieve the first-thrown dummy, send him for the last-thrown one – this not only helps to teach him direction but also stimulates his memory. Repeat this exercise of 'double dummies' until he always goes in the desired direction. He is now sufficiently advanced for you to try him on three dummies – one at either side of him and one in front. Direct him to whichever dummy you wish him to retrieve, and he will quickly learn that an arm waved in a par-ticular direction indicates that there is something to hunt for and retrieve. The distance of the retrieve should gradually be increased and you should now have reached the stage where you are able to stop him and redirect him if he should get too far away from the dummy.

Having perfected this exercise, the next step is to hide the dummies before bringing the dog out, and by signals to direct him to collect whichever you want. By now you presumably have sufficient control over him to stop him at any desired place and he should be able to respond to all your hand signals. When he has become completely steady to the 'stop' whistle when ranging out at varying distances, the discipline of sitting can be dispensed with and he need only stop and look at you for his directions.

To be able to send your dog to retrieve in the desired direction and to exercise control from a distance can, as well as looking spectacular, save many precious minutes when you are out shooting and require him to take the line of a runner which he has not seen, for you are thus able to get him to the fall as quickly as possible.

STEADINESS

It is most important to instil 'steadiness' into the dog at an early age, i.e. he should be taught that he must not 'run in' to gun-fire, or falling game, and should not chase fur or feather, or indeed any domestic animal or bird. To this end, in his early lessons he should be accustomed to seeing several dummies thrown around him without making any unbidden move to retrieve them, and he should also be familiar with the sight of dummies being thrown when he is actually retrieving. If you have free access to fields or woods known to contain game this part of the training is, of course, made much easier. The dog may be walked through these, on a slip-leash, and should he show any sign of making a move from the 'heel' position when any game is disturbed, correct him instantly by blowing the 'stop' whistle, giving the leash a good tug, and rating him soundly. If his earlier lessons of obedience have been well learned you will soon be able to dispense with the slip-leash, and your whistle will be sufficient to ensure instant obedience. A headstrong dog may need firmer handling to stop him from chasing. Such a dog should be put on a check-cord (described earlier) and allowed to get a few yards away, then at the same time as the whistle is blown he should be brought to a sudden halt by throwing sufficient weight on the check-cord to stop him suddenly. This experience shakes him, and he will not be likely to repeat the offence.

It considerably facilitates this steadiness-training for the dog to be taken into an enclosure containing several rabbits – on the leash at first – for then the slightest inclination to chase can be checked instantly, and the dog soon becomes used to seeing the rabbits running around him. When he can safely be walked in the rabbit pen off the leash, then the dummy may be thrown in for him to retrieve.

RETRIEVING FROM WATER
Goldens generally love swimming and only very few of them need to be persuaded to go into water. Introduce your young dog to water at about six months of age, preferably at a place with easy access, and with an older dog who will plunge straight in. The youngster will usually follow, and enjoy swimming about with him, but if he should be reluctant to enter, throw a dummy into the water, just out of his reach, for this will usually tempt him. If this fails, try walking in a little way yourself and encourage him to follow. Should he be a 'paddler' and dislike actual swimming, this can generally be overcome by waiting for a suitable opportunity to go in for a swim yourself, when he will almost certainly follow, for he will not want to be left behind.

Having got your dog into water, he should be given retrieves from there, and also the dummy should be thrown across a narrow stream on to the opposite bank and he should be sent to retrieve it. The difficulty of this exercise can be increased by throwing the dummy into thick cover over the stream, and, further, by throwing two dummies over and sending him for each in turn. The final step in this water-training is taken by hiding 'unseen' dummies on the far side of the stream and getting him across it to hunt for them. This necessitates the exercising of a considerable amount of control, for the dog will be inclined to expect to find something in the water, and will be loth to get out over the stream, without the incentive of seeing something fall.

JUMPING
Young puppies, with their undeveloped muscles and soft bones, should not be allowed to jump, so wait until his training proper is well advanced, and he is partly matured, before

introducing him to jumps. Probably the easiest way to teach him to tackle jumps is to erect several suitable obstacles, which should be quite low, in a narrow cul-de-sac. These first jumps are made easy so that the dog will not have to put much effort into getting over them. Nothing puts a young dog off more than a jump which wobbles or collapses when he is attempting to get over it, so whatever is erected must be quite firm. Throw the dummy over one of the jumps in full view of the dog, give the command 'Get over' and provided that the obstacle is not too difficult to negotiate he will in all probability not hesitate to either jump or scramble over. If he should refuse to get over, climb over it yourself and encourage him to follow. As he becomes accustomed to jumping these low hurdles, etc., you can gradually increase the height and vary the type of jump, so that he will happily negotiate all types of obstacles likely to be encountered when actually out shooting or in a trial. After sufficient time has been devoted to these exercises you should be able to stand well back from the jump and send him to retrieve over it on command.

RETRIEVING GAME

A partridge or small hen pheasant which has been freshly shot, but allowed to get cold, is the ideal type of game for a young dog's first retrieves, for neither is too heavy, and either is easy for him to carry. Pigeons should not be used in the early stages, for the feathers tend to come out too easily. Before introducing the bird it is advisable to bind the wings to the body, to prevent his picking it up by a wing – this fault once indulged in may be difficult to eradicate.

Take the dog out to his usual training ground, make him 'drop', and throw the bird a short distance. Most Goldens will instantly pick the bird and come straight back with it, but if he should be dubious about picking it, encourage him with 'Hie lost'. Do not worry if he should drop it when retrieving, for he will soon learn by experience how to carry it properly. Should he completely refuse to pick the bird, put it in his mouth. As soon as he will hold it, walk a few steps backwards, calling him to you, then gently take it from him. This should work in the same way as it did for the dummy, for having once got the dog to carry the bird, he will usually pick it up when next it is thrown. Very occasionally there is the dog who refuses to co-operate – I had one such who was accustomed to retrieving dummies with the previous season's pheasant wings tied round them, and it was only after I had put these old wings from a dummy round a bird that she would retrieve it. I removed these additional wings one by one from the pheasant, and after this she was prepared to retrieve all types of game.

When the dog has learnt to carry small birds satisfactorily he should be introduced to cock pheasants, and other types of game, including rabbits and hares.

TAKING A LINE

The dog having been taught to retrieve dead game must now learn to follow the line of wounded game, in order that the injured creature may be brought to hand as soon as possible. This is taught by dragging a dead bird along the ground to leave a scent trail, and placing it at the end of the trail. The dog is sent to hunt near the beginning of the 'line', and is encouraged to follow it. To ensure that he does not follow his master's footsteps, as well as the scent of the game, attach the bird to the centre of a long rope. Hold one end of the rope yourself and have someone else hold the other end. Stretch the rope to its full length, but allow the game to trail on the ground. Now both persons walk forward together, dragging it. When the scent trail has been laid, detach the bird and leave it at the end of the line. Do not walk across the ground on which you have laid the trail, for this will mask the scent and distract the dog as he follows the line. This exercise teaches the dog to make good use of his nose, so that when taken out with the gun he will be able to be directed to hunt for a runner, follow its scent and collect it.

THE SHOOTING DAY

If the dog has performed the training exercises satisfactorily he should now be sufficiently advanced to undertake his first outing with the gun. It is helpful if someone else does the shooting, so that you can concentrate on him without distractions and be ready to check any sign of transgression. Do not allow him to retrieve everything he sees shot, and make certain that he only retrieves dead game on his first few outings. He should not be sent for a runner too soon in his actual shooting experience, as this may unsteady him, and he may take to chasing, or become hard-mouthed (a hard-mouthed dog is one which crushes the ribs of, or badly damages, the game he retrieves). A young soft-mouthed dog sometimes finds difficulty in collecting freshly shot game, and may drop it once or twice to get a better hold. This is usually overcome with experience, and a clean pick-up and good delivery to hand should soon come.

If all the basic lessons of obedience, together with the later training, have been instilled, you should now have a useful gundog, who is a credit to you, and who will give you much pleasure to work. He will be an asset to any shooting party, for he should be able speedily to find lost game which falls in dense cover, over streams, etc., and to collect runners, and be controlled in all circumstances, and generally help to fill the bag.

FIELD TRIALS

Many who have successfully trained their dogs to the gun will want to do competitive work, and for this there are many Field Trials run by various societies all over the country during the shooting season.

One of the essentials in a trial dog is that it should be perfectly steady to both fur and feather, for a dog which 'runs in' is automatically eliminated. Another important requisite for the trial dog is that of being soft-mouthed, for judges examine all game retrieved for signs of crushed ribs, and any dog known to have bitten its game is put out of the trial. Other eliminating faults are whining or barking.

Other important qualities necessary to a dog running in trials are game-finding ability combined with drive, style and perseverance, and for these the dog must possess a good nose, be a good marker and be capable of ranging well away from his handler, and must be at all times under complete control, and capable of being directed to any desired spot.

Field Trials are held under very strict Kennel Club rules and are graded into several differing categories according to the amount of winning by dog or handler, such as Puppy, Non-Winner, Novice and Open or All-Aged. There may be various combinations of these, such as Puppy and Non-Winners, or Novice Dog and Novice Handler, etc.

A Puppy Stake is one which is confined to dogs whelped not earlier than 1st of January in the year preceding that in which the trial is run, thus, dogs under twelve months old and up to nearly two years old are eligible to compete for such a stake. The definitions of Non-Winners and Novice Stakes vary with the societies running the trials, but a typical definition of a Non-Winners Trial is one in which any dog having won a first prize in any type of trial is ineligible to compete. A popular definition of a Novice Stake is one limited to dogs who have not won a first, second or third prize in any trial.

Open Stakes are those which are open to all dogs of a named breed, without restriction as to variety, age, etc. (i.e. if the stake is a Retriever one, this will be open to all varieties of Retrievers – Labradors, Goldens, Flat-Coats and Curly-Coats). An All-Aged Stake is similar to an Open one, but is restricted by the regulations of the promoting society. Thus a society may run a trial which restricts neither the amount of winning nor the age of the dogs, but specifies one variety of Retriever only, and this must be called an All-Aged Stake.

Winners in the most important of these Open or All-Aged Stakes 'qualify' to run in the Retriever Championship Stake, which is run annually in December, and sees the cream of the Field Trial winning Retrievers of all varieties competing. The qualifications necessary for a dog to compete in this Championship vary from time to time, and are now rather complicated, and are graded into A, B and C categories.

In order to qualify for the Retriever Championship a dog must win the following in Open or All-Aged Stakes:

A—1st in Open or All-Aged 2-day Stake (16 or more runners)

B—2nd in Open or All-Aged 2-day Stake (16 or more runners)

C—3rd in Open or All-Aged 2-day Stake (16 or more runners)

B—1st in Open or All-Aged 1-day Stake (8 or more runners)

C—2nd in Open or all-Aged 1-day Stake (8 or more runners)

To run in the Championship, dogs must have obtained one of the following qualifications:

a. 1 qualification *A*.
b. 2 qualifications *B*.
c. 4 qualifications *C*.
d. 1 qualification *B* and 2 qualifications *C*.

The winner of the previous year's Championship, and any dog which gains its F.T. Ch. title during the current season, is automatically eligible to compete.

The winner of the Retriever Championship automatically becomes a Field Trial Champion, as does a dog which wins two Open or All-aged Stakes for twenty-four dogs, or one twenty-four and one twelve dog Stakes, or three twelve dog Stakes – one win must be in a stake open to all breeds of Retrievers.

In order to enter your dog in a Field Trial you must apply for a 'nomination', which must be in the hands of the secretary of the society running the trial by a given date. These 'nominations' usually far exceed the number of places, so are balloted for, the dogs to compete being allotted numbers. Those successful in drawing a place must then send in an entry naming the dog it is intended to run.

Trials take place on much the same lines as those of the usual shooting day, except that the first consideration is that of the dog work. The conditions vary according to the ground, some trials having most of the work done with the dogs and handlers walking up in line, others having the game driven over the dogs, while others have a little of both types of work. If circumstances permit, it is also usual to have a water test.

There are usually three judges, each of whom have two dogs in the line with them at the same time, and they also have two guns allocated to them. The right-hand judge starts with Nos. 1 and 2 dogs in line with him. The centre judge has Nos. 3 and 4, and the left-hand judge Nos. 5 and 6, and each judge sends his lowest-numbered dog to retrieve first. When a judge has tried out a dog to his satisfaction – each one being given two retrieves if game permits – he calls another higher-numbered dog into the line. Not until all the competitors have been tested under one judge are others recalled into the line under a different one. When all have been tested under two judges it is usual for those dogs which have done the best work to be brought into line again to decide the final placings. Occasionally there are four judges, who work in pairs. In this case there are only four dogs in the line at a time – two dogs with each pair of judges.

Some of the qualities which the Kennel Club recommend Field Trial judges to look for are natural game-finding ability and initiative (they are instructed that dogs who show these should be placed above those which need handling on to their game), good marking, walking steadily to heel, a good pick-up and fast return, obedience to handler's signals, and being under control at all times.

All dogs, except puppies, are expected to pick fur as well as feather, and refusal to pick any type of game eliminates the dog from the trial. The Kennel Club recommendations to trial judges also point out that a dog which fails to find game subsequently retrieved by another dog (has its 'eye wiped') should be penalised. Judges are also advised to request their guns not to shoot at all when a dog is out working in Puppy, Novice and Non-Winners Stakes, and not to shoot directly over a dog out working in Open or All-Aged Stakes, and to ensure that wounded game is collected as quickly as possible.

As well as first, second, third and fourth prizes there is generally a reserve place given, and Certificates of Merit are awarded at the judges' discretion to dogs which do not get into the prize money but complete a satisfactory trial. In Open and All-Aged Stakes Awards of Honour may be given to dogs not in the first four but who have merited more than a Certificate of Merit.

GUNDOG WORKING TESTS

These are held by the various gundog-training societies who run regular classes at which both handler and dog are taught all the aspects of gun-training. These tests are usually divided into those for Puppies and Non-Winners, and Open tests, and the rules of eligibility are similar to those of actual trials. These tests are unofficial and are not recognised by the Kennel Club.

They take place with the use of dummies or occasionally with cold game, and consist of several set exercises in which each dog is tested in turn, so that each has an equal opportunity. The exercises are designed to coincide with the sort of things the dog would be required to do when out shooting, or in a trial, e.g. walking in line, dummies being thrown to accompanying gun-fire and each dog being sent in turn to retrieve. Other typical tests are retrieving an unseen dummy from cover after gun-fire, over a three-foot jump, or retrieving an unseen dummy over water. More difficult tests are given in the Open Stakes, such as 'double dummy' exercises, in which a dummy is thrown up and fired at, after which the dog is sent to retrieve an unseen one in another direction.

These tests prove excellent stepping-off grounds for Field Trials, and many are the Working Test winners who have gone on to win high honours in trials.

CHAPTER 11

GOLDENS OVERSEAS

This chapter gives as much information about the breed in other countries as it has been possible to collect, and I am indebted to Golden owners in these various countries for their help in collating this.

There have been Goldens exported from this country to France, Germany, Belgium and other European countries throughout the years, but the breed has not, as yet, become very popular in those places. However their numbers are increasing in the countries of their adoption. Those which have gone to these countries have gone there either as gundogs or as companions. Very few have been shown or bred from, and there are few Golden Retriever organisations in any of the European countries other than Holland and the Scandinavian countries.

Other countries also have imported Goldens from England, though in small numbers, but some of these dogs have brought credit to their owners and breeders both in the show ring and as gundogs. These countries are Sri Lanka, Finland, Hong Kong, Pakistan, Singapore, South America and the West Indies.

In all the countries referred to later in this chapter the adopted Standard of the breed is that of the Kennel Club of the British Isles unless otherwise stated.

There seems to be some confusion amongst breeders and judges in various countries on certain points, and I would draw the attention of those living in countries which adopt the English Standard to the fact that this permits 'all shades of gold or cream' – this includes the palest of cream and the deepest of gold, and only bars red or mahogany (this being Irish Setter colour, not very often seen in a Golden). It has also been pointed out to me that in some countries judges penalise wavy coats. Again I draw their attention to the Standard which permits a wavy coat – and, indeed, to my mind, it is most attractive. I have several Goldens in my kennel with wavy coats, and I think that they are much more attractive than the straight ones, and they are usually much more water-resisting and have the desired dense undercoat.

SOUTHERN IRELAND (EIRE)

The Irish Kennel Club holds jurisdiction over show and trial activities in Eire, and all dogs competing in these must be registered with it. It is an entirely separate body from the British Kennel Club, therefore wins at shows and trials held under the jurisdiction of the British Kennel Club (which covers Northern Ireland) do not count towards Irish titles.

The first Goldens known to have been registered with the Irish Kennel Club (in 1925) were Mrs B. Escombe's Cubbington Beauty (bred by Mr F. Rodgers by Thaxted Binks out of Stagden Cross Gleam) whelped in 1923, and Cubbington Drake (bred by Mr W. S. Hunt by Triumph out of Ottershaw Honey) whelped in 1921. It is not known for certain whether or not these two were in fact shown or run in trials, but as Mrs Escombe lived in England, this may possibly have been the reason for their being registered with the Irish Kennel Club.

Mrs W. S. Charlesworth was in Ireland for a time, and had some of her Noranby Goldens with her, which she worked on private shoots in that country. They too, may have been shown or run in Irish trials, but this is not known for certain either.

It was not until after the Second World War that Goldens started to become popular there. The first owner to show them was Mrs C. Twist (honorary secretary of the All-Ireland Golden Retriever Club) in 1946. She piloted her Pennard Golden David, which she imported from England from Mrs R. Thompson, to his Irish title of champion. Later Mrs Twist imported Irish Ch. Westhyde Rona from Mr Peter Fraser, and Irish Ch. Bryanstown Diplomat of Ulvin from Mrs Ulyatt.

Mrs D. Metcalfe was the next to exhibit Goldens, and took the title of Irish Champion with her Tullynore Linda. Then came Mr S. Brown, who exhibited his Stubbings Golden Verbena, imported from Mrs S. Winston (*née* Nairn). A few years later Miss L. Ross started showing, and had great success with her famous English Ch. and F.T. Ch. and Irish Ch. and F.T. Ch. David of Westley.

Other Goldens to have taken the title of Irish Champion are Mr E. Orton's English and Irish Ch. Mossbridge Challenger, Mr J. Green's English and Irish Ch. Jeanaras Blond Boy of Sektuny, Mrs Z. Moriarty's English and Irish Ch. Cabus Cadet, Mr J. Stewart's Irish Gh. Weeton Witch of Ouzedale, Mr J. Twohig's Irish Ch. Leygore Calcharm, Mrs Harkness's Irish Ch. Mandingo Buidhe Colum and Mrs C. Twist's Irish Ch. Bryanstown Camrose Gail and several others since that time.

In 1952 Goldens started their successes at Field Trials in Eire. The first to go to the top in this sphere was the previously mentioned Int. Dual Ch. David of Westley, handled throughout his trial career by Mr Jim Cranston. He was joined in trials in 1953 by Mr and Mrs Twist's Titania of Bryanstown, and in 1954 by their Irish Ch. Bryanstown Diplomat of Ulvin, both of whom competed successfully. Next came Mr Dobson's Irish F.T. Ch. Holway Legato, and from then on Goldens went on to win many awards in trials and more competed each year. Others to attain their Irish F.T. Ch. title are Miss Ross's F.T. Ch. Stubblesdown Vanda (later exported to Canada), Mrs Barron's Irish F.T. Ch. Moonbeam of Anbria (sold later and trialled by Major Currie) and Mr Blossom's Irish F.T. Ch David of Corrievern.

In 1964 the Irish Kennel Club held its first Retriever Championship Stake which was won by Irish F.T. Ch. David of Corrievern, another Golden, Irish F.T. Ch. Holway Legato, taking second place. Again in 1965 Goldens did well in the Irish Retriever Championship, taking third place and two Certificates of Merit.

Entries at shows at which Irish Green Stars (which are valued at one, three or four points, according to the average nuber of exhibits at shows) are offered do not compare at all favourably with those at English shows, and the most dogs entered at any show are very few, when compared with those in the United Kingdom.

The All-Ireland Golden Retriever Club was formed in 1953,

and the membership has steadily grown, but there are at present not many kennels of Goldens in this country, not many litters are bred, most of the breeding stock being imported from England, and as the present nucleus is mostly from good strains, Southern Ireland will undoubtedly produce increasing numbers of Goldens in the fairly near future.

IRISH KENNEL CLUB TITLES

CHAMPION. To become an Irish Champion a dog must win 'Green Stars' to a minimum total of fifteen points. These must include at least one four-point Green Star, or two three-point Green Stars. These Green Stars may all be won under one judge or under different judges. A second three- or four-point Green Star, however, won under a judge who has previously awarded the dog a three- or four-point Green Star, counts only one point.

The dog must also win an award at a Field Trial or be granted a Working Certificate at a Field Trial held under Irish Kennel Club rules. The dog is only eligible to enter for the Working Certificate after winning one or more Green Stars. In order to obtain this qualifying certificate the dog must prove that he is not gun-shy, that he will hunt and retrieve tenderly and, where this is possible, he will be given a water test.

IRISH FIELD TRIAL CHAMPION. To be come an Irish Field Trial Champion the dog must win at least two four-point Green Stars in two Open Stakes at two different Field Trials held under the Irish Kennel Club rules, provided there were at least eight dogs competing in each stake and that the wins were gained under different judges. Before the dog may be granted the title of Field Trial Champion he must also win a first, second or third prize in a Graduate, Limit or Open Class at a show at which Green Stars or Challenge Certificates were awarded for the breed.

DUAL CHAMPION. This title is awarded when a dog has become both a Champion at shows and a Field Trial Champion.

HOLLAND

The first Golden Retrievers were imported into Holland in the 1930s from the Noranby, Heydown and Avishays kennels in England. They were required mainly for work, and were seldom shown. Few descendants were left by these dogs, who had established an excellent reputation for their working qualities.

In 1946 Mrs van Schelle (*née* s'Jacob) founded her Staverden kennel by importing the litter-sisters Pennard Golden Garland and Pennard Golden Genista (Stubbings Golden Nicholas × Pennard Golden Gem). Garland became a Dutch Champion, and the dam of several Champions. Later Mrs van Schelle imported Masterstroke of Yeo (litter-brother to F.T. Ch. Musicmaker of Yeo), who also gained his title, proved an excellent worker and was a good sire. Another Golden to be imported about the same time was Melody Abess (in whelp to Ch. Colin of Rosecott), who went to Mrs van Mourik and became a Dutch Champion.

At that time the breed was still rare in Holland, and only very few were shown, most of them being bred and used mainly for work. Some Goldens of purely working strains were imported from France, but they have left little stock behind them, so their blood has died out.

It was not until 1956 that several owners, led by Baroness Snouckaert van Schauberg and Mrs C. van Crevel, founded the Golden Retriever Club of the Netherlands, and this was recognised by the Dutch Kennel Club the following year. The club is very active – it has now well over 2000 members – and it assists members in the breeding of dual-purpose Goldens by advising them on points of training. It encourages them to show their dogs and helps them with the general care of them and to find suitable homes for the pups.

Since the formation of the club many Goldens have been imported from England, several of them have become Dutch Champions, and many more have won c.c.s and Field Trial awards. Those who have attained their title of Dutch Champion are the two mentioned earlier. Pennard Golden Garland and Masterstroke of Yeo, then came Bosco Brit with the unequalled record of fourteen c.c.s. Others to gain their title are

Echo of Ulvin, Happy Lass of Ulvin, Chieftain of Ulvin, Weyland Curfew, Whamstead Gaye, Alresford Lovely Lady, Lindys Mary Rose and Lindys Lysander.

The growth of the breed is also reflected in the number of entries at an All-Breed Championship show, from the one or two Goldens shown in the late 1940s to about eighty nowadays. An entry of over 300 in a club show is not surprising anymore.

There are five or six All-Breed Championship shows a year, and the Golden Retriever Club of the Netherlands was granted its first Championship show in 1966.

To become a Dutch champion a dog must win four c.c.s – at least one of which must be won after the age of twenty-seven months – and a c.c. won at the annual 'Winner' show at Amsterdam counts double, as does one gained at a Specialist Club's Championship show. In Holland it is not necessary to gain a working qualification before taking the Champion title.

To become an International Champion in Europe a dog must win c.c.s in three countries, and also a first, second or third in an International Open Field event.

To become a Dual Champion a dog must win two c.c.s in a show and two c.c.s in an International Field event.

As well as having about twenty Dutch-bred Champions in 1965, Holland can boast of having a Dutch-bred Dual Champion (Andy van Sparrenrode owned by Mrs C. van Crevel) and one International Champion, namely Cindy fan it Foksehoal, also Dutch-bred and owned by Mr Th. Pennings. All these Champions stem from imported dogs.

There are only two Retriever Trials (both for all varieties) held each year in Holland. One takes place in roots, and the other on the dunes along the coast. On nearly every shoot there is water, so that gundogs in Holland must be equally good in water and on land.

FRANCE

Until quite recently there has been very little interest in Goldens in this country, but now there are quite a few breeders who have imported good stock from England and there are now several who have taken the European Champion title, as well as their Championships in various countries on the Continent. The lines from which they come are Westley, Gyrima and Telmah.

To become a French Champion a dog must win 3 c.c.s, one of which must have been won at a Club Show or the French Championship (both held once a year), and it must obtain a certificate of merit at a Field Trial.

SWITZERLAND

Goldens are becoming increasingly popular in Switzerland, and in 1978 231 puppies were registered at the Swiss Kennel Club. Quite a few are shown and others are being trained for mountain rescue and avalanche rescue work (one such dog, who has been awarded several rescue degrees is Dr Bult's Swiss Ch. Camrose Listrander).

The only early breeder of Goldens in this country who is still active is Mr Scheidegger, whose association with the breed stretches for about twenty years. He and Mr Thöenen were two of the first to breed. Mr Thöenen started with Angus of Gresham and Camrose Gypsy (sister to Ch. Camrose Jessica), who had several litters.

Most of the present-day show dogs stem from the Yeo, Deerflite, Rooftreetop, Thenford and Gyrima kennels, and there are now several enthusiastic breeders.

To become a Swiss Champion a Golden must obtain three c.c.s under at least two different judges, in a period of not less than twelve months. The dog must also hold a breeding pass i.e. must be tested in temperament, hip dysplasia, and conformity to the breed Standard.

DENMARK

As far as I can ascertain, the first Goldens to be bred from in this country were those imported from England about the year 1958 by Mr Albrechtson, namely Vagabond of Coldharbour and Empshott Charming Lady. Mated together these two produced the two International Champions, Tais Philips Flapore and Philips Kiwi. A few years later Mr Albrechtson also imported a daughter of Ch. Simon of Westley from Miss Joan Gill, called Helen of Westley (bred by Mrs Hughes), and one from Mrs L. A. Harry's Colchis kennel.

Early Champions in Denmark came from the Wessex kennel of Miss Lizzie Broderson, and that of Mr Carl Bauder. Miss Broderson, who was in England for several years, took back with her Anbria Joriemour Lizbeth (English Ch. Camrose Nicolas of Westley × Joriemour Anbria Liana), and Anbria Tarlatan (English Ch. Camrose Tallyrand of Anbria × Anbria Laurel), both of whom became Danish Champions. Miss Broderson also took back Anbria Laurel, and from these three she has produced many winners for herself and others. Mr Bauder's Field Trial winning Danish Ch. Camrose Quixote has also sired much good show and working stock.

It is from these that the early Goldens in Denmark today stem, though there have been many others imported since which appear at shows and are used as gundogs, or kept as companions. The number of registrations with the Danish Kennel Club for this breed now is quite high.

Before being able to compete in the 'Winners' class at a show (and thus to compete for the c.c.) the dog must have taken a Working Test first prize. This test is a type of obedience test in which the dog must walk to heel off the leash, sit and stay whilst the owner goes out of sight. It must also retrieve twice and show that it is not gun-shy.

In order to qualify for the title of champion the dog must also have at·least a second prize in a Field Trial – the trials being run on dead game or dummies.

NORWAY

Goldens do not appear to have been bred or shown in Norway until recently. It was not until 1954, when three were imported from England, namely Prinmere Alisdair, Pennard Golden Tosca and Mellow Golden Jester, that any interest in the breed appears to have been shown.

In 1959, a bitch Redstead Belinda (Arbrook Alresford Eclipse × Ecstasy of Arbrook), was imported and produced two litters, the first by Danish Ch. Tais Philips Flapore (Vaga-

bond of Coldharbour× Empshott Charming Lass), the other
by Tais Griff (Danish Ch. Camrose Quixote × Danish Ch.
Philips Kiwi). In the same year Seaspel of Boyers, also
imported from England, was mated to Danish Ch. Tais Philips
Flapore.

In 1961 Camrose Una was imported by Mrs Norah
Bleutecher, and this bitch took her Norwegian title of Champion. Also in 1961 about eight puppies were imported from
Denmark, sired by Danish Ch. Camrose Quixote, and several
from Sweden from the Apport and Hedetorpet kennels. In
1962 two more Goldens were imported from England, Boltby
Brigand and Drexholme Chrysler Venture – the latter to
become the first Norwegian Champion of this breed.

The dogs mentioned above laid the foundations of the
breed in Norway, and they have produced much winning
stock. There are now many title-holders from more recently
imported dogs and bitches (Norwegian Ch. Camrose Voravey,
for instance, has proved a very influential sire). There are
other Norwegian Champions, domiciled in the other Scandinavian countries, for dogs are frequently shown in all three
Scandinavian countries.

The breed is becoming increasingly popular, for in 1961
there were only four members of the Norwegian Retriever
Club (any variety) who owned Goldens, whereas several years
later there are many 'Golden' members, and it is not unusual
for between 100 and 150 dogs to be entered at a Show.

To become a Norwegian Champion a dog must win three
c.c.s under three different judges within a period of not less
than two years.

Field Trials at which Retrievers can compete are very new to
this country and so far no Goldens have taken awards at
them.

SWEDEN

There have been Goldens in Sweden since about 1930, but
little is known of them or their activities before the Second
World War, except that one, probably imported from
England, was a good working dog.

The first two to be bred from were imported in 1950 by Mr

K. G. Zetterstén (kennel Borghälla) and Mr and Mrs Nilsson (Hedetorpet). These were Stubblesdown Tinker (Stubblesdown Torrdale Trueman × Stubblesdown Countess) and Barthill Fanny (Sandy of Westcroftley ×Barthill Brumblitz). Fanny was imported in whelp to Strelley Starlight, and one of the puppies was Borghällas Star, who was later mated to Stubblesdown Tinker. Mrs M. Lilliehöök (Apports) had her foundation bitch (Borghällas Golden Sannie) from the resulting litter in 1953.

In 1958 Mrs Lilliehöök imported Stubblesdown Begay in whelp to English Field Trial Ch. Stubblesdown Larry. This litter produced Finnish and Norwegian Ch. Apports Larry, who had a great influence on the breed. Mrs Lilliehöök's other great stud dog of the 1960s was Norwegian and Finnish Ch. Wessex Timmy Tinker, imported from Denmark. He was a great winner-producer and helped his breeder to improve her great line of winners.

Of other early kennels which are still influencing the breed is that of Mrs Ylva Braunahjelm (Sandemars), whose kennel has had much success with imported dogs, starting with Whamstead Queen, Int. Nordic Ch. Glennessa Waterbird of Stenbury, Norwegian Ch. Glennessa Helmsman and Int. Ch. Synspur Iona. Later she imported Swedish Ch. Cabus Clipper and Eng. Sh. Ch. and Norwegian Ch. Glenavis Barman and Norwegian Ch. Caliph of Yeo, all of which proved good sires.

Mr and Mrs Ulle and Sune Nilsson (Hedertorpets) started breeding in the 1950s and have had great success with many Champions. Their first import was Int. Swedish and Norwegian Ch. Whamstead Jess, and later came Stolford Sea Bird and Larkspur, but their most influential dog was the Danish-bred Int. Scandinavian Ch. and F.T. Ch. Coxy.

Newer breeders to start successful strains are Mr Filip Johnsson (Daintys), whose Davern Fergus has been an influential sire, and Mrs Karin Ericksson (Knegartens) whose Norwegian and Finnish Ch. Deremar Donald has many winning progeny.

Mr Henric Fryckstrand (Dewmar) has not only made up Champions, but has made an intensive pedigree research, and has delved extensively into breed history in his country.

Top-winning Golden in Sweden in 1977 and 1978 was Int.

Swedish and Norwegian Ch. Pengelli Lysander, owned by Mr
and Mrs Strandbrinck.

There have been quite a few Dual Champions made up, and
the most famous of the F.T. Chs is Duckflight Dik-Dik, who
has done much for the Golden's image in Trials.

Goldens increase in popularity all the time and in 1978
there were nearly 3000 registered with the Swedish Kennel
Club. Average entries at shows in the late 1970s were of about
100 dogs (the record was of 225 at the Club's annual show in
1979). To become a Champion in Sweden is no easy thing, for
as well as winning his three c.c.s, the dog must also take at least
a second prize in an Open Class Field Trial. To win in a trial
the dog has to pass three set tests, such as following a blood
scent, execute five retrieves of dead game and to retrieve from
water. The tests are given over specified distances, and there
are certain conditions for the handler to obey.

UNITED STATES OF AMERICA

The Standard of the Golden Retriever in America was
originally that of the Golden Retriever Club (or Britain), but
this was revised in 1953, and again later, and that of the
American Kennel Club and the Golden Retriever Club of
America (1983) is given below. As will be seen this is a much
more comprehensive standard than that of the U.K.

General Appearance. A symmetrical, powerful active dog,
sound and well put together, not clumsy nor long in the
leg, displaying a kindly expression and possessing a
personality that is eager, alert and self-confident. Primarily
a hunting dog, he should be shown in hard working condition. Over-all appearance, balance, gait and purpose to
be given more emphasis than any of his component
parts.

Head. Broad in skull, slightly arched laterally and longitudinally without prominence of frontal bones (forehead)
or occipital bones. Stop well defined but not abrupt.
Foreface deep and wide, nearly as long as skull. Muzzle
straight in profile, blending smoothly and strongly into
skull; when viewed in profile or from above, slightly
deeper and wider at stop than at tip. No heaviness in
flews. Removal of whiskers is permitted but not

preferred.

Eyes. Friendly and intelligent in expression, medium large with dark close-fitting rims, set well apart and reasonably deep in sockets. Colour preferably dark brown, medium brown acceptable. Slant eyes and narrow, triangular eyes detract from correct expression and are to be faulted. No white or haw visible when looking straight ahead. Dogs showing functional abnormality of eyelids or eyelashes (such, but not limited to, trichiasis, entropion, ectropion, or distichiasis) are to be excused from the ring.

Nose. Black or brownish black, though fading to a lighter shade in cold weather not serious. Pink nose or one seriously lacking in pigmentation to be faulted.

Ears. Rather short with front edge attached well behind and just above the eye and falling close to cheek. When pulled forward, tip of ear should just cover the eye. Low, hound-like ear set to be faulted.

Neck. Medium long, merging gradually into well laid back shoulders, giving sturdy muscular appearance. Untrimmed natural ruff. No throatiness.

Body. Well-balanced, short coupled, deep through chest. Chest between forelegs at least as wide as a man's closed hand including thumb, with well-developed forechest.

Brisket extends to elbows. Ribs long and well-sprung but not barrel shaped, extending well towards hindquarters. Loin short, muscular, wide and deep, with very little tuck-up. Back line strong and level from withers to slightly sloping croup whether standing or moving. Slab-sidedness, narrow chest, lack of depth in brisket, sloping back line, roach or sway back, excessive tuck-up, flat or steep croup to be faulted.

Forequarters. Muscular, well co-ordinated with hindquarters and capable of free movement. Shoulder blades long and well laid back with upper tips fairly close together at withers. Upper arms appear about the same length as the blades, setting the elbows back beneath the upper tip of the blades, close to the ribs without looseness. Legs, viewed from the front, straight with good bone, but not to the point of coarseness. Pasterns short and strong, sloping slightly with no suggestion of weakness.

Hindquarters. Broad and strongly muscled. Profile of croup slopes slightly; the pelvic bone slopes at a slightly greater angle (approximately 30 degrees from horizontal). In a natural stance, the femur joins the pelvis at approximately a 90-degree angle; stifles well bent; hocks well let down with short, strong rear pasterns. Legs straight when viewed from rear. Cow hocks, spread hocks and sickle hocks to be faulted.

Feet. Medium size, round, and compact and well knuckled, with thick pads. Excess hair may be trimmed to show natural size and contour. Dewclaws on forelegs may be removed, but are normally left on. Splay or hare-feet to be faulted.

Tail. Well set on, thick and muscular at base, following the natural line of the croup. Tail bones extend to, but not below, the point of hock. Carried with merry action, level or with some moderate upward curve, never curled over back nor between legs.

Coat. Dense and water repellent with good undercoat. Outer coat firm and resilient, neither coarse nor silky, lying close to body; may be straight or wavy. Moderate feathering on back of forelegs and on under-body; heavier feathering on front of neck, back of thighs and underside of tail. Coat on head, paws, and front of legs is short and even. Excessive length, open coats, and limp, soft coats are very undesirable. Feet may be trimmed and stray hairs neatened, but the natural appearance of coat or outline should not be altered by cutting or clipping.

Colour. Rich, lustrous golden of various shades. Feathering may be lighter than rest of coat. With the exception of greying or whitening of face or body due to age, any white marking, other than a few white hairs on chest, should be penalised according to its extent. Allowable light shadings are not to be confused with white markings. Predominant body colour which is extremely pale or extremely dark is undesirable. Some latitude should be given to the light puppy whose colouring shows promise of deepening with maturity. Any noticeable area of black or other off-colour hair is a serious fault.

Gait. When trotting, gait is free, smooth, powerful and well co-ordinated, showing good reach. Viewed from any position, legs turn neither in nor out, nor do feet cross or interfere with each other. As speed increases, feet tend to converge toward centre line of balance. It is recommended that dogs be shown on a loose lead to reflect true gait.

Size. Males 23–24 in. in height at withers; females 21½–22½ in. Dogs of up to one inch above or below standard size should be proportionately penalised. Deviation in height of more than one inch from the standard shall disqualify. Length from breastbone to point of buttocks slightly greater than height at withers in ratio of 12:11. Weight for dogs 65–75 lb.; bitches 55–65 lb.

Temperament. Friendly, reliable, and trustworthy. Quarrelsomeness or hostility towards other dogs or people in normal situations, or an unwarranted show of timidity or nervousness, is not in keeping with Golden Retriever character. Such actions should be penalised according to their significance.

Faults. Any departure from the described ideal shall be considered faulty to the degree to which it interferes with the breed's purpose or is contrary to breed character.

Disqualifications.

1. Deviation in height of more than one inch from standard either way.
2. Undershot or overshot bite.

(Approved 13 October, 1981)

The Golden Retriever Club of America came into being in 1938, but there had been considerable interest in the breed prior to this, and I am most grateful to Mrs Rachel Elliott for giving me much of the following information. It would seem that the first Golden Retriever to go to the American continent was Lady, an ancestress of Lord Harcourt's Culham Brass and Culham Rossa, who in 1881 went with the Hon. Archie Marjoribanks, Lord Tweedmouth's son, to his Rocking Chair Ranch, located in Collingsworth County, Texas. He also had with him Sol, a great-grandson of Nous and Belle. Sol died in Texas, but Lady accompanied the Hon. Archie when he later visited his sister, the Marchioness of Aberdeen, whose husband was Governor General of Canada and lived in Vernon, British Columbia. Lady must have been a great favourite, for she appears in numerous photographs of the Aberdeen family during their years in Canada.

Another of Lord Tweedmouth's sons, Coutts Marjoribanks, lived in Towner, North Dakota, and he probably had Goldens also, so it may be that some of the progeny were distributed amongst their friends. But none of these earlier dogs played any great part in establishing the breed on the American continent, and little else is known of Goldens there until they were imported two or three decades later. It was not until 1932 that the breed was recognised by the American Kennel Club.

In the early 1930s Mr B. M. Armstrong, referred to in Chapter 2 (Part II), of Winnipeg, who founded the Gilnockie kennel, and had dogs of this breed, corresponded with Mrs Charlesworth, who was then secretary of the Golden Retriever Club (in England), enquiring about the prospects of developing the breed in North America, including Canada. He asked for guidance from the club on the correct height and weight of a Golden, and as a result of his enquiries, prominent breeders in England were asked to ascertain the average height and weight of their best dogs and bitches. These findings were passed on to him, and were subsequently added to our English Standard of the breed.

It was largely through Mr Armstrong and Mr Christopher Burton of Vancouver, who had shot over Goldens in England and thereby had become an enthusiast of the breed, that Colonel S. S. Magoffin's interest in Goldens was aroused. He decided to breed them as gundogs for himself and his friends, and it is to Colonel Magoffin that the breed in America and Canada owes much of its early success, and it was principally through his efforts that the Golden Retriever Club of America was formed. He it was who imported the great American and Canadian Champion Speedwell Pluto – English Ch. Michael of Moreton × Speedwell Emerald (*Sh Ch*) – from Mr and Mrs Evers-Swindell. This dog was the first Golden Champion in the U.S.A. He later became a Canadian Champion and also played a great part in founding the breed on the American continent, for, being a prepotent sire, he was able to transmit his great qualities to his progeny. The bitches on which Colonel Magoffin founded his kennel were Saffron Chipmonk and Saffron Penelope (both by English Ch. Haulstone Dan), whose offspring by Speedwell Pluto started his strain. When Mr Armstrong died, Colonel Magoffin acquired the Gilnockie kennel, and from this and his own Rockhaven kennels have stemmed many of the leading Goldens of today.

In 1932 another enthusiast of the breed, Dr Charles H. Large, visited England and made contact with the Golden Retriever Club here. Following his visit he imported Goldens into the U.S.A. and started his Frantelle kennels. The following year he wrote to the club, informing them of the proposal to form a Golden Retriever Club of America. This proposal was welcomed by the club here, which expressed the hope that the future club would adopt, and adhere strictly to, the British Standard. Later, when the club was formed, this Standard was adopted, and used until 1953, when it was completely revised, and the new and more comprehensive Standard was adopted.

Interest in the breed soon became widespread. The usefulness of Goldens as gundogs, their beauty and their excellence as companions quickly became recognised. Many more were imported from England, and these formed the nucleus of the breeding stock from which the present-day Goldens in America are descended. Imported dogs who gained their titles in the country of their adoption in the period before the Second World War are Am. and Canadian Ch. Speedwell Pluto (breeding given earlier); Am. Ch. Wilderness Tangerine (Speedwell Barley × Eng. Ch. Wilderness Maud); Am. Ch. Alaisdair of Highstead (Eng. Ch. Anningsley Crakers × Eng. Ch. Anningsley Beatrice); Am. Ch. Lady Burns (Eng. Ch. Bruar Scot × Abbots Amber); Am. Ch. Ottershaw Colette (Ottershaw Sunclad × Ottershaw Electra); Am. and English Ch. Vesta of Woolley (English Ch. Cubbington Diver × English Ch. Vic of Woolley); Am. Ch. Speedwell Tango (Corney of Rivey × Sheena of Ricketts); Am. Ch. Sprite of Aldgrove (English Ch. Kelso of Aldgrove × Rorina of Aldgrove); Am. and English Ch. Bingo of Yelme (Beppo of Yelme × Alveley Biddy).

During the early 1940s there were many others who started

to breed Goldens. Some of these early kennels whose names appear behind many present-day dogs are Mr Henry Norton's Tonkahof kennels, Mr and Mrs Theo Rehm's Taramar kennels, Mrs Mariel King's Kingswere kennels, Mr Charles Snell's Oakcreek kennels and Mrs James Austin's Catawba kennels.

The first Golden to do well in trials was Nero of Roedare (Mr R. Ryan), who was the first of the breed to be placed in an Open All-Age Stake. In 1939 the first Field Champion – Rip – was made up. Rip was from the English-bred parents Speedwell Reuben and American Ch. Speedwell Tango. This dog also has the distinction of having won sixty-three Field Championship points – a record equalled by only one other Retriever.

In 1941 the first-ever National Championship Retriever Trial was run, and was won by the Golden, Field Ch. King Midas of Woodend. Another Golden, Field Ch. Shelter Cove Beauty, won this same award in 1944.

The year 1946 saw the first two Dual Champions in the breed, namely the dog Dual Ch. Stilrovin Rip's Pride (a son of the famous matron Gilnockie Coquette, the dam of two Dual Champions, three Bench Champions and two Field Champions). The other was the bitch Dual Ch. Tonkahof Esther Belle. Since then there have been four other American Dual Champions – Stilrovin Nitro Express (another of Gilnockie Coquette's children), Squawkie Hill Dapper Dexter (who was also an American Amateur Field Ch.), Cresta Gold Rip (also an American Amateur Field Ch.) and Craigmar Dustrack, yet another to have the title of American Amateur Field Ch.

Another outstanding Golden who won in three spheres in the mid-1950s was Lorelei's Golden Rockbottom. He not only won the title of Bench Ch. and Amateur Field Ch. but also an Obedience U.D. The first Golden to win this Obedience degree of 'Utility Dog' was, however, Goldwood Toby in 1946, and the first 'Utility Dog Tracker' was his son Featherquest Trigger in 1950. Since then other Obedience degrees have been won, including that of C.D. (Companion Dog).

Goldens are now popular all over the country, and during 1964 U.S. registrations totalled 3993 – a very different situation from that of 1932 when only twenty were registered with the American Kennel Club. The number of Goldens entered at shows does not compare favourably with that at our Championship shows in England, where it is unusual not to see over 200 dogs competing – and at the larger shows, such as Crufts and the Golden Retriever Club Breed show, well over 200 dogs compete annually. At present, shows in the United States at which points towards the title of Champion are awarded average twenty to thirty Goldens in competition, and it is only at some of the Specialty shows run by the Golden Retriever Club of America where entries top the 100 mark. Because of the vastness of the country this club now holds Specialties in several different areas, and in conjunction with these 'beauty' shows, Field and Obedience Trials are often scheduled.

There have been many outstanding dogs produced over the years, and the famous kennels are too many to list. A few of these kennels which started prior to 1950 and have consequently produced many of the forbears of today's American Goldens, are Mr R.M. Bischoff's Lorelei kennels; Mr Ben Boalt's Gunnerman (formerly Beavertail); Mr R. Boalt (Stilrovin); Mr and Mrs H. B. Christian (Goldwood); Dr and Mrs M. Elliott (Featherquest); Dr L. M. Evans (Beautywood); Mrs G. H. Flinn (Tigathoe); Mr B. Foster (Des Lacs); the Misses and Mr E. Johnson (Wildwood); Mr and Mrs M. MacNaught (Marshgrass); Dr and Mrs O. C. Olson (Craigmar); Mr C. H. Overvold (Krystolida); Mr and Mrs R. S. Peterson (Golden Knoll's); the Misses D. and G. Rowley (Wessala); Mr E. Shaul (Feather Fetch); Mr C. S. Snell (Oakcreek) and Mr M. C. Zwang (Sprucewood).

During the post-war period there have been quite a few Goldens imported from England, some of which have done well in trials, and others have gained their bench titles, but the outstanding dog of the 1970s was the American-bred U.S.A., Canadian and Bermudan Ch. Cummings Goldrush Charlie who won many Groups and Best in Shows.

AMERICAN KENNEL CLUB TITLES
Up to the middle of the 1960s there have been six Dual Champions, well over 700 Champions, over seventy Field Champions, and many Goldens which have taken Obedience Degrees.

CHAMPION. To become a Bench Champion in America a dog must win fifteen points which are accumulated according to the number of 'class' dogs (not Champions) defeated at each show. At least six of these points must be won at two shows with a rating of three or more championship points each, and under two different judges. Five is the maximum number of points that can be won at any one time. (Example: one point . . . two dogs or bitches present; two points . . . five dogs or four bitches; three points. . . eight dogs or seven bitches; four points . . . thirteen dogs or ten bitches; five points . . . seventeen dogs or fourteen bitches.) Ratings vary according to the breeds.

There are 'Specials Only' classes, in which only Champions compete, therefore a dog looking for its title does not come into competition with existing champions. It is not necessary for a dog to gain any field qualification before attaining the Champion title, but to encourage owners to retain the working instincts of the breed the Golden Retriever Club of America offers 'Working Certificates' to dogs which prove that they are capable of doing the work of a gundog.

FIELD CHAMPION. At present to earn this title a Retriever must win a total of ten Open All-Age points. These may be acquired in either Open All-Age, Limited All-Age or Special All-Age Stakes, in which there are at least twelve starters, each of which is a 'point' dog, or eligible for entry in a Limited All-Age Stake. Not more than five points of the required ten may be acquired in trials open only to one breed of Retrievers, and of the total points five must be won through placing first in any one of the above-mentioned stakes.

> 1st place counts 5 points
> 2nd place counts 3 points
> 3rd place counts 1 point
> 4th place counts ½ point

AMATEUR FIELD CHAMPION. To earn this title a Retriever must win a total of fifteen points which may be acquired through placing in any of the stakes listed above, or in Amateur All-Age

Stakes, where there are at least twelve starters, each of which is eligible for entry in a Limited All-Age Stake. The handler must be an amateur. Before acquiring a championship, a dog must win a first place, and acquire five points in at least one Open All-Age, Limited All-Age, Special All-Age or Amateur All-Age Stake open to all breeds of Retrievers, and not more than five points of the required fifteen shall be won in trials not open to all breeds of Retrievers.

> 1st place counts 5 points
> 2nd place counts 3 points
> 3rd place counts 1 point
> 4th place counts ½ point

DUAL CHAMPION This title applies to a dog which has won a Bench and Field Championship. It does not apply to a dog which has won a Bench and Amateur Field Championship.

FIELD TRIALS IN AMERICA
These are run on different lines from those of our British ones, for the tests give each dog competing as nearly as possible uniform cover and 'falls' – similar to our Gundog Working Tests in England. To ensure this uniformity, game is thrown into the air and then shot, rather than flushed from varying locations. To test marking ability, double and triple retrieves on land and water are set. Often judges require a test that calls for a short 'confuser' bird near the line, while one or more longer birds are shot further out. This short bird will sometimes be a thrown dead bird, so that it falls roughly in the same place each time.

Certain 'blind' retrieves are called for in order to simulate the conditions of an ordinary shooting day, when a runner falls far out and the dog has not been able to mark it. In these tests over land or water a freshly killed bird is placed from 100 to 200 yards (occasionally even further) from the line without the dog seeing it. He is then required to find and retrieve that bird, which tests his response to the signals and directions of his handler, who must remain on the line.

Thrown birds in American trials are given an instantaneous start at top speed, and, unless shot quickly, will pull very

rapidly out of gun range. Since equal falls under these conditions are required, only the top guns in the country are
invited to shoot at important trials.

The Standard of the breed for this country was exactly the
same as the American one before it was revised in 1981 and is
given below:

General Appearance. A symmetrical, powerful, active dog,
  sound and well put together, not clumsy nor long in the
  leg, displaying a kindly expression and possessing a personality that is eager, alert and self-confident. Primarily a
  hunting dog, he should be shown in hard working condition. Overall appearance, balance, gait and purpose to be
  given more emphasis than any of his component
  parts.

Size. Males 23–24 in. in height at the withers, females
  21½–22½ in. Length from breastbone to buttocks slightly
  greater than height at withers in ratio of 12:11. Weight for
  dogs, 65–75 lb.; bitches 60–70 lb.

Head. Broad in skull, slightly arched laterally and
  longitudinally without prominence of frontal or occipital
  bones. Good stop. Foreface deep and wide, nearly as long
  as skull. Muzzle when viewed in profile, slightly deeper at
  stop than at tip; when viewed from above, slightly wider
  at stop than at tip. No heaviness in flews. Removal of
  whiskers for show purposes optional.

Eyes. Friendly and intelligent, medium large with dark rims,
  set well apart and reasonably deep in sockets. Colour
  preferably dark brown, never lighter than colour of coat.
  No white or haw visible when looking straight ahead.

Teeth. Scissors bite with lower incisors touching inside of
  upper incisors.

Nose. Black or dark brown, though lighter shade in cold
  weather not serious. Dudley nose (pink without pigmentation) to be faulted.

Ears. Rather short, hanging flat against head and with
  rounded tips slightly below jaw. Forward edge attached

well behind and just above eye with rear edge slightly below eye. Low, hound-like ear set to be faulted.

Neck. Medium long, sloping well back into shoulders, giving sturdy, muscular appearance with untrimmed natural ruff. No throatiness.

Body. Well balanced, short coupled, deep through the heart. Chest at least as wide as a man's hand, including thumb. Brisket extends to elbows. Ribs long and well sprung but not barrel shaped, extending well to rear of body. Loin, short, muscular, wide and deep, with very little tuck-up. Topline level from withers to croup, whether standing or moving. Croup slopes gently. Slab-sidedness, narrow chest, lack of depth in brisket, excessive tuck-up, roach or sway back to be faulted.

Forequarters. Forequarters well co-ordinated with hind-quarters and capable of free movement. Shoulder blades wide, long and muscular, showing angulation with upper arm of approximately 90 degrees. Legs straight with good bone. Pasterns short and strong, sloping slightly forward with no suggestion of weakness.

Hindquarters. Well-bent stifles (angulation between femur and pelvis approximately 90 degrees). With hocks well let down, legs straight when viewed from rear. Cow hocks and sickle hocks to be faulted.

Feet. Medium size, round and compact with thick pads. Excess hair may be trimmed to show natural size and contour. Open or splayed feet to be faulted.

Tail. Well set on, neither too high nor too low, following natural line of croup. Length extends to hock. Carried with merry action with some upward curve but never curled over back or between legs.

Coat and Colour. Dense and water repellent with good under-coat. Texture not as hard as that of a short-haired dog nor silky as that of a setter. Lies flat against body and may be straight or wavy. Moderate feathering on back of forelegs and heavier feathering on front of neck, back of thighs, and underside of tail. Feathering may be lighter than rest of coat. Colour lustrous golden of various shades. A few white hairs on chest permissible but not desirable. Further white markings to be faulted.

Gait. When trotting, gait is free, smooth, powerful and well co-ordinated. Viewed from front or rear, legs turn neither in nor out, nor do feet cross or interfere with each other. Increased speed causes feet to converge towards centre line of gravity.

Disqualifications. Deviation in height of more than 1 in. from Standard, either way. Monorchism or cryptorchism. Undershot or overshot bite. This condition not to be confused with misalignment of teeth. Trichiasis (abnormal position or direction of the eyelashes).

Standard of Golden Retriever Club of Canada

The Golden Retriever Club of Ontario was formed in 1958 by some seven enthusiasts of the breed. It soon grew, and in 1960 became the Golden Retriever Club of Canada (to whose secretary, Mrs D. Sprunt, I am most grateful for her efforts in collecting information for me), which now has directors and members throughout the whole of Canada.

It is not certain in which year the breed was introduced into Canada, but it is thought likely that the first Goldens came with the first Lord Tweedmouth's sons and daughter as early as the 1890s, as is mentioned in the part of this chapter dealing with U.S.A. Mr Christopher Burton, for whose help I am also indebted, is at the present time investigating the background of the early dogs, for it is thought that some were probably also brought into the country by retired naval and army officers from England, and possibly from India, Hong Kong and Malay, long before the breed was officially recognised by the Canadian Kennel Club.

The first reference to Golden Retrievers as such, in the Canadian Kennel Club Stud Books, appears in the year 1927, but it seems most likely that others were registered before this, for until that year all Retrievers were grouped together in these Stud Books without any reference to the particular variety.

In 1928 Mr B.M. Armstrong of Winnipeg, who owned Goldens for several years and did much to promote interest in the breed, registered his kennel name of Gilnockie. After his death his kennel was transferred to Colonel S. S. Magoffin in 1932, as previously stated.

The first recorded Golden to become a Canadian Champion is Foxbury Peter, who took his title in 1928. He was sired by English Dual Ch. Balcombe Boy × Wonder Duchess (both tracing back to Culham Copper). The next Champion was Mr Vernon's Dame Daphne in 1931. This bitch was imported from England in whelp to English Ch. Haulstone Dan, and two of the resulting litter, Saffron Chipmonk and Saffron Penelope, were the first bitches on which Colonel Magoffin's Rockhaven kennel was founded.

It was partly through Mr Christopher Burton that in 1932 Colonel Magoffin imported American and Canadian Ch. Speedwell Pluto, who, as was reported earlier in this chapter, was destined to have such an influence on the breed. (Mr Burton's love of Goldens dates from his boyhood, as he had come into contact with and often shot over those owned by his brother-in-law in England.) Colonel Magoffin's Rockhaven kennels, founded in North Vancouver, and later his Gilnockie kennels, were principally responsible for the interest developing in Goldens in North America, for he kept large numbers of the breed – indeed, at one time his Rockhaven kennel housed as many as ninety-eight Goldens – and from them many of the best of today's Goldens both in Canada and the United States owe their descent. It is interesting to note that of the twenty-one Champions in the show ring between 1928 and 1939, only four were not from the Rockhaven or Gilnockie kennels!

Since 1945 there have been about 150 Champions, fourteen Field Champions, and nearly 100 Goldens who have received Obedience degrees – though they are not, of course, all Canadian-bred.

The first Canadian Field Champion was the bitch Stalingrad Express, owned by Mr Charles Snell, which was made up in 1947. The first Field Champion dog was Oakcreek's Van Cleve, who belonged to the famous Canadian trainer the late Mr Charles Bunker. This dog's record was noteworthy, for he was a Canadian National Champion, Canadian Field Ch., American Field Ch. and American Amateur Field Ch. He amassed seventy-eight and a half points in Open Trials and forty-six and a half in Amateur Trials. Another outstanding dog was Colonel Magoffin's Canadian Dual Ch., American Field Ch. and American Amateur Field Ch. Rockhaven

Raynard of Fo-Go-Ta. A more recent notable dog, who has won awards in three different spheres, is Dr and Mrs D. Croll's Stonegates Golden Tamarack, who holds the titles of Canadian Dual Ch., American Field Ch. and is a C.D. in both Canada and the U.S.A.

Some of those excelling in the Obedience sphere who have taken more than one degree are Mrs P. R. Mayo's Lorelei's Tulachard Katrinka, C.D., T.D.; Mr D. T. Holland's Holland's Red Shadow, C.D., C.D.X., T.D., U.D.; Mr S. J. Pollock's Marshgrass Golden Topper, C.D., C.D.X., U.D.; Mr and Mrs Moss's Ch. Mossbank's Golden Honey, C.D., C.D.X., T.D., U.D.; Mr A. E. Munneke's Ch. Sundance's Rusticana, C.D., C.D.X., U.D. and Mr J. Smith's Quamorly's Golden Sasha, C.D., T.D.

The following are a few of the prominent kennels in this country: Colonel and Mrs S. S. Magoffin's Rockhaven kennel and Mr and Mrs L. H. Baker's Northlands kennel (both of which have now ceased to operate but produced outstanding dogs in the past). Others, given alphabetically, are Cmdr and Mrs Beardmore (Wayfarer's); Mrs V. Cochran (Sunnyknoll); Mr G. V. Joyce (Krooked Kreek); Mr N. C. McDonald (Shadywell); Mr and Mrs D. McKenzie (Anjamar); Mr G. N. Mehlenbacher (Mel-Bach), Mr and Mrs F. M. Moss (Mossbank); Mr R. J. Reid (Goldrange); Mr S. F. D. Roe (Roedare); Mr M. J. Seguin (Seg-Mar); Mr and Mrs W. Stewart (Whinbrae); Mr A. G. Wilson (Wilsonia).

There have been many Goldens exported from the British Isles since the war who have gained their Champion titles in Canada, and many more breeders who have come into prominence during the 1970s, and the popularity of the breed increases all the time.

CANADIAN KENNEL CLUB TITLES

CHAMPION. To become a Canadian Champion a dog must win ten points under at least three different judges. The points are awarded according to the number of dogs competing in the breed, and the maximum number of points awarded at one show is five. The points for each breed vary according to the particular part of Canada in which the show is held.

FIELD CHAMPION. To gain this title a dog must win ten points, five of which must be won by taking first prize in an Open All-Age Stake (not more than five points may be acquired in Limited Stakes). The points are awarded as follows:

> 1st place counts 5 points
> 2nd place counts 3 points
> 3rd place counts 1 point
> 4th place counts ½ point

DUAL CHAMPION. The dog must become a Champion on the show bench and in the field.

FIELD TRIALS

These are run on somewhat similar lines to those run in the United States, there being set exercises for each dog, thus giving more or less equal opportunities to all dogs. Equal importance is attached to work in water as to that on land. Dead game is thrown, rather than being shot over the dogs, and in the case of an 'unseen' retrieve the game is placed in a given spot. Mostly pheasants and ducks are used, and occasionally pigeons.

SOUTH AFRICA

The breed is not new to South Africa, but of recent years there have been very few imports. It would seem that the first Goldens there were those taken out by Commander Frank Wild when he settled in South Africa. This was the Commander Wild of Antarctic fame – he it was who took over the command of the *Quest* when Shackleton died. He had purchased Peter and Wendy of Dewstraw from Major Ayton-Blake in 1929, and gave them his kennel name of Quest. These two were bred from, and a dog from the litter was bought by the family of Miss M. Webb, who also imported Golden Anne of Dewstraw from Major Ayton-Blake in 1939. Miss Webb herself later imported a dog and bitch from my Camrose kennel in the 1950s. They both took their South African Championships. The dog was a litter-brother of English Ch. Camrose Nicolas of Westley, namely Camrose Nelson, and the bitch, Camrose Tamara, was a daughter of Ch. Camrose Fantango.

Another to become enthusiastic about Goldens at about the same time was the Rev. French, who imported Wanderer of Brambletyne (also by Ch. Camrose Fantango) from Mr and Mrs F. Tripptree. This dog, too, became a South African Champion, as did a later English import to the same kennel, Chablis of Carloway. Another to be imported by the Rev. French was Buyile Thembalisha, who took her title in 1965. These three have founded the Thembalisha kennel of Goldens in the Transvaal, which produced a number of litters for the Rev. French before his departure to the U.S.A.

During 1962, 1963 and 1964 there were about thirty-five Goldens registered with the Kennel Union of South Africa, and though there are quite a number of Goldens in Rhodesia, and the Transvaal, the Cape, Natal and the Free State, there are few breeders, and hardly any Goldens appear at shows.

To become a South African Champion the dog must win a c.c. in three different provinces.

INDIA

The first registrations of Golden Retrievers with the Indian Kennel Club were in the year 1924, and it is believed that the first dogs of this breed to arrive in India were those of His Highness the Maharaja Dhiraj of Patiala, who imported English Ch. Flight of Kentford (born in 1921), later to become an Indian Dual Champion, from the Hon. Mrs Giff, and Cubbington Jan from Mrs Cottingham. Others were to join the Maharaja's kennels and were to compete successfully at trials. Mr Brunt, head keeper to Lord Rank, was with the Maharaja from 1929 to 1935, during which time he remembers running one of the Goldens, Marigold, with success in trials.

H.H. the Maharaja presented an elegant trophy to the Golden Retriever Club (in England), which is competed for at the annual Championship show, and is awarded to the best dog or bitch at the show which has won at least a Certificate of Merit at a recognised trial.

In 1928 Colonel E. Cobb, of the Indian Political Service,

took with him to India a bitch from Mrs Coverdale-Butterwick (Ruebury) registered as Ingleby Vesta, who was mated to Colonel Sutherland's Treacle which had been given to him by the Maharaja, and these two were thought to be the only Goldens in the country, other than those in Patiala. Vesta's litter produced some good gundogs, and one – Sancho Panza – which was given by Colonel Cobb to his brother General Eddy Cobb, was later exhibited at the All India Delhi Championship show by Miss V. Wood of the Kolahoi prefix, where he was Best of Breed.

Later, Vesta was mated to Eng. Ch. and Indian Dual Ch. Flight of Kentford and also to Cubbington Jan, and on both occasions had large litters, all of which were distributed among friends and acquaintances in the north of India, so the breed became more widely known. Colonel Sutherland's wife imported Cubbington Jickey (Ch. Cubbington Diver × Cubbington Bunty), who was mated to one of Ingleby Vesta's sons (Stirling Stringer), and Brigadier W. E. H. Grylls (whose Funtington prefix has been to the fore at English shows and trials) had one of this litter (Funtington Dinah) which he used mainly for duck shooting.

Miss V. Wood's own dogs did much to popularise the breed, for in 1938 she exported Quook (Stubbings Golden Nimbus × Stubbings Golden Sincerity) to Colonel Fraser, Resident of Kashmir. A bitch, Chaudi (Stubbings Golden Jacobite× Stubbings Golden Quietude), soon joined the same owner. In 1939, Miss Wood herself went to India and had the dog Mountaineer of Mintika from a litter by Quook out of Chaudi (both Indian Champions). Miss Wood also had an Indian-bred bitch which produced several litters to Mountaineer. Puppies from these litters were sold to the Nawab of Dir, the Raja Harendra Singh of Baroda, and others to Europeans. Mountaineer was accompanying Miss Wood back to England, but unfortunately was poisoned *en route*.

Many Goldens have followed from these early beginnings, and the number of registrations during the forty years of their existence in India have totalled about 2000, and there have been about ten Champions.

It is well known that Goldens held a special place in the affections of President Nehru and his family. Madhu – Rusty of Maling – was his own particular favourite, and the Prime

Minister, the Hon. Mrs Indira Gandhi (President Nehru's daughter), kept Madhu and several others. This dog was named Madhu (which means 'honey') because, according to an extract from a letter from the Hon. Mrs Indira Gandhi to Colonel Cobb, 'he looked like a huge drop of honey when he came to us as a tiny puppy'.

There have been several others exported to India from this country since the war, amongst which those belonging to Major and Mrs J. Lawrence had much success. They imported Indian Ch. Alresford Countryman (full-brother to Ch. Alresford Advertiser) from Mrs L. Pilkington, and Kestrina of Kuldana (Ch. Dorcas Glorious of Slat × Ch. Katrina of Kuldana) from Mrs G. Medhurst early in the 1950s. Mrs L. Anderson sent Indian Ch. Legend of Lindys to Mr M. S. Advani, and in 1962 Camrose Zinnia (Ch. Simon of Westley× Ch. Camrose Jessica) went from my kennel to Mr Wright of Calcutta. Mrs S. Gill, who lived in India for a short time, made Mermaid of Anbria into an Indian Champion before bringing her back to England.

Some other owners of Indian Champions are Colonel and Mrs R. N. Sen, Mr Prakash Krishna, Mr D. Cottle, Mr and Mrs R. H. Stuart, Mrs L. J. MacFadyan, Mr A. S. Mani, the Maharana of Sant and Mr M. S. Advani.

INDIAN KENNEL CLUB TITLES

CHAMPION. A Champion Certificate is issued on application for a dog which has won three c.c.s under three different judges.

FIELD TRIAL CHAMPION. The title is awarded to a dog which has won two first prizes in Field Trials in that country.

DUAL CHAMPION. A Champion on the show bench and at Field Trials.

AUSTRALIA

Information on early Goldens in Australia is somewhat scanty, but it seems likely that some were imported from England prior to 1939, for Grackle of Tone (from Miss Newton-

Deakin's English kennel) became an Australian Champion, and appears in the background of several New Zealand dogs, as does another Australian Champion, Temeraire.

Two early post-war exports from England to South Australia were those which went to Mrs Arnfield, namely Kristina of Kuldana (Ch. Dorcas Glorious of Slat × Ch. Katrina of Kuldana) from Mrs G. Medhurst, and a dog, Alexander of Arbrook (Stubbings Golden Dandylyon × Honeyflower of Arbrook), from Mrs M. Wills. These two both became Australian Champions.

It is possible that the next Golden to come to this country was Molyneux Gina Edwina (whelped in 1949), who founded Mrs Elsie Dodd's kennel in Queensland. This bitch, mostly of Stubbings breeding, became an Australian Champion, and, mated to Aus. Ch. Manyung Masterpiece of Melbourne (bred from New Zealand stock), produced Molyneux Melody, who in her turn has continued the winning line. It was mainly through Mrs Dodd's efforts that the governing body in Queensland eventually listed Goldens as a separate breed in 1954.

In this same year Mrs V. L. Reid (Leoline) bought a bitch from Mrs Dodd's first litter, and later added another to her kennel, namely Débutante of Silverpeaks (imported from New Zealand but of English breeding), who became an Australian Champion. Mated to Aus. Ch. Kyvalley Kyva (all English blood-lines), Débutante produced Aus. Ch. Leoline Golden Lorilee.

Two imports into Australia at about this time (1954) were to have far-reaching effects on the breed, for many kennels have been founded on their offspring. These were Boltby Comet (Ch. Boltby Skylon × Goldawn Brandy) from Mrs R. Harrison's kennel, and Halsham Hazel (Major of Elsiville (*Sh. Ch.*) × Halsham Merrie Maid) from Mrs I. Broomhall. Both were to take their titles in the ownership of the late Mr Spencer (Bonspiel) of New South Wales, and were to breed five Champions for him. After Mr Spencer's death Comet and Hazel went to Mr W. Davis, and produced more winners under his kennel name of Edmay, most notable of which were Aus. Ch. Edmay Day Dawn, Aus. Ch. Edmay Brandy and Aus. Ch. Edmay Donna. So few were the available stud dogs that Comet was mated to several of his daughters, and the resulting progeny have again been closely in-bred to.

Just before Mr Spencer died, Mr R. H. Philp bought two bitches from him (Aus. Chs Bonspiel Goldglint and Bonspiel Goldgleam), and later bought Aus. Ch. Edmay Day Dawn from Mr W. Davis. All three were from the Comet × Hazel mating, and from them he founded his influential Kyvalley kennel, which has produced nearly twenty Champions for himself and for others, a few of which are Kyvalley Kyva, Kyvalley Bobbie (owned by Mr A. Pickering), Kyvalley Fairsky, Kyvalley Cameron (owned by Mr and Mrs K. Webber), Kyvalley Honey Bun (owned by Mrs A. Bridgford), Kyvalley Sallie (owned by Mr Hughes), Kyvalley Skipper, winner of the obedience degree, C.D. ex. (owned by Mr B. Nelson and Mrs G. Deckert), Kyvalley Kym C.D. (owned by Mrs M. E. Grant).

After a time Mr Philp introduced an outcross into his line by using the English-bred Benedict of Golconda (Dorcas Quicksilver × Jyntee of Golconda), bred by Miss F. Gallop and owned by Mr Edwards, and through this mating to Aus. Ch. Bonspeil Goldglint he produced the afore-mentioned Aus. Ch. Kyvalley Kyva, who had an excellent show career and has sired many Champion progeny. Benedict was not long in Australia but his stock has had much influence on the breed.

In 1958 Mrs A. Bridgford added a Golden to her Taumac kennel of other gundogs. This was Kyvalley Honey Bun from Mr Philp's kennel – by Boltby Comet out of his daughter Aus. Ch. Bonspiel Goldglint – who became an Aus. Ch. Honey was mated back to her sire (Comet) and produced Aus. Ch. Taumac Golden Nectar, and later when mated to her half-brother Honey produced Aus. Ch. Taumac Golden Marksman.

Another of the Comet × Hazel daughters mentioned earlier, Aus. Ch. Edmay Donna, has produced some outstanding progeny through her mating to Mr Lee Pithie's Aus. Ch. Alresford Major (imported from Mrs L. Pilkington), of which Mr B. Nelson's Aus. Ch. and Ob. Ch. Whythouse Rip and Aus. Ch. Whythouse Madonna are two. Major also has many other winning children and grandchildren.

Late in the 1950s Mrs Morris imported Lindys Fable (Ch.

Camrose Lucius × Lindys Sarah of Westley) from Mrs L. Anderson. Unfortunately this dog soon met with a fatal accident, and during his short life sired only one litter from which Mr and Mrs Lenihan had a son of his, and early in the 1960s bought a bitch from Mrs Ledingham, Sundials Damask, from which to found their kennel.

Other kennels which have had a great influence on the breed in Western Australia are those of Mrs M. E. Grant (Karadoc) and Mrs G. M. Ledingham (Sundials). In 1961 Mrs Grant imported from Mrs M. Woodbridge the Field Trial winning English Ch. Iris of Essendene (Ch. Nickodemus of Cleavers × Folly of Essendene), who was to become an Australian Champion and had many successes in Field Trials in that country. Mrs Grant also imported Holway Mandolin from Mrs J. Atkinson and this dog became a winner in trials. During 1961 Mr and Mrs Ledingham arrived in Perth from England with their two Goldens, Storm of Sundials and Sonia of Winchendon. During the next three years these two kennels bred about 200 Goldens. Storm of Sundials soon gained his title and proved an excellent sire, as well as a good worker. These two kennels combining their blood-lines have produced many good dual-purpose dogs. In 1965, Mr and Mrs Ledingham returned to England, bringing some of their dogs with them.

Mr and Mrs K. Webber started their kennel with a bitch Aus. Ch. Sundials Aquila, from Mrs Ledingham, which has had an impressive show career, and they have also had great success with their dog Aus. Ch. Kyvalley Cameron.

Another successful breeder is Mr B. Nelson, who is chief trainer of the South Australian Obedience Club. His Aus. Ch. and Ob. Ch. Whythouse Rip C.D.ex, referred to earlier, Aus. Ch. and Ob. Ch. Sundials Alchemist and Aus. Ch. and Ob. Ch. Kyvalley Skipper C.D. (owned in partnership with Mrs G. Deckert), have all been successful both in the show ring and Obedience.

Mr and Mrs Hughes of New South Wales own the Australian-bred Ch. Kyvalley Sallie, and have imported other Goldens from Mrs L. Sawtell's Yeo kennel to bring in fresh blood-lines to the country.

Another import from England which has done well at

shows is Mrs Maundrell's Fergus of Westley (sired by Daniel of Westley).

Mr and Mrs R. Jenner, whose Nutmeg Sheba is closely line-bred to Boltby Comet, have imported New Zealand stock to introduce fresh blood-lines, and Mr and Mrs R. Trowse have two Aus. Chs – one with Stubblesdown breeding in his background is Bindarra Golden Duke, whilst Nutmeg Golden Gem is another which is line-bred to Aus. Ch. Boltby Comet.

In 1964 the Golden Retriever Club was formed, with Mr Philp as its President, and it has so far held two Championship shows, and is rapidly growing – the membership already being well over 100.

It is only within the last few years that Goldens have competed at Field Trials, and up to 1967 only one Golden has attained the F.T. Ch. title. Entries at shows naturally do not compare favourably with those in England – distances are so vast that breeders are not able to cover many shows. Entries therefore vary from about fifteen at the smaller shows to between thirty and forty at the Sydney Royal and Melbourne shows.

AUSTRALIAN KENNEL CLUB TITLES
Each of the six States in Australia has its own separate Kennel Club, and dogs must be registered with the Kennel Club of each State in which they are shown or run in trials. All the six Kennel Clubs are affiliated to the Australian National Kennel Council.

CHAMPION. This title is awarded on a points system, 100 of which are needed to become a Champion. One c.c. gives five points plus a bonus of one point for every dog (or bitch, if it is a bitch c.c.) beaten, up to a maximum of twenty-five points. Another bonus of up to twenty-five points is given for a Group winner.

RETRIEVING TRIAL CHAMPION AND FIELD TRIAL CHAMPION. Nine points are needed for the title and are won as follows:
    1st Championship Stake counts 9 points
    2nd Championship Stake counts 4 points

> 1st Open counts 4 points
> 2nd Open counts 2 points
> 3rd Open counts 1 point
> 1st Novice counts 2 points

FIELD TRIALS

These take place on similar lines to those of our English Gun-dog Working Tests, and freshly killed pigeons are mostly used. There are seven set exercises, which may be given, and thus each dog has equal opportunities. These trials are divided into four different categories:

PUPPY TRIAL. At which one single retrieve from water and one single retrieve on land is given.

NOVICE TRIAL. One single retrieve from water, one single retrieve across water and one single retrieve on land.

OPEN TRIAL. Any three of the seven different set exercises.

CHAMPIONSHIP TRIAL. Any four of the different exercises.

NEW ZEALAND

It appears that the first Goldens were imported into this country in 1926 or 1927, but from which kennels they came is not known. However, some English-bred dogs appear in the pedigrees of some of the early post-war dogs as far back as the third and fourth generations. These are Fair Gypsy of Nutwood, Grackle of Tone and Temeraire, the latter two being Australian Champions – so presumably some of the early dogs were imported from Australia but were of English origin.

Towards the end of the Second World War the purity of the breed was marred by an Irish Setter cross, and the very dark colour and Settery type which resulted is still apparent in many of the Goldens descended from this cross.

The Golden Retriever Club of New Zealand was formed in 1948 by Mr R. T. Willan of Christchurch, South Island, whose prefix of Huntingdon became most famous. Mr Willan was president of the club until the end of his life in 1957, after which time this office was taken on by Mr J. Tucker.

One of the early club members was Miss Hueston of the Gisborne kennel, who imported New Zealand Champion Pennard Golden Grania from Mrs R. Thompson in the latter part of the 1940s. Other Goldens to go to this country between the late 1940s and the early 1950s were New Zealand Ch. Roundwood Charm (bred by Mrs H.M. Watson) to Mr and Mrs G. Bremner, and New Zealand Ch. Alresford Standard (bred by Mrs L. Pilkington) to Mr N. Brown, and Beauchasse Furze (bred by Mr W. D. Barwise) to Mr R. T. Willan.

There have been three New Zealand Dual Champions, all from the Chelsea kennel of Mr and Mrs G. Bremner of the North Island. The first was New Zealand Dual Ch. Gold Laddie of Huntingdon, bought from Mr Willan. This dog became a New Zealand Champion, then took his Field Trial title in 1954 – at the age of seven. The next Dual Champion was one of Laddie's son, Chelsea Battue, bred and owned by Mr and Mrs Bremner. He too, became a New Zealand Champion first, then, in 1957, like his sire, he took his Field Trial title at the age of seven. The third dual Champion was Chelsea Dancing Lady, whose sire and dam were both post-war imports from England (N.Z. Ch. Alresford Standard × N.Z. Ch. Roundwood Charm). Dancing Lady was owned by Mr L. W. Morris-Denby, who trained and handled her in trials. She took her final Field Trial point in 1962, at the age of nine.

During the 1950s there were several more English imports, most of which have produced winning descendants and have helped to popularise the breed. Mrs D. Randall took with her from England Mishtair Rustic and Farthingdown Festive (both of whom became N.Z. Champions). Rustic's daughter, N.Z. Ch. and N.Z. Obedience Champion Pytchley Annabelle C.D.ex. (owned by Mrs H. White), was the first New Zealand Champion of all breeds to take the Obedience title. Mrs H. White also owns Annabelle's daughter, who also holds both these titles, namely N.Z. Ch. and N.Z. Ob. Ch. April of Laurelia C.D.ex.

Another dog of the early 1950s to go to New Zealand, and produce Champion descendants, was N.Z. Ch. Diver of Ipsden. During this decade Mr and Mrs Tucker, who already had a Beauchasse dog, imported Jonathan of Cleavers (Ch. Camrose Fantango× Ch. Lakol of Yelme) from Mr and Mrs G. Search. This dog was to have an outstanding career at shows, becoming a Champion at an early age, and having many successes in group competitions. He has proved himself an excellent stud force, producing several Champions and good gundogs. Mr and Mrs Tucker, whose kennel name is Lakenheath, also had a New Zealand-bred bitch (of all-English breeding) who was a daughter of N.Z. Dual Ch. Chelsea Dancing Lady. Later they imported from me Camrose Rosatanya (a daughter of Ch. Camrose Nicolas of Westley× Ch. Camrose Tamarisk), and from these beginnings have built up a winning line, which has produced several Champions, notably Mr and Mrs P. B. C. Pirani's N.Z. Ch. Lakenheath Bernhard. A later import to this kennel is Camrose Brambletyne Phantom, bred by Mr and Mrs F. Tripptree.

Mrs M. Hill-Smith emigrated to New Zealand in the late 1950s, taking with her two bitches (Tangueny Tangee and Idsall Amanda) and a young dog later to become N.Z. Ch. Camrose Terrie (Ch. Camrose Lucius × Castelnau Melody). Although dying at an early age, this dog left several Champion offspring. Later Mrs Hill-Smith imported another dog from me, and he too was to take his title – this was Camrose Xanthos, half-brother to Terrie – and she also imported a bitch from Mrs G. Barron, Anbria Feodora (a daughter of Ch. Melody of Anbria). These two mated together have produced several Champion offspring for the Tangueny kennel.

In the late 1950s Mr and Mrs J. A. Tennyson (Gorregan) imported N.Z. Ch. Stubblesdown Hesta (Stubblesdown Dewmist Chieftain× Stubblesdown Kandy) from Mr W. Hickmott, and she was to produce litters to Chelsea Mighty Fine (N.Z. Ch. Diver of Ipsden× N.Z. Ch. Roundwood Charm) and N.Z. Ch. Jonathan of Cleavers, mentioned earlier. Bitches from these two litters, Gorregan Britannia and Gorregan Jane, have founded Mr and Mrs Pirani's Willowglen kennel, which has successfully worked and shown them, and produced winning stock from them, as well as from their N.Z. Ch. Lakenheath Bernhard.

From 1957 the Golden Retriever Club of New Zealand was

inactive for ten years, but in 1967 a surge of popularity for the breed in the Auckland area brought about the revival of the Club, this time with an Auckland-based Committee, and with Club activities centred there for several years.

However, by 1975 the breed had reached eighteenth place in the Kennel Club's table of registrations, and it became obvious that there was sufficient interest to justify the formation of other clubs, so late in 1976 two new clubs emerged, the Southern Golden Retriever Club in Christchurch, and the Central Golden Retriever Club in Wellington.

All three Golden clubs in New Zealand continue to thrive and each encourage participation in field and obedience activities, and in fact the Southern Club is a recognised Obedience club as well as a specialist breed club. Each club has about 200 members, and an increasing number of dogs, mainly New Zealand-bred now, but still with occasional imports from Great Britain and Australia.

In 1978 Golden Retrievers occupied eleventh place in the registration table, and the Golden is now very much a contender for top placings in all fields of competition, and to date a total of five New Zealand Goldens have earned Obedience Champion status, the first in 1958 and the most recent in 1978.

NEW ZEALAND KENNEL CLUB TITLES

CHAMPION. To be awarded the title of Champion a dog must win eight c.c.s, under at least five different judges; at least one of which must be awarded after twelve months old. No field qualification is required.

FIELD TRIAL CHAMPION. To gain this title a gundog has to obtain six Challenge points under at least two separate judges (one at least of these points has to be won away from its owner's home clubs). These points are graded according to the type of trial run, with five points being awarded to the winner of the National All-Breeds Championship stake, and three, two or one points for wins in trials of lesser importance.

OBEDIENCE CHAMPION. To become an Obedience Champion a dog must win three Obedience Challenge Certificates, under three different judges.

DUAL CHAMPION. A Dual Champion is a dog which has won the titles of both Champion and Field Trial Champion.

CHAPTER 12

COMMON AILMENTS

Goldens are quite hardy dogs and no more prone to ailments than other breeds. The normal temperature of a healthy dog is 101.5°F. (38.5°C.) (to take the temperature a blunt-ended thermometer should be inserted into the rectum), his eyes are bright and clear from discharge, he is lively, has a good appetite and a general air of well-being. Any rise in temperature over 102.5°F. (39°C.), coupled with any 'off-colour' symptoms, indicates the need for veterinary advice. The temperature often rises after exercise, travelling or other forms of excitement, therefore it is not advisable to take the temperature immediately following these activities. Very loose motions, vomiting, listlessness or the refusal of food are all primary indications that all is not well.

ANAL GLANDS. These glands, situated at either side of the anus, occasionally become overfilled with secretion. The indications are rubbing the rear on the ground or licking the anus. In this case they should be squeezed out with finger and thumb.

BITES. Injuries sustained as a result of attack by another dog should be treated by cutting away the hair around the affected area and thoroughly washing it with a mild antiseptic solution of Dettol, T.C.P. or similar preparation. If the injuries are severe watch for symptoms of shock. If any stiffness or swelling occurs in the first twenty-four hours this is indicative of a septic condition.

BURNS. Use acriflavin as a first-aid measure. If severe, call your vet because of the likelihood of shock. Keep the dog quiet and warm. Watch for several days, as severe burn symptoms can be delayed.

CANKER. See Otitis.

CATARACT. Hereditary cataracts may possibly cause an obvious dense total cataract in young dogs and bitches, causing blindness as early as twelve to fifteen months of age (sometimes even earlier). A considerable amount of research into this disease has been done by Dr Keith C. Barnett, Ph.D., B.Sc., M.R.C.V.S., who has found that this hereditary type of cataract may also take the form of a small spot at the back of the lens. It is not obvious, and indeed can only be discovered when examined with an ophthalmoscope by a veterinary surgeon who specialises in eye diseases. This second form may not progress in later life, but when bred from these dogs may produce progeny which become blind. Research has not definitely ascertained the exact mode of inheritance but it is believed to be transmitted by a dominant gene with incomplete penetrance. It follows that no dog which has any degree of hereditary cataract should be bred from.

There is a British Veterinary Association Kennel Club scheme whereby certificates are issued for freedom from Hereditary Cataract, and these are issued by an ophthalmologist on the Eye Panel, and must be renewed each year.

CHOREA. A condition in which groups of muscles in any part of the body may twitch with a regular rhythm – nearly always the aftermath of distemper.

CONJUNCTIVITIS. Inflammation of the conjunctavae (membrane surrounding the eye), caused by an infection, or an irritant such as grit, or corneal damage. It is associated with distemper and entropion. The membranes appear swollen and the sclera (white of the eye) appear reddened. The eyes may be half closed, and the dog may rub the eye on the ground, or with its paw. There may be a discharge. If this is greenish yellow and catarrhal it is indicative of distemper, particularly if accompanied by a rise in temperature, diarrhoea or any other sign that the dog is unwell. If a bluish film forms this can indicate corneal ulcer or hepatitis. Treat with Golden Eye Ointment or some other oily substance, e.g. cod-liver oil.

CONSTIPATION. This occurs sometimes in old or wrongly fed dogs, and is also associated with feeding bones. Alter the diet so that it contains laxative foods, e.g. liver, All-Bran, liquid paraffin (one dessertspoonful daily), and if the condition continues, seek expert advice.

COUGH. Coughing occurs in distemper, pneumonia, bronchitis, emphysema and heart trouble, and is, of course, evident in kennel cough. It can be symptomatic of many conditions, so it is advisable to seek early advice. To alleviate the cough give one codeine tablet every four hours.

CRYPTORCHIDISM. This is a hereditary condition in which either one or both testicles are absent, or are retained in the abdomen, or in or near the inguinal canal. A dog with only one testicle descended is called a monorchid. Any dog which is not 'entire' may be penalised by a judge when competing at shows. The Kennel Club also insists on a veterinary certificate to the effect that the dog is entire before issuing an export pedigree – or, if the dog is not entire, a certificate that the purchaser is aware of the fact. A dog which has neither testicle descended into the scrotum is incapable of siring puppies, but the monorchid may possibly be able to do so. If both testicles are not descended by six months old, seek veterinary advice.

CYSTITIS. Inflammation of the bladder, generally caused by an infection, stones or a growth. Urine is passed more frequently than usual, there may be straining, and the dog may adopt the urinating position without passing water, and there is often blood present. Veterinary treatment is required to remove the cause of infection.

DIARRHOEA. This may be the result of eating something unsuitable, a sudden change of diet, incorrect feeding or during certain infections. It is often accompanied by vomiting. If the dog has a rise in temperature over 102.5°F. (39°C.), or seems unwell, or blood is present in the motions, contact your vet, as the cause may be a virus, bacteria or parasitic infestation – all requiring specialised attention. Feed little and often, and increase the starch intake, e.g. boiled rice, arrowroot or cornflour. Do not feed offal, red meat or undiluted milk. Give one tablespoonful of kaolin powder, mixed in water, three times a day, for a grown Golden.

DISTEMPER. A specific infectious disease caused by a virus. It is imperative that all puppies should be inoculated against this, and other virus infections, by about three months of age. Symptoms of distemper are very variable, and may change from year to year. The classic form starts with a hard, dry cough, running eyes and nose. Temperature rises to 103°F. (39.5°C.), the tonsils become inflamed, glands enlarged and the sclera reddened. There will be depression and loss of appetite. The first indications may be vomiting and diarrhoea and a temperature rise of up to 104°F. (40°C.) It occasionally occurs in a very mild form in which the early stages go unnoticed. A severe case of distemper may last up to eight weeks and may possibly result in permanent damage to the nervous system, manifesting itself in fits, paralysis or chorea. Expert advice in the earliest stages is essential.

ECLAMPSIA (milk fever). A sudden drop in blood calcium associated with whelping and lactation. The most common time of occurrence is during the first three days after whelping, but it can occur at any time during lactation. In the early stages the bitch appears restless and apprehensive and the litter also may become restless. In the later stages the bitch may collapse and have convulsions. Prompt veterinary attention is essential, for the course of the disease is rapid. Treatment is with injections of calcium, and, if given in time, effects a complete recovery. Care should always be taken throughout lactation, for the condition may recur.

ECZEMA. This is a non-specific term used to cover various skin diseases.

1. WET ECZEMA. This trouble starts with an inflamed area together with eruptions. It soon exudes moisture, the hair dis-

appears due to the constant nibbling or scratching, and the exudate forms a crust over the affected parts. These patches occur most commonly at the base of the tail, on the tail, along the back, on the face and behind the ears. It is more common in summer than at any other time, and though the cause is not always obvious, it includes such agents as fleas and irritant substances. What may cause one dog to have wet eczema will leave another unaffected. The treatment is to cut away all the hair around the area, bath with Seleen once daily and dress with calamine lotion thrice daily, until the condition clears.

2. DRY ECZEMA. With this complaint the skin becomes reddened, sometimes blackened, and there is partial loss of hair, and irritation. It is most commonly seen on the tummy, flanks and legs, and is thought to be associated with demodectic mange. Bath in Seleen, and repeat after five days. If the condition is not alleviated after this, seek veterinary advice.

ENTROPION. A condition whereby the eyelids roll inwards (in this breed it is usually the lower lids), causing irritation and weeping of the eyes. If it is allowed to remain long there is a considerable possibility that there may be permanent damage to the cornea, leading eventually to blindness. A minor operation is necessary to rectify the condition. This is a hereditary defect (which is transmitted by a recessive gene), therefore no dog possessing this fault should be bred from. It is occasionally acquired as the result of certain long-standing eye troubles.

FITS. Fits are the result of a variety of causes, such as distemper, worms, abdominal pain, teething, and, in bitches, by the suppression of the season. The indications are that the dog suddenly collapses, the jaws are clamped and the limbs are extended and rigid. There is frothing at the mouth and the bladder and bowels may be emptied involuntarily. As the fit progresses, the dog may cry out regularly, and 'paddle' its feet. Recovery usually starts from one to thirty minutes from the onset. The dog may appear dazed when consciousness is regained and full vision may not return at once. Keep the dog warm and completely quiet after the fit, in a darkened room. Do not attempt to administer medicine until the dog is completely conscious. A little brandy may be helpful on recovery and a sedative should be given, and veterinary help sought in order to diagnose the cause.

FLEAS (see Parasites).

FRACTURES AND DISLOCATIONS. Simple and compound fractures and dislocations generally need early veterinary attention.

1. FRACTURE. Breaking of a bone anywhere along its length. A bone can fracture in almost any direction. The commonest fractures are of the jaw, any limb bone, the ribs and the pelvis. They can occur at any age, and in very young dogs they are often near the ends of bones, or are only partial (greenstick). With a simple fracture the skin is not broken, nor is the bone showing, but with a compound fracture the skin is broken and the bone is protruding.

2. DISLOCATION. This describes the alteration in relative positions of bones at their joints, and is generally, as with fractures, the result of injury. It is most commonly found in hip, jaw and toe joints.

   Any sudden severe lameness with pain should be regarded as a suspected fracture or dislocation. There may be swelling at the site of the injury, with obvious changes in the shape of the limbs or body. Keep the dog as still as possible, and in the warm. If there is evidence of pain, give two aspirins. If the dog has to be moved, support the damaged part as much as possible. Get veterinary assistance and do not attempt to apply bandages or splints yourself.

GASTRITIS. Gastritis is the result of inflammation of the lining of the stomach caused by irritant substances or infection. Frequent vomiting occurs, and after all the food has been vomited the dog will continue bringing up a clear fluid or froth, which may be white or yellow, or tinged with blood. A mixture of one teaspoonful of brandy, one teaspoonful of sugar, one tablespoonful of water should be made, and one teaspoonful of this mixture should be given every fifteen minutes until it is all used up. If this fails to alleviate the condition, expert advice should be sought, for these symptoms may indicate trouble of a more serious nature. To stop the vomiting another good remedy is a mixture of kaolin and chlorodine (as made up by chemists for human disorders), and one tablespoonful of this should be given every four hours. Solid food should be withheld, and the dog allowed only one tablespoonful of boiled water every hour.

GASTRO-ENTERITIS. This is, as its name suggests, a combination of gastritis and enteritis in which there is both vomiting and diarrhoea, possibly accompanied by a rise in temperature. If this should rise to about 102.5°F. (39°C.), get veterinary help for this may indicate a virus infection. There is quite a common form of infectious forty-eight-hour gastro-enteritis. The treatment is the same as for gastritis and diarrhoea.

GROWTHS. These are either benign or malignant, and may range from simple wart-like skin growths to internal conditions of a serious nature. The commonest types of growth are the mammary tumours. These manifest themselves as hard lumps under the skin in one or more of the mammary glands. Immediate advice should be sought whenever growths are suspected.

HARD-PAD. This is the term given to a specific virus infection related to distemper (inoculation against this is given at about three months of age). It is not always possible to distinguish between these two diseases, for the hardening of the pads is not a reliable symptom, as it does not occur until late in the disease (see Distemper).

HARVEST MITES (see Parasites).

HEART ATTACK. The incidence of heart attack is, of course, greatest among middle-aged and old dogs. Its indication is sudden collapse, and the dog may appear to be dead. Recovery usually takes place within about five minutes. There may be involuntary evacuation of bladder and bowels, and the eyes may be rotated upwards. Keep the dog quiet and warm and in a subdued light, and leave him alone during the actual attack. Afterwards administer brandy as a mild stimulant and secure expert treatment.

HEPATITIS. This is another specific virus infection with variable symptoms. There is a very effective inoculation which can be given with that for distemper and hard-pad. The disease often takes a rapid and fatal course in puppies. There may be a rise in temperature short in duration, together with vomiting, diarrhoea, pneumonia and convulsions. Keep the patient warm and quiet and get veterinary assistance. In adults it may take a mild form with no symptoms other than a tummy upset, which may be followed some days later by a blue film on the surface of the eyes.

HICCOUGHS. Puppies frequently suffer from these, which are most likely to occur after food, and which may be associated with worm infestation. Generally they are not serious and can be alleviated by giving one teaspoonful of gripe water.

HIP-DYSPLASIA. This is a hereditary malformation of the hip joint, mild cases of which may show no symptoms. In severe cases, however, the animal will show hindleg lameness, pain and difficulty in rising from a sitting position. The only certain way of diagnosis is by X-ray. Because of the increasing number of dogs with this malformation in many breeds, the Kennel Club has now brought into operation a scheme, in conjunction with the British Veterinary Association, in an attempt to curtail the spread of the disease. Under this scheme, X-rays are submitted to members of a panel of experts for scrutiny, and these are 'scored', left and right hips separately, and the best score is one which has a total of 0, the breed average just over two years since the scoring scheme was started being just over eighteen, but the worst affected dogs can score over 100. As this is primarily an inherited defect no dog should be bred from which has a high score, i.e. one showing serious radiographic evidence of hip dysplasia.

LEPTOSPIROSIS

1. LEPTOSPIRAL CANICOLA. An infection caused by the leptospira germ, commonly leading to nephritis (see paragraph on this complaint).

2. LEPTOSPIRAL ICTEROHAEMORRAGIAE. Cause of leptospiral jaundice. It is generally contracted from the urine of infected rats, and its early symptoms are loss of appetite, vomiting and loss of condition. There is no sign of jaundice in the early stages. To detect jaundice, examine the subject in bright natural light for yellow colour in the whites of the eyes, and in the membranes of the cheek, and the gums. The acute form of this infection is often fatal within forty-eight hours and is characterised by frequent vomiting of blood and the passage of vile-smelling bloody diarrhoea. This virulent form is known as haemorrhagic enteritis. Professional treatment is, of course, vital for both these diseases.

There is, however, a most effective vaccine available for both these infections, and this may be given to puppies as young as eight weeks old, and is usually given in conjunction with inoculation for distemper and hard-pad.

LICE (see Parasites).

MANGE. Mange is a skin complaint caused by one of the mange mites burrowing into the skin which can only be specifically identified by having skin scrapings examined.

1. SARCOPTIC MANGE (Mite Sarcoptes). Occurs usually on the underside of the body, the armpits, inside of thighs, around the head, neck and ears, and is highly contagious. It is characterised by reddening of the skin, slightly raised red pimples, loss of hair and severe irritation. Its later stages may cause wrinkling of the skin, accompanied by a 'doggy' smell. The treatment is to bath the dog with Seleen or Alugan, Derris or Gammexane suspension every four days for at least one month. For obstinate cases there is now a preparation, given orally, which can be prescribed by your veterinary surgeon.

2. DEMODECTIC MANGE. This is caused by the mite Demodectes, and occurs most commonly on the underside of the body, armpits, insides of the thighs and down the legs. It produces dry, hairless areas, which may become excessively pigmented and reddened. Though less contagious than sarcoptic mange, it is frequently associated with general skin

health. The same treatment should be followed as for sarcoptic mange, but it should be continued for at least two months if the condition has become well established.

MASTITIS. Inflammation of the milk glands caused by bacterial multiplication. This may take the form of an abscess, and may attack only one gland. The symptoms are the reddening and the hardening of the milk glands, and it may be painful. The temperature may also be raised. Hot fomentations should be applied and the milk drawn off, and should the condition not respond quickly, antibiotic injections may be necessary. (Often erroneously known as milk fever.)

METRITIS. Inflammation of the uterus. This is a bacterial multiplication due to a number of causes – streptococcal and staphylococcal infection, retained afterbirths, dead foetuses or infection introduced during parturition. Variable symptoms may be shown, but any malaise appearing a few days after whelping must be regarded with suspicion. Temperature is usually raised, there may be an evil-smelling discharge, containing pus, from the vulva, but this is not always present. Milk production is affected and may dry up. Veterinary attention is essential.

MILK FEVER (see Eclampsia).

MONORCHIDISM (see Cryptorchidism).

NEPHRITIS. A disease of the kidneys, which may be acute or chronic. Most commonly due to Leptospiral Canicola infection, though a few poisonous substances can cause it, i.e. petrol and paraffin. The symptoms are: *Acute.* Great thirst, vomiting, back pains and a rise in temperature. *Chronic.* This form is insidious in onset. There is thirst, loss of condition and the breath smells 'fishy'. The diet must be altered to contain very little protein, and small quantities of food should be given at frequent intervals. The fluid intake must also be regulated, and barley water substituted for ordinary water (this should be made as follows: one pint of boiling water, two rounded tablespoonsful of pearl barley stirred together, allowed to cool and strained).

OTITIS. The term for inflammation of the ear. The simple form appears as an ear irritation, made obvious by the shaking of the head, scratching the ears, holding the head and ears on one side, or rubbing the affected ear on the ground, and is accompanied by a reddish-brown discharge. Treat this condition by cleaning the ear with warm water and Cetavlon (one teaspoonful of Cetavlon to one teacupful of warm water) squeezed into the ear with cotton wool. Dry by putting a swab of cotton wool on the finger, and, putting this inside the ear, and gently drying it out – do not push the finger down too far. Repeat twice daily for three days, and if no improvement is noticed consult your vet.

OTODECTIC MANGE. This infection is another form of ear trouble, formerly known as canker. It is frequently caught from cats, and is caused by mites, which may be seen in severe cases. There may be severe irritation of the ears accompanied by a discharge, which is usally hard and dry and very dark coloured. Clean out the affected ear with Cetavlon solution (as described earlier) and use an insecticidal treatment, such as Otodex. If this condition does not improve after three days seek expert advice.

The least sign of evil-smelling discharge or pus must also be regarded as needing urgent attention, as must any sign of sudden violent irritation of the ear, without discharge, occurring between July and October, for this is suggestive of grass seeds having penetrated the ear passages.

PARASITES (external).

1. FLEAS. Dog fleas are reddish brown in colour and move quickly through the coat. They can be found anywhere on the body, but most commonly on the head and face, along the back and at the base of the tail. They may cause severe irritation and may lead to a form of dry eczema. They are one of the intermediate hosts of the common canine tapeworm. They are most prevalent during a long, dry summer. Treat by

dusting the coat all over with a form of insecticide (such as Alugan) powder every four days until about a week after all signs have disappeared. It is also advisable to sprinkle this powder on bedding, and all kennels must be well cleaned out to ensure that no infestation remains.

2. HARVEST MITES. These occur in chalky country from July to October and appear as clusters of minute orange dots close to the skin. Two favourite sites are between the toes and in the ear sockets, but they can occur anywhere, and cause severe irritation. Treat by giving two baths of Alugan dip or Quellada at an interval of five days.

3. LICE. These are very small, hardly discernible insects which move very slowly. They are most usually found on the insides of the thighs, on the sides of the body, under the armpits and round the ears, and they cause intense irritation. Treat either with an insecticidal powder, as for fleas, or, to ensure complete freedom from these parasites, give two baths of Quellada at intervals of five days. Again, bedding and kennels must be thoroughly cleaned out and powdered.

4. TICKS. These are sucking parasites which feed by sucking blood from their host. They then swell and appear as a slate-grey blister on the skin. They are found anywhere on the animal, but most commonly on head, neck and shoulders, from early spring to late summer, and are firmly attached by the mouth. To remove these parasites, use cotton wool dampened with surgical spirit or methylated spirit. Hold the cotton wool on the tick for about five minutes, then pull it gently off with tweezers, being careful to remove all the tick, for if the mouth is left in the skin a sore place may develop. For heavy infestations bath in Seleen.

PARASITES (internal).

1. ROUND WORMS (Ascarids). These are round in cross-section, pointed at both ends and from ½ to 3 in. long. They are white in colour, though their intestines may be visible if filled with the blood of the host. Round worms can be found in dogs of

any age but are most common in animals up to four years old, and they are most likely to cause symptoms in puppies under six months old. One particular form of round worm (Toxo-cara) can be passed via the placenta from the dam to her off-spring before birth. Symptoms of the presence of round worms are poor condition, depraved or capricious appetite, intermittent vomiting and diarrhoea, pot-belly, fits and hic-coughs. Infestation with Toxocara will sometimes produce a cough due to the migration of the larval stage through the lungs. Treat with one of the worming preparations containing piperazine citrate. It is most important to ascertain accurately the weight of the dog, for an overdose may upset the animal, and underdosing on several occasions may lead to a resistance to the preparation. Repeat the dose in about a week.

2. TAPEWORMS. These are flat in cross-section, containing many segments of about ½ in. long. In the common tapeworm in dogs (Dipylidium) these segments are usually voided in the motions rather than the complete worm. They often appear stuck to the coat round the hindquarters, and they are white, and rather like rice grains. Tapeworms occur in dogs of any age, but are most common in young adults. They are not passed directly from dog to dog, but spend part of their life-cycle in dog fleas and lice. Treat this condition with tablets containing dichlorophen, strictly according to the instructions.

3. HOOK WORMS. These are very small and not usually visible to the naked eye. They are usually only discovered by testing the motions. They may occur in young dogs and nursing bitches, and generally show the same symptoms as round worms. Veterinary treatment is required, as there is frequently a general debility.

4. WHIP WORMS. Again these are very small and only diagnosed by testing a sample of the motions. They are most usual in puppies and young adults. Though not very prevalent in Britain at present, there appear to be more cases appearing of late. The symptoms are variable – occasional vomiting, soft

motions, loss of condition. Effective treatment is not available to the layman, therefore veterinary treatment is essential.

PARVOVIRUS. This killer disease, which has been known in this country since 1978, is one which affects very young puppies (from about three–four weeks of age) and older dogs.

Puppies soon produce blood in their motions and it is essential that veterinary help is sought immediately. The puppy will soon dehydrate unless given 'Lectade', either orally or from a drip, to restore the body fluids and minerals which will be lost. It will also immediately need a strong course of antibiotics.

All puppies and adult dogs should be vaccinated against this disease and given regular boosters. Veterinary advice is needed immediately the dog shows signs of this illness.

PHANTOM PREGNANCY. This condition occasionally occurs after a bitch has been in season, though she may not have been mated. At about six weeks after the end of the season there may be listlessness, loss of appetite, an increased thirst and an increase in the size of the abdomen. There is also a swelling of the vulva, and enlarging and soreness of the mammary glands, which may contain milk. At such time as a litter would have been born the bitch may produce symptoms suggestive of whelping and lactation, such as making her bed, as though to suggest the onset of labour. A phantom pregnancy may last up to eight weeks if not checked. The treatment is to substitute fish or white meat for red meat, and to replace half the biscuit ration by All-Bran. Cut down her fluids and give one teaspoonful of Epsom Salts daily with the main meal. If the symptoms persist after one week on this diet, or if the bitch appears ill, seek professional advice, for in older bitches this can be the forerunner of more serious conditions.

POISONS. If there is the slightest indication that a poisonous substance has been ingested, veterinary advice should be sought as quickly as possible, but first-aid measures taken immediately will help to relieve suffering and may save life. Some common poisons are listed below, together with the suggested measures to be taken:

1. ALCOHOL. Apply cold water to the head and neck. Keep the extremities warm. Give smelling salts to inhale.

2. STRONG ACIDS (sulphuric, hydrochloric, nitric)). Do not use an emetic. Administer weak alkalis, i.e. either one tablespoonful of bicarbonate of soda mixed with water, or one tablespoonful of lime water, or one tablespoonful of Aludrox. Also give olive oil, milk and eggs.

3. STRYCHNINE. Give an emetic (a piece of washing soda about the size of a walnut, or a strong saline solution) and any sedative or narcotics that may be available, e.g. phenobarbitone (up to two grains) or tranquilliser tablets. Veterinary attention urgent.

4. TURPENTINE. Administer an emetic and a purgative, e.g. castor oil, one dessertspoonful. Feed only milk and eggs.

5. RAT POISONS. It is essential to obtain veterinary advice immediately.

PROGRESSIVE RETINAL ATROPHY. This is a hereditary eye defect which can afflict Goldens. The retina becomes affected causing eventual blindness. There is a BVA/KC scheme for certifying clarity from this disease, and the dog must be annually examined by a specialist on the Eye Panel.

PYOMETRA. This is a form of metritis in which a quantity of pus collects in the womb. It is common in bitches over six years old, maiden bitches and those which have only had one litter, and is thought to be glandular in origin. Pyometra can take two forms:

1. CLOSED. In which the womb is closed and no pus escapes. The symptoms are listlessness, loss of appetite, increased thirst, raised temperature, increase in the size of the abdomen and vomiting.

2. OPEN. Where the womb is open and pus escapes through the vulva, causing a discharge which may be yellow, pink,

brown or red, and sometimes is evil-smelling. Symptoms are the same as for a 'closed' case, but less severe. It usually appears four to twelve weeks after the end of the bitch's season, in bitches whose seasons are abnormal or irregular, and who frequently have phantom pregnancies. Seek immediate advice, for it may rapidly become serious, and the need for surgery is frequently indicated.

RINGWORM. A skin disease caused by a fungus which can occur anywhere on the dog. It starts as a raised red irritating lump, and as it progresses a scale forms over this, the reddened area increases in size and the hair is lost round the lesion. As the centre of the lesion improves, the reddened scaly area spreads out to form a ring. If untreated, these lesions may become quite large and join up with others. This condition is most common during the summer months. Veterinary treatment is necessary, as this complaint is contagious to humans, cats and other dogs.

SCALDS (as for burns).

SKIN TROUBLES (see Mange, Eczema, Ringworm).

SNAKE BITES. Adders are the only poisonous snakes in this country. They are found over wide areas, but are most numerous in dry, heathy areas, particularly in the south and south-west of the country. Adders are about 2 ft. long, slate-grey in colour, with a rather thick body and a short tail. Their bite is serious to dogs, but is rarely fatal, though it is particularly dangerous if it occurs in the region of the mouth or throat. Veterinary advice is needed as soon as possible, for an anti-snake serum is required. First-aid treatment is to cut the hair round the region of the bite to a depth of about ¼ in. and then to rub on crystals of potassium permanganate. If the bite occurs on the leg, ligate the limb above the bite.

STINGS. Any sudden reddened swelling is suggestive of a sting, and sometimes the actual sting shows up as a dark red spot in the swelling. Insect stings are not usually dangerous, and the effects wear off in a few hours. However, a very few dogs may be allergic to them. If the sting is in the region of the mouth or throat it may be dangerous if there is marked swelling. If there is difficulty in breathing, contact your vet.

1. BEE-STINGS. The sting is usually left in, and must be removed with tweezers. Apply an alkali such as washing soda (dissolve one teaspoonful of washing soda in a teacupful of water), or bicarbonate of soda made up in a similar solution, to the sting area with cotton wool.

2. WASP-STINGS. Treat with a weak acid such as vinegar or a cut lemon.

TICKS (See Parasites).

TONSILLITIS. Inflammation of the tonsils, which are situated at the back of the throat, at either side of the root of the tongue, in a fold of mucous membrane. They can be seen by opening the mouth to the fullest extent and depressing the back of the tongue. It is caused in distemper, kennel cough, and other infections, and the symptoms are coughing, frequent swallowing and refusal of food. Tonsillitis is frequently accompanied by a rise in the temperature. Because this is symptomatic of various infectious diseases it is important to consult your veterinary surgeon.

URTICARIA (Nettle Rash). An allergy to certain foodstuffs, which is most common in young adults. It appears as a round raised area on the skin, particularly round the lips and eyelids. Give one aspirin as soon as the symptoms are noticed, but if there is no improvement within an hour, or if the dog shows any signs of distress, seek expert advice. This condition may recur.

WORMS (see Parasites).

WOUNDS. These can be classified as follows:
    a. Incised – a clean cut, such as that caused by a very sharp knife or a razor blade. May need stitching if large.
    b. Lacerated – caused by tearing and crushing, e.g. by glass,

barbed wire, etc. May also need stitching, and heals better if this is done within a short time.

c. Contused – wounds accompanied by bruising.

d. Punctured – small deep wounds, e.g. dog bites. Often need veterinary attention, as they bleed very little and are prone to sepsis and abscess formation.

GENERAL TREATMENT. Cut away hair round the wound. Remove the dirt with warm water. Bathe the wound with mild antiseptic, e.g. T.C.P. or Dettol (one part to five parts water).

BLEEDING. If only capillary blood vessels are damaged, bleeding will stop quickly. If it should persist, hold a cloth, thoroughly wetted in cold water, over the wound.

When the bleeding comes from a vein, dark red blood pours from the wound (usually on the limbs or the tail), and this should be treated by applying a pressure bandage over the wound.

In arterial bleeding, bright red blood spurts with a pulsating rhythm from the wound (this is again usually on the limbs and the tail), and this, too, should be treated with a pressure bandage.

If this treatment fails to control the haemorrhage apply a tourniquet above the wound, if this is possible, and tighten slowly until the bleeding just stops. After twenty minutes release for a few moments, to prevent circulatory damage, then re-tie. In both these instances call veterinary help.

POST-WAR REGISTRATIONS
OF GOLDEN RETRIEVERS

1946	2207	1961	2881	1975	5950
1947	2652	1962	2846	1976[1]	1926
1948	2132	1963	3078	1977	1474
1949	2396	1964	3040	1978[2]	4940
1950	2414	1965	3323	1979	8616
1951	2128	1966	3358	1980	10,274
1952	1750	1967	3872	1981	8837
1953	1679	1968	4251	1982	9702
1954	1745	1969	4751	1983	10,270
1955	2090	1970	5189	1984	10,448
1956	1852	1971	4766	1985	11,451
1957	2136	1972	5760	1986	11,948
1958	2222	1973	5913	1987	11,290
1959	2359	1974	6107	1988	10,278
1960	2551				

[1] A new system came into force.
[2] Another new system came into force during this year.

SPECIALIST CLUBS IN BRITISH ISLES

Golden Retriever Club
Hon Sec: Mrs T. Theed, Squirrelsmead Cottage, Fivehead, Taunton, Somerset TA3 6QY.

Northern Golden Retriever Association
Hon Sec: Mrs U. Spratt, Cliff Cottage, Lincoln Road, Boothby Graffoe, Lincoln, LN5 0LB.

Golden Retriever Club of Scotland
Hon Sec: Mr E. Fogg, 7 Pitcullen Terrace, Perth PH2 7EQ.

All-Ireland Golden Retriever Club
Hon Sec: Mrs E. Harkness, Greenmount, 2 Church Road, Portadown, Co. Armagh, Northern Ireland.

Golden Retriever Club of Wales
Hon Sec: Mr R. J. Edwards, 3 Hollywell Road, Tonteg, Pontypridd, Mid-Glamorgan.

Golden Retriever Club of Northern Ireland
Hon Sec: Mrs M. Neill, 'Alma Rosa', 49 Brackagh Moss Road, Portadown, Northern Ireland.

South Western Golden Retriever Club
Hon Sec: Mr R. Coward, Green Acres, Ibsley Drive, Nr. Ringwood, Hants.

Midland Golden Retriever Club
Hon Sec: Mr R. Hibbs, 8 Overdale Road, New Mills, Nr. Stockport, Cheshire.

Southern Golden Retriever Society
Hon Sec: Mrs G. Clark, Stocks Green Cottage, Rings Hill, Hildenborough, Kent.

Eastern Counties Golden Retriever Club
Acting Hon Sec: Mrs B. Webb, 116 Cambridge Road, Great Shelford, Cambs CB2 5JS.

Golden Retriever Club of Northumbria
Hon Sec: Mrs J. Hay, 12 Hedley Road, Holywell, Whitley Bay, Tyne and Wear.

Berkshire Downs and Chilterns Golden Retriever Club
Hon Sec: Mrs M. Iles, Crofters Heron, Fox, Amport, Andover, Hants.

North Western Golden Retriever Club
Hon Sec: Mrs J. Robinson, 32 Meadowcroft, Buxton, Chorley, Lancs.

APPENDIX C

GUNDOG CLUBS RUNNING TRAINING CLASSES AND WORKING TESTS FOR ALL VARIETIES OF RETRIEVERS

United Retriever Club
Hon Sec: Mrs D. E. Compton, Fox Close, Stonely, Huntingdon PE18 0EH.

South Eastern Gundog Society
Hon Secs: Mr & Mrs C. M. O'Brien, Furzedown, Grubb Street, Limpsfield, Oxted, Surrey.

Mid-Western Gundog Society
Hon Sec: Mr R. Hall Jones, The Captains, Castle Morton, Malvern, Worcs.

Midland Gundog Society
Hon Sec: Mrs J. Heywood, 171 Baginton Road, Styvechale, Coventry.

POST-WAR TITLE-HOLDERS

1. DUAL CHAMPIONS

Name	Sex	Sire	Dam	Owner	Breeder	Born
Dual Ch. Stubblesdown Golden Lass	B	Stubbings Golden Garry	Stubbings Golden Olympia	Mr W. E. Hickmott	Mr F. D. Jessamy	24.12.44
Dual Ch. Noranby Destiny	B	Bristle of Tone	Noranby Dumpling	Mrs W. Charlesworth	Mrs W. Charlesworth	19.11.43
Dual Ch. and Irish Dual Ch. David of Westley	D	Ch. Dorcas Glorious of Slat	Ch. Susan of Westley	Miss L. Ross	Miss J. Gill	6. 6.51

2. CHAMPIONS

Name	Sex	Sire	Dam	Owner	Breeder	Born
Ch. Torrdale Happy Lad	D	Torrdale Sandyboy	Ch. Dukeries Dancing Lady	Mrs I. Parsons	Mrs I. Parsons	18. 5.45
Ch. Alexander of Elsiville	D	Torrdale Tinker	Zena of Elsiville	Mrs E. L. Ford	Mrs E. L. Ford	15. 5.44
Ch. Culzean Sulia	B	Culzean Simba	Culzean Sanda	Mrs V. Porter	Lady Angus Kennedy	12. 4.44
Ch. Susan of Westley	B	Gazeon Golden Krasha	Linda of Hazelfax	Miss J. Gill	Miss L. Dixon	3. 6.45
Ch. Dorcas Glorious of Slat	D	Dorcas Bruin	Stella of Slat	Mrs H. T. Stonex	Mrs R. K. Pope	4. 7.43
Ch. Golden Girl of Morinda	B	Duke of Elsiville	Sandra of Ingledene	Mrs E. Saunders	B. Davies	19. 9.43
Ch. Dorcas Gardenia	B	Stubbings Golden Nicholas	Dorcas Lorelia	Mrs H. T. Stonex	Mrs H. T. Stonex	25. 8.45
Ch. Colin of Rosecott	D	Sh. Ch. Roger of Rosecott	Dawn of Rosecott	Miss R. Clark	Miss R. Clark	12. 3.46
Ch. Prince Victor of Dewstraw	D	Pasha of Dewstraw	Magic of Dewstraw	Major J. Ayton Blake	Major J. Ayton Blake	2. 7.46
Ch. Braconlea Gaiety	B	Dorcas Bruin	Stubbings Golden Olympia	Mr W. E. Hickmott	Mr F. D. Jessamy	8. 8.46

Name	Sex	Sire	Dam	Breeder	Owner	Date
Ch. Alresford Mall	B	Alresford Last Laugh	Windward Honeyat	Mrs L. Pilkington	Mrs E. Cuffe-Adams	3.10.47
Ch. Dernar of Yelme	D	Quilder of Yelme	Sunar	Mrs M. K. Wentworth Smith	Miss E. Todd	16.11.47
Ch. Nickolai of Elsiville	D	Tim of Elsiville	Nesta of Elsiville	Mrs E. L. Ford	Mrs E. L. Ford	23. 2.47
Ch. Royal Son of Dewstraw	D	Pasha of Dewstraw	Magic of Dewstraw	Major J. Ayton Blake	Major J. Ayton Blake	26. 4.47
Ch. William of Westley	D	Spar of Yelme	Ch. Susan of Westley	Miss J. Gill	Miss J. Gill	11. 1.47
Ch. Oakwin Gentle Maid	B	Oakwin Major	Rossbourne Quicksilver	Mr R. Panther	Mr R. Panther	2. 1.49
Ch. Charming of Stenbury	B	Torrdale Don Juan	Laughter of Stenbury	Mrs E. Minter	Mrs E. Minter	21. 9.46
Ch. Beauchasse Dominie	D	Ch. Torrdale Happy Lad	Sh. Ch. Beauchasse Bergamot	Mr W. D. Barwise	Mr W. D. Barwise	17. 9.47
Ch. Scaurend Susannah	B	Rum	Amber	Mr J. Baptie	Unknown	-. 6.44
Ch. Mossbridge Challenger (and Irish Ch.)	D	Buster of Gordonville	Aurea Barcarolle	Mr E. Orton	Mr E. Orton	1.10.49
Ch. Masterpiece of Yeo	D	Ch. Anningsley Fox	Princess of Slat	Mrs W. H. Sawtell	Mrs W. H. Sawtell	27. 7.42
Ch. Weyland Varley	D	Weyland Venturer	Ch. Culzean Sulia	Mrs H. J. Morgan	Mrs V. Porter	13. 5.49
Ch. Gaiety Girl of Stenbury	B	Sh. Ch. Torrdale Kim of Stenbury	Laughter of Stenbury	Mr & Mrs D. Hamilton	Mrs E. Minter	21. 4.48
Ch. Torrdale Faithful	D	Ch. Torrdale Happy Lad	Torrdale Chenilles Marigold	Mrs J. Wood	Mrs I. Parsons	9. 6.48
Ch. Alresford Advertiser	D	Ch. Alexander of Elsiville	Ch. Alresford Mall	Mrs L Pilkington	Mrs L Pilkington	15. 4.51
Ch. Westhyde Remus	D	Pennard Rusty of Yeo	Westhyde Waxwing	Mrs P. Fraser	Mrs P. Fraser	1. 6.50
Ch. Boltby Moonraker	D	Boltby Kymba	Boltby Sunshine	Mrs R. Harrison	Mrs R. Harrison	26.12.49
Ch. Fiona of Maidafield	B	Ch. Beauchasse Dominie	Sh. Ch. Torrdale Maida	Miss J. Murray	Miss J. Murray	20. 8.50
Ch. Katrina of Kuldana	B	Stubbings Golden Dandylyon	Honeysuckle of Rosecott	Mrs G. Medhurst	Mrs G. Medhurst	4. 3.46

Name	Sex	Sire	Dam	Owner	Breeder	Born
Ch. Pennard Golden Jolly	D	Dorcas Timberscombe Topper	Pennard Golden Gem	Mrs R. Thompson	Mrs R. Thompson	11. 6.50
Ch. Boltby Skylon	D	Boltby Kymba	Boltby Sweet Melody	Mrs R. Harrison	Mrs R. Harrison	3. 7.51
Ch. Camrose Anthea	B	Ch. Colin of Rosecott	Golden Camrose Tess	Mrs J. Tudor	Mrs J. Tudor	3. 6.48
Ch. Bramble of Essendene	B	Ch. Colin of Rosecott	Essendene Anna of Glenshaw	Mrs M. Woodbridge	Mrs M. Woodbridge	27. 7.48
Ch. Charming of Ulvin	B	Ch. Colin of Rosecott	Bewitching Maid of Ulvin	Mrs L. Ulyatt	Mrs L. Ulyatt	13. 5.51
Ch. Czarina of Cronethills	B	Countryside Monty	Harry's Choice	Mr A. M. Nicholls	Mr A. M. Nicholls	19. 7.48
Ch. Mefus Morning Light	B	Dorcas Timberscombe Topper	Torrdale Dorrie	Mr K. Hounsell	Mrs E. E. Dodd	27.10.48
Ch. William of Westmartin	D	Ch. Colin of Rosecott	Sandra of Westmartin	Miss B. Martin	Miss B. Martin	10. 5.47
Ch. Briar of Arbrook	B	Ch. Dorcas Glorious of Slat	Heatherbell of Arbrook	Mrs G. Barron	Mrs W. Wills	30. 8.49
Ch. Gay of Peradenia	B	Beau Laddie	Peradenia	Mr W. R. Jacobs	Mr W. R. Jacobs	7. 3.48
Ch. Camrose Tantara	B	Camrose Antony	Timberscombe Tansy	Mrs J. Tudor	Mrs D. Wyn	10. 3.50
Ch. Boltby Annabel (and Am. Ch.)	B	Ch. Boltby Moonraker	Boltby Sweet Melody	Mrs R. Harrison	Mrs R. Harrison	12.10.52
Ch. Kolahoi Willow of Westley	B	Dorcas Timberscombe Topper	Westley Frolic of Yelme	Miss V. Wood	Miss J. Gill	18. 6.49
Ch. Memory of Morinda	B	Joker of Morinda	Sherry of Morinda	Mrs E. Saunders	Mrs E. Saunders	12.11.49
Ch. Chip of Butlers	D	Golden Wag of Restville	Tess of Hatchett	Lt Col. M. B. Allsebrook	Mrs Q. M. Allen	3.10.49
Ch. Rushlight Roger	D	Rex of Rushmere	Goldgrain Brumas	Mrs M. Williamson	Mrs M. Williamson	23. 8.51
Ch. Sally of Westley	B	Dorcas Timberscombe Topper	Westley Frolic of Yelme	Miss J. Gill	Miss J. Gill	18. 6.49

Name	Sex	Sire	Dam			Date
Ch. Simon of Westley	D	Ch. Camrose Fantango	Westley Frolic of Yelme	Miss J. Gill	Miss J. Gill	23. 4.53
Ch. Beauchasse Gaiety	B	Ch. Beauchasse Dominie	Dorcas Leola	Miss J. Brison	Mr W. D. Barwise	11. 8.50
Ch. Camrose Fantango	D	Dorcas Timbers-combe Topper	Golden Camrose Tess	Mrs J. Tudor	Mrs J. Tudor	11.11.50
Ch. Lakol of Yelme	B	Ch. Nikolai of Elsiville	Later of Yelme	Mr G. Search	Mrs M. K. Westworth Smith	2. 2.50
Ch. Mossbridge Diadem	B	Int. Ch. Mossbridge Challenger	Fair Dinkum	Mr & Mrs J. Gregory	Mr M. McBride	26. 3.53
Ch. Bard of Cleavers	D	Ch. Colin of Rosecott	Ch. Lakol of Yelme	Mr G. Search	Mr G. Search	4. 7.53
Ch. Deerflite Delilah	B	Sh Ch Sonnet	Celia of Stenbury	Mrs F. E. Borrow	Mrs M. E. Denning	6. 9.51
Ch. Boltby Mystral	B	Ch. Boltby Moonraker	Denes Daydream	Mrs R. Harrison	Mr P. Whitworth	17. 4.54
Ch. Jane of Anbria	B	Ch. William of Westley	Ch. Briar of Arbrook	Mrs G. Barron	Mrs G. Barron	30. 6.52
Ch. Jacqueline of Hughenden	B	Cracker of Hughenden	Susan of Amber	Mrs L. Bacon	Mrs I. C. Fitzpatrick	10. 4.53
Ch. Crusader of Carthew	D	Ch. Camrose Fantango	Caona of Carthew	Mr P. Baird	Mrs A. Welch	8. 2.54
Ch. Heatherdell Gay Boy	D	Dorcas Peter Paul	Heatherdell Katrina	Miss M. M. Clarke	Mrs J. Tyzack	4. 3.52
Ch. Pennard Golden Primrose	B	Ch. Dorcas Glorious of Slat	Pennard Golden Pride	Mrs R. Thompson	Mrs R. Thompson	22.10.49
Ch. Alresford Atom	B	Ch. Alresford Advertiser	Alresford Emblem	Mrs L Pilkington	Mrs L Pilkington	28. 2.55
Ch. Nickodemus of Cleavers	D	Ch. Colin of Rosecott	Ch. Lakol of Yelme	Mr G. Search	Mr G. Search	4. 7.53
Ch. Camrose Lucius	D	Mishtair Destin	Ch. Camrose Tantara	Mrs J. Tudor	Mrs J. Tudor	24. 5.56
Ch. Avonvale Brandy	D	Sh Ch Sonnet	Wyckwold Golden Bunty	Mrs F. E. Borrow	Mrs R. Rowe	24. 1.54

Name	Sex	Sire	Dam	Owner	Breeder	Born
Ch. Fordvale Gay Moonlynne	B	Ch. Boltby Moonraker	Ch. Beauchasse Gaiety	Miss J. Brison	Miss J. Brison	11. 2.55
Ch. Miss Rebecca	B	Kiaora Royalist	Amber of Binfield	Mr F. Tripptree	Mr F. Tripptree	25. 5.53
Ch. Flax of Wham	B	Wyckwold Desperado	Stubblesdown Greeba	Mrs E. Gostyn	Miss Loake	15. 4.54
Ch. Simon of Fionafield	D	Ch. Torrdale Faithful	Ch. Fiona of Maidafield	Mr J. Carney	Miss J. Murray	12. 5.54
Ch. Miranda of Anbria	B	Ch. Camrose Fantango	Ch. Jane of Anbria	Mrs G. Barron	Mrs G. Barron	11. 5.54
Ch. Chalice of Altarnun	B	Sabaka of Altarnun	Glorious Dawn of Altarnun	Miss J. Chamberlain	Miss J. Chamberlain	15. 5.55
Ch. Rivertrees Susan	B	Ch. William of Westley	Nicola of Westley	Mr R. Walker	Mrs V. Dunn	24. 8.56
Ch. Camrose Nicolas of Westley	D	Ch. William of Westley	Ch. Camrose Jessica	Miss J. Gill	Mrs J. Tudor	31.10.57
Ch. Iris of Essendene	B	Ch. Nickodemus of Cleavers	Folly of Essendene	Mrs M. Woodbridge	Mrs M. Woodbridge	24. 5.57
Ch. Fillip of Yelme	D	Gilick of Yelme	Trafalgar Beechvale	Mrs M. K. Wentwor Smith	Hon. J. Nelson	24. 4.53
Ch. Kasanova of Kuldana	D	Kim of Kuldana	Kathryn of Kuldana	Mrs G. Medhurst	Mrs G. Medhurst	12.10.55
Ch. Dai of Yarlow	D	Int. Dual Ch. David of Westley	Sider of Yarlaw	Mrs R. Hutton	Mrs R. Hutton	8. 3.57
Ch. Samdor Nimble Nick	D	Stubblesdown Ladis	Golden Patricia Mayfree	Mrs J. Hendley	Mr F. Bodiam	21. 6.54
Ch. Jeanara's Blond Boy of Sektuny (and Irish Ch.)	D	Stubblesdown Glenilla	Dinah of Sektuny	Mr J. Green	Mrs E. D. Pearce	23. 2.53
Ch. Camrose Loretta	B	Mishtair Destin	Ch. Camrose Tantara	Mr A. Stewart	Mrs J. Tudor	24. 5.56

Name	Sex	Sire	Dam	Breeder	Owner	Date
Ch. Whamstead Diana	B	Whamstead Meteor	Whamstead Lavender of Janville	Mrs E. Gostyn	Mrs E. Gostyn	1.12.58
Ch. Battanropie Rissa	B	Ringmaster of Yeo	Battanropie Jane	Miss A. Baker	Miss A. Baker	18. 3.60
Ch. Camrose Jessica	B	Ch. Camrose Fantango	Ch. Camrose Tantara	Mrs J. Tudor	Mrs J. Tudor	7. 8.54
Ch. Deerflite Headline	D	Ch. Avonvale Brandy	Ch. Deerflite Delilah	Mrs F. E. Borrow	Mrs F. E. Borrow	31. 5.60
Ch. Cabus Cadet (and Irish Ch.)	D	Beauchasse Jason	Brecklands Tamaris	Mrs Z. Moriarty	Mrs Harding	1.12.59
Ch. Drexholme Herb Robert	D	Ch. Boltby Skylon	Hill of Hambleton	Miss M. Peart	Miss M. Peart	16. 2.56
Ch. Camrose Tallyrand of Anbria	D	Ch. Camrose Fantango	Ch. Jane of Anbria	Mrs J. Tudor	Mrs G. Barron	20. 4.60
Ch. Ulvin Vintage of Yelme	D	Ch. Dernar of Yelme	Ch. Charming of Ulvin	Mrs M. K. Wentworth Smith	Mrs L Ulyatt	20.11.56
Ch. Figaro of Yeo (and Am. Ch.)	D	Ringmaster of Yeo	Alresford Badminton	Mrs W. H. Sawtell	Miss Cocks	7.11.59
Ch. Gavotte of Altarnun	B	Camrose Fantasy of Rosecott	Ch. Chalice of Altarnun	Miss J. Chamberlain	Miss J. Chamberlain	8. 1.59
Ch. Glennessa Amber Amanda	B	Ringmaster of Yeo	Glennessa Claire	Mrs P. C. Dennis	Mrs K. M. B. Rogers	16. 7.59
Ch. Sharland The Scot	D	Ch. Nickodemus of Cleavers	Sharland Skiffle	Mrs J. Munday	Mrs J. Munday	6. 4.61
Ch. Gladiator of Ulvin	D	Ch. Dernar of Yelme	Daddsdog of Ulvin	Mrs L Ulyatt	Mrs L Ulyatt	4. 7.56
Ch. Melody of Anbria	B	Bart of Anbria	Irish F.T. Ch. Moonbeam of Anbria	Mrs G. Barron	Mrs G. Barron	13.11.57
Ch. Crouchers Bambina	B	Ch. Kasanova of Kuldana	Crouchers Brackengold Ranee	Mrs E. C. Melville	Mrs E. C. Melville	3. 6.59
Ch. Kenbara Castelnau Nonet	B	Ch. Camrose Lucius	Castelnau Motif	Miss M. Baker	Miss M. Baker	24.12.59
Ch. Camrose Tamarisk	B	Ch. Camrose Lucius	Lindys Sarah of Westley	Mrs J. Tudor	Mrs L Anderson	10. 3.58

Name	Sex	Sire	Dam	Owner	Breeder	Born
Ch. Synspur Lunik	D	Ch. Camrose Lucius	Synspur Bracken	Mrs K. Graham-White	Mrs K. Graham-White	8. 1.60
Ch. Toddytavern Kummel of Yeo	D	Ringmaster of Yeo	Toddytavern Henassy	Mrs W. H. Sawtell	Miss Constant	22. 8.61
Ch. Shadow of Rosecott	B	Ch. Nickodemus of Cleavers	Rosetta of Rosecott	Miss R. Clark	Miss R. Clark	17. 3.59
Ch. Boltby Felicity of Brierford	B	Int. Ch. Cabus Cadet	Sh. Ch. Boltby Sugar Bush	Mrs I. Wragg	Mrs R. Harrison	22.11.62
Ch. Cabus Boltby Combine (and Irish Ch.)	D	Int. Ch. Cabus Cadet	Sh. Ch. Boltby Sugar Bush	Mrs Z. Moriarty	Mrs R. Harrison	22.11.62
Ch. Anatas Gypsy Dancer	B	Anbria Linkboy	Sonnblick Fantasy	Mrs J. Sweetenham	Mrs J. Sweetenham	12. 7.61
Ch. Duckflight Greylay	D	Samdor Gamble in Gold	Byxfield Tess	Mr J. Noel	Mrs J. Noel	13. 6.59
Ch. Jenny of Aldercarr	B	Ringmaster of Yeo	Goldcrest of Aldercarr	Mrs J. F. French	Mrs J. F. French	5. 4.62
Ch. Glennessa Seasprite of Stenbury	B	Glennessa Crofter of Empshott	Sh. Ch. Watersonnet of Stenbury	Mrs M. Iles	Mrs E. Minter	23. 1.63
Ch. Pippa of Westley	B	Ch. Camrose Nicolas of Westley	Echo of Westley	Miss J. Gill	Miss J. Gill	8. 5.63
Ch. Bellemount Contoul Commanche	D	Int. Ch. Cabus Boltby Combine	Contoul Cherokee	Mr F. Hayton	Mr M. Constable	17. 2.66
Ch. Camrose Wistura	B	Ch. Camrose Tallyrand of Anbria	Ch. Camrose Loretta	Mrs J. Tudor	Mrs J. Tudor	28.11.61
Ch. Camrose Gay Delight of Sladeham	B	Ch. Camrose Lucius	Kerry Jane of Kuldana	Mrs J. Tudor	Mr M. Askew	13.11.63
Ch. Cabus Janville Defender	D	Int. Ch. Cabus Cadet	Sh. Ch. Janville Renown	Mrs Z. Moriarty	Mrs J. Harrison	23. 4.64

Name	Sex	Sire	Dam	Breeder	Owner	Date
Ch. Pinecrest Topper	D	Ch. Camrose Nicolas of Westley	Broadwaters Geraldine	Mr & Mrs Balaam	Mr & Mrs Balaam	5.11.64
Ch. Mandingo Buidhe Colum (& Irish Ch.)	D	Alresford Nice Fella	Buidhe Dearg	Mrs Sawtell & Mrs Harkness	Miss L. Ross	8. 8.63
Ch. Sansue Camrose Phoenix	D	Int. Ch. Cabus Cadet	Camrose Wistansy	Mrs V. Birkin	Mrs J. Tudor	11.11.65
Ch. Glennessa Seashanta	B	Glennessa Crofter of Empshott	Waterminx of Stenbury	Mrs M. Iles	Mrs Iles & Mrs Minter	7.10.65
Ch. Lindys Olivia	B	Ch. Camrose Nicolas of Westley	Lindys Linaria	Mrs W. Anderson	Mrs W. Anderson	7. 7.66
Ch. Brambleyne Boyd	D	Brambleyne Twig	Nellie of Westwood	Mr F. Tripptree	Mr A. Boyd-Gibbins	14. 4.64
Ch. Camrose Pruella of Davern	B	Int. Ch. Cabus Cadet	Camrose Wistansy	Mr & Mrs C. Lowe	Mrs J. Tudor	11.11.65
Ch. Bryanstown Gale Warning (& Irish Ch.)	D	Irish Ch. Bryanstown Shannon of Yeo	Irish Ch. Camrose Gail	Mrs C. Twist	Mr & Mrs Twist	28. 6.67
Ch. Anbria Joriemour Marigold	B	Sh. Ch. Anbria Tantalus	Joriemour Lily Marlene	Mrs G. Barron	Mrs M. Clark	25. 1.65
Ch. Crouchers Leo	D	Crouchers Joriemour Lucky Star	Crouchers Camrose Elsie	Mrs E. Melville	Mrs E. Melville	11. 1.67
Ch. Camrose Cabus Christopher	D	Ch. Camrose Tallyrand of Anbria	Cabus Boltby Charmer	Mrs J. Tudor	Mrs Z. Moriarty	17. 9.67
Ch. Cabus Caruso	D	Ch. Camrose Tallyrand of Anbria	Cabus Boltby Charmer	Mrs Z. Moriarty	Mrs Z. Moriarty	5. 7.66
Ch. Deerflite Endeavour of Yeo	B	Mandingo Beau Geste of Yeo	Sh. Ch. Deerflite Rainfall	Mrs L Sawtell	Mrs F. E. Borrow	10. 2.69
Ch. Sansue Saracen of Westley	D	Ch. Camrose Nicolas of Westley	Sansue Latisha	Miss J. Gill & Mrs D. Philpott	Mrs V. Birkin	25. 9.68
Ch. Deremar Rosemary	B	Ch. Camrose Cabus Christopher	Deremar Tess of Farmcott	Mrs D. J. Price-Harding	Mr D. J. Price-Harding	3. 2.70
Ch. Sutton Rudy	D	Charwards Simon of Stokeford	Rawlstone Sherry	Mr & Mrs C. Lowe	Mrs E. Herbert	24.11.62

Name	Sex	Sire	Dam	Owner	Breeder	Born
Ch. Stubblesdown Jester of Steddles	D	Ch. Sharland the Scot	Stubblesdown Verbena	Mrs R. Hodgson	Mr W. Hickmott	2. 5.65
Ch. Brierford Briar of Bessram	D	Ch. Camrose Tallyrand of Anbria	Ch. Boltby Felicity of Brierford	Mr H. W. Ingram	Mr A. Gribbin & Miss M. Gregory	29. 8.69
Ch. Hughenden Cabus Columba	D	Ch. Camrose Tallyrand of Anbria	Ch. Cabus Boltby Charmer	Mrs L. Bacon	Mrs Z. Moriarty	5. 7.66
Ch. Greenwards Latin Boy of Kirkton	D	Greenwards Cabus Celtic	Greenwards Fiona	Mr A. Simpson	Mrs B. P. Jenkinson	1.10.67
Ch. Anbria Schumac	D	Sh. Ch. Anbria Tantalus	Joriemour Lily Marlene	Mrs M. Barron	Mrs M. L. Clark	18. 7.67
Ch. Chiming Bells of Cressex	B	Ch. Camrose Nicolas of Westley	Gamebird Donshella of Cressex	Mrs M. Burden	Mrs M. Burden	4. 6.69
Ch. Brambletyne Carrock Fell of Daryock	D	Brambletyne Castelnau Intermezzo	Brambletyne Scroll	Mr F. Tripptree	Mrs Ackroyd	6. 3.69
Ch. Clarissa of Westley	B	Ch. Sansue Camrose Phoenix	Ch. Pippa of Westley	Miss Gill and Mrs Philpott	Miss Gill	18. 4.68
Westley Jacquetta	B	Ch. Crouchers Leo	Samantha of Westley	Miss Gill and Mrs Philpott	Miss Gill and Mrs Philpott	13. 7.70
Ch. Styal Sibella	B	Ch. Camrose Nicolas of Westley	Camrose Gilda	Mrs H. Hinks	Mrs H. Hinks	21.12.65
Ch. Teecon Ambassador	D	Sh. Ch. Gamebird Debonair of Teecon	Sh. Ch. Peatling Stella of Teecon	Mr & Mrs J. Tiranti	Mr & Mrs J. Tiranti	18. 4.68
Ch. Sansue Tobias	D	Ch. Camrose Tallyrand of Anbria	Sansue Camrose Justeresa	Mrs V. Birkin	Mrs V. Birkin	27. 3.71
Ch. Stolford Happy Lad	D	Stolford Playboy	Prystina of Wymondham	Mrs P. Robertson	Mr Ranger	14. 5.69

Name	Sex	Sire	Dam	Owner	Breeder	Date
Ch. Nomis Portia of Stenbury		Glennessa Grigore	Nomis Nina	Mrs E. Minter	Mrs Edwards	8. 2.72
Ch. Styal Susila	B	Ch. Camrose Cabus Christopher	Ch. Styal Sibella	Mrs H. Hinks	Mrs H. Hinks	6. 7.73
Ch. Styal Stefanie of Camrose	B	Ch. Camrose Cabus Christopher	Ch. Styal Sibella	Mrs J. Tudor & Miss R. Wilcock	Mrs H. Hinks	6. 7.73
Ch. Royal Pal of Catcombe	B	Mandingo Beau Geste of Yeo	Patsy Adams	Mr & Mrs Andrews	Mrs Pole	14. 4.68
Ch. Tranquility Token of Regina	D	Synspur Stolford Andriscus	Mytonvale Nell Ganna	Mr & Mrs P. A. Nowell	Miss P. Furniss	19.11.69
Ch. Crouchers Pinecrest Melissa	B	Ch. Crouchers Leo	Pinecrest Serena of Westley	Mrs E. Melville	Mrs M. Balaam	9. 4.69
Ch. Westley Victoria	B	Ch. Sansue Camrose Phoenix	Ch. Westley Jacquetta	Mr M. Philpott	Miss Gill & Mrs Philpott	2. 4.73
Ch. Gyrima Pipparanda	B	Ch. Camrose Cabus Christopher	Styal Sonnet of Gyrima	Mrs H. Morris	Mrs M. Timson	22. 4.70
Ch. Gyrima Pippalina	B	Ch. Camrose Cabus Christopher	Styal Sonnet of Gyrima	Mrs V. Jones	Mrs M. Timson	22. 4.70
Ch. Camrose Evenparol (& Bermudan & Canadian Ch.)	D	Ch. Camrose Cabus Christopher	Camrose Kertrude	Mr R. Johnson	Mrs J. Tudor	30.11.68
Ch. Cressex Czar of Teecon	D	Sh. Ch. Gamebird Debonair of Teecon	Gamebird Donshella of Cressex	Mr & Mrs J. Tiranti	Mrs M. Burden	20. 6.72
Ch. Ardinia Barcarolle	B	Ch. Stolford Happy Lad	Ardinia Athelfleda	Mr & Mrs Hardie	Mr & Mrs Hardie	8.11.72
Ch. Streamrise Tina	B	Synspur Stolford Andriscus	Greatoaks Tara of Streamrise	Mr R. Hadwen	Mr R. Hadwen	29.10.70
Ch. Jescott Galahad	D	Ch. Cabus Janville Defender	Jescott Jess	Mr J. P. McKenna	Mrs Richards	25. 7.70
Ch. Davern Figaro	D	Ch. Camrose Tallyrand of Anbria	Ch. Camrose Pruella of Davern	Mr & Mrs C. Lowe	Mr & Mrs C. Lowe	2. 6.71

Name	Sex	Sire	Dam	Owner	Breeder	Born
Ch. Camrose Fabius Tarquin	D	Ch. Camrose Cabus Christopher	Sh. Ch. Camrose Matilda	Mrs Tudor & Miss Wilcock	Mrs Tudor & Miss Wilcock	7. 3.75
Ch. Westley Topic of Sansue	D	Ch. Camrose Cabus Christopher	Ch. Westley Victoria	Mrs V. Birkin	Mr M. Philpott	5. 6.75
Ch. Braconcot Alcide	D	Ch. Teecon Ambassador	Amber of Aldercar	Mrs Barclay	Mrs Barclay	17. 6.72
Ch. Scotangus of Mossburn	D	Mossburn Sandpiper	Elsa of Kindaruma	Miss S. H. Pounds	Mrs M. Rowland	19.12.74
Ch. Pinecrest Salvador	D	Ch. Davern Figaro	Pinecrest Patricia	Mr & Mrs D. Balaam	Mr & Mrs D. Balaam	11. 5.74
Ch. Moorquest Mugwump	D	Deerflite Tradition of Janville	Caprice of Yeo	Mrs S. Crick	Mrs S. Crick	10. 9.76
Ch. Brensham Audacity	D	Ch. Stolford Happy Lad	Moonswell Dora of Brensham	Mrs M. Wood	Mrs M. Wood	16. 3.76
Ch. Challenger of Yeo Glengilde	D	Nor. Ch. & Sh. Ch. Glenavis Barman	Caravelle of Yeo	Mr & Mrs R. Scholes	Mrs W. H. Sawtell	19. 9.74
Ch. Stolford Merienda	B	Ch. Stolford Happy Lad	Stolford Sherry	Mrs S. Nowell	Mrs P. Robertson	6. 4.73
Ch. Catcombe Charm	B	Ch. Brackengold Max	Ambercharm of Catcombe	Mr & Mrs D. Andrews	Mr & Mrs D. Andrews	1. 8.75
Ch. Stradcot Simon of Crouchers	D	Clipper of Davern	Stradcot Cameo	Mrs E. Melville	Mrs J. Davis	6. 7.74
Ch. Nortonwood Faunus	D	Ch. Camrose Cabus Christopher	Nortonwood Fantasy of Milo	Mr & Mrs R. Bradbury	Mr & Mrs R. Bradbury	15. 2.74
Ch. Westrose La Reinah	B	Sh. Ch. Concord of Yeo	Heronsmarch Duchess	Mrs M. C. Owen	Mrs M. C. Owen	23. 1.74
Ch. Deremar Dinah	B	Ch. Davern Figaro	Ch. Deremar Rosemary	Mrs D. Price-Harding	Mrs D. Price-Harding	25. 7.74
Ch. Bryanstown Gaucho	D	Ch. Stolford Happy Lad	Janacre Gaiety of Bryanstown	Mr & Mrs M. Twist	Mr & Mrs M. Twist	12. 4.77

Name	Sex	Sire	Dam	Breeder	Owner	Date
Ch. Kuldana Kordelia	B	Ch. Camrose Cabus Christopher	Kabella of Kuldana	Mrs G. Medhurst & Miss J. Hopkins	Mrs G. Medhurst	2. 6.76
Ch. Sansue Cressida of Manoan	B	Ch. Camrose Cabus Christopher	Sansue Camrose Justeresa	Mrs J. Peck	Mrs V. Birkin	2. 2.74
Ch. Mousseglen Mayguy of Saxavord	D	Brett of Corrievern	Mousseglen Marguerite	Miss A. Moncrieff	Miss I. Cuthill	13. 5.76
Ch. Stenbury Sea Tristram of Camrose	D	Ch. Camrose Cabus Christopher	Ch. Nomis Portia of Stenbury	Mrs J. Tudor & Miss R. Wilcock	Mrs E. Minter	22. 4.77
Ch. Styal Scott of Glengilde	D	Ch. Nortonwood Faunus	Ch. Styal Susila	Mr & Mrs R. Scholes	Mrs H. Hinks	28.11.78
Ch. Westley Martha	B	Ch. Nortonwood Faunus	Ch. Westley Victoria	Miss J. Gill & Mrs D. Philpott	Mr M. Philpott	2.11.78
Ch. Arbutus Kinsella	B	Ch. Pinecrest Salvador	Arbutus Peppercorn	Mrs S. Almey	Mrs S. Almey	29.12.76
Ch. Stolford Sheralee of Talleego	B	Ch. Stolford Happy Lad	Stolford Sherry	Mr & Mrs N. Leary	Mrs P. Robertson	26. 3.77
Ch. Okus Buccaneer	D	Ch. Moorquest Mugwump	Saffron Dawn of Okus	Mrs C. Gilbert	Mrs C. Gilbert	22. 4.80
Ch. Ninell Franchesca	B	Ch. Nortonwood Faunus	Ninell Adelina	Mrs V. Jones	Mrs V. Jones	20. 6.77
Ch. Westley Mabella	B	Ch. Nortonwood Faunus	Ch. Westley Victoria	Mr M. Philpott	Mr M. Philpott	2.11.78
Ch. Odart Arabella	B	Sh. Ch. Brackengold Max	Avonpine Ashwater Governess	Mr T. Palethorpe	Mr T. Palethorpe	4.10.78
Ch. Camrose Waterlyric of Beldonburn	B	Ch. Stenbury Sea Tristram of Camrose	Camrose O'Tangey	Mrs A. Weeks	Mrs J. Tudor	3. 7.78
Ch. Oystergold Pandorina of Vinecroft	D	Glennessa Kingpin	Starlance Aquila of Oystergold	Mrs S. Medhurst	Mr D. Linter	23.10.78

Name	Sex	Sire	Dam	Owner	Breeder	Born
Ch. Gaineda Consolidator of Sansue	D	Glennessa Escapade	Sh. Ch. Rachenco Charnez of Gaineda	Mrs V. Birkin	Mrs M. Anderson	28. 9.78
Ch. Standerwick Thomasina	B	F.T. Ch. Holway Spinner	Strathcarron Seil of Standerwick	Miss J. Gill & Mrs D. Philpott	Miss J. Gill & Mrs D. Philpott	15. 3.79
Ch. Nortonwood Marx	D	Mark of Westley	Nortonwood Mischief	Mrs M. Johnson	Mr & Mrs F. Bradbury	23. 2.79
Ch. Tugwood Viking	D	Ch. Brensham Audacity	Tugwood Paula	Mr & Mrs A. Axe	Mr & Mrs A. Axe	7. 5.79
Ch. Sansue Pepper of Lovehayne	B	Ch. Gaineda Consolidator of Sansue	Sh. Ch. Sansue Wrainbow	Mr & Mrs R. Edwards	Mrs V. Birkin	2. 1.80
Ch. Sherida Sirdar	D	Ch. Pinecrest Salvador	Glennessa Carrissima of Sherida	Mrs P. Cooke	Mrs P. Cooke	4. 9.80
Ch. Bethrob Bracken	D	Kimsgold Dean	Garbank Golden Oriole	Mrs G. Crosbie	Mr & Mrs R. Humphries	8. 9.80
Ch. & Irish Ch. Mytonvale Jessica of Glenavis	B	Sh. Ch. Styal Shakespeare	Sh. Ch. Greta of Mytonvale	Mrs H. Avis	Mrs M. Guest	9. 5.81
Ch. Darris Double Diamond	D	Sh. Ch. Westley Munro of Nortonwood	Sh. Ch. Sandusky Brigitta of Darris	Mrs C. Gray	Mrs H. Morris & Mrs N. Day	8. 8.81
Ch. Lark of Lestronde	B	Sh. Ch. Stolford Likely Lad	Lestronde Waveney	Mrs B. Baskett & Mrs B. Wolton	Mrs B. Wolton	25. 9.82
Ch. Westley Samuel	D	Ch. Nortonwood Faunus	Ch. Westley Victoria	Miss J. Gill & Mrs D. Philpott	Mr M. Philpott	8. 5.81
Ch. Raylees Reema	D	Sebastian of Eidrah	Raylees Spring Song	Mrs C. Hardie	Mrs C. Hardie	2. 5.81
Ch. Canina Winter Berry	D	Ch. Tranquility Token of Regina	Teecon Infatuation of Canina	Mr & Mrs R. Sillence	Mr & Mrs R. Sillence	12. 2.80

Name	Sex	Sire	Dam	Breeder	Owner	Date
Ch. Gwelo Sinbad of Tamsbrook	D	Shandeen Sportsman of Pinecrest	Gwelo Tarella	Mrs P. Tuck	Mr J. Brittain	12. 4.83
Ch. Coomstock Disco Dancer	D	Ch. Okus Buccaneer	Coombstock Fashion	Mrs J. Newton	Mrs J. Newton	29. 3.83
Ch. Westley Felicia of Siatham	B	Sh. Ch. Lacons Enterprise	Ch. Westley Mabella	Mrs A. Falconer	Mr M. Philpott	4. 5.82
Ch. Pinecrest Susannah	B	Ch. Pinecrest Salvador	Westley Nerissa of Pinecrest	Mr & Mrs D. Balaam	Mr & Mrs D. Balaam	6. 7.80
Ch. Sansue Golden Ruler	D	Ch. Gaineda Consolidator of Sansue	Sh. Ch. Sansue Wrainbow	Mrs V. Birkin	Mrs V. Birkin	12. 1.84
Ch. Meant to be at Moorquest	D	Ch. Moorquest Mugwump	Orantique Outstep	Mrs S. Crick	Mrs W. Barnsey	9.10.82
Ch. Janacre Hogan	D	Ch. Bryanstown Gaucho	Littlecombs Hebe of Janacre	Mrs A. Woods	Mrs A. Woods	18. 5.81
Ch. Gatchells Sky at Night	D	Ch. Camrose Fabius Tarquin	Gatchells Superkay	Mrs G. Cowen	Mrs. G. Cowen	29.11.82
Ch. & Irish Ch. Garbank Special Edition of Lislone	D	Ch. Camrose Fabius Tarquin	Sh. Ch. Garbank Charming Cindy	Mrs C. Black	Mr J. Crosbie	20.10.81
Ch. Okus Jallina of Kerrien	B	Ch. Okus Buccaneer	Gay Jessica of Okus	Mrs S. Jolly	Mrs C. Gilbert	2. 3.83
Ch. Westley Ramona	B	Ch. Gaineda Consolidator of Sansue	Ch. Westley Martha	Dr & Mrs E. Caisley	Miss J. Gill & Mrs D. Philpott	22. 2.86
Ch. Ninell Morwenna	B	Sh. Ch. Gyrima Oliver	Ch. Ninell Franchesca	Mrs V. Jones	Mrs V. Jones	29.12.82
Ch. Moonsprite Mermaid of Carasan	B	Sh. Ch. Rossbourne Harvest Gold	Janville Ladybird	Mr B. Bargh	Mrs J. O'Hanlon	21. 1.84

3. FIELD TRIAL CHAMPIONS

Name	Sex	Sire	Dam	Breeder	Owner	Date
F.T. Ch. Musicmaker of Yeo	B	Ch. Masterpiece of Yeo	Sandy Girl	Mrs J. Atkinson	Mr S. Hodnott	29. 5.47
F.T. Ch. Westhyde Stubblesdown Major	D	Stubblesdown Riot	Dual Ch. Stubblesdown Golden Lass	Mr P. Fraser	Mr W. E. Hickmott	1. 5.50

Name	Sex	Sire	Dam	Owner	Breeder	Born
F.T. Ch. Treunair Cala	D	Treunair Lunga or Treunair Ciabbach	Gay Vandra	Mrs J. Lumsden	Mrs J. Lumsden	11.12.48
F.T. Ch. Haulstone Meg	B	Tanatside Bruce	Haulstone Madge	Mrs P. Eccles	Mrs P. Eccles	10. 6.49
F.T. Ch. Mazurka of Wynford	D	F.T. Ch. Westhyde Stubblesdown Major	F.T. Ch. Musicmaker of Yeo	Mrs J. Atkinson	Mrs J. Atkinson	29. 4.52
F.T. Ch. Stubblesdown Larry	D	Ch. Dorcas Glorious of Slat	Dual Ch. Stubblesdown Golden Lass	Mr W. E. Hickmott	Mr W. E. Hickmott	18. 2.49
F.T. Ch. Haulstone Bobby	D	Haulstone Bron	Haulstone Judith	Mrs P. Eccles	Mrs P. Eccles	7. 9.48
F.T. Ch. Holway Zest	D	F.T. Ch. Mazurka of Wynford	Holway Lyric	Mrs J. Atkinson	Mrs J. Atkinson	8. 6.56
F.T. Ch. Holway Bonnie	B	F.T. Ch. Haulstone Bobby	Holway Melodymaker of Wynford	Mrs J. Atkinson	Mrs J. Atkinson	17. 3.57
F.T. Ch. Holway Lancer	D	F.T. Ch. Stubblesdown Larry	Holway Melodymaker of Wynford	Mrs J. Atkinson	Mrs J. Atkinson	21. 5.59
F.T. Ch. Treunair Texa	D	Stubblesdown Kite	Gay Vandra	Sir Lansdale Train	Mrs J. Lumsden	19. 5.59
F.T. Ch. Holway Flush of Yeo	B	F.T. Ch. Mazurka of Wynford	Picture of Yeo	Mrs J. Atkinson	Mrs W. H. Sawtell	6. 6.60
F.T. Ch. Holway Teal of Westley	D	F.T. Ch. Holway Lancer	Echo of Westley	Mr E. Baldwin	Miss J. Gill	6. 7.62
F.T. Ch. Palgrave Holway Harmony	B	F.T. Ch. Holway Lancer	Holway Sally	Mr E. Baldwin	Mr M. Atkinson	23. 6.61
F.T. Ch. Westhyde Zenith	D	F.T. Ch. Holway Zest	Westhyde Merry Lass	Miss J. Pilling	Mrs P. Fraser	3. 7.65
F.T. Ch. Holway Westhyde Zeus	D	F.T. Ch. Holway Zest	Westhyde Merry Lass	Mrs J. Atkinson	Mrs P. Fraser	3. 7.65
F.T. Ch. Palgrave Holway Folly	D	Holway Lackey	F.T. Ch. Holway Flush of Yeo	Mr E. Baldwin	Mrs J. Atkinson	15. 3.65

F.T. Ch. Palgrave Fern of Ardyle	B	Palgrave Rivertrees MacAndrew	Palgrave Donna of Westley	Mr R. Taylor	Mr E. Baldwin	11. 9.66
F.T. Ch. Westhyde Zurka	D	F.T. Ch. Holway Zest	Westhyde Merry Lass	Mr K. Scandrett	Mrs P. Fraser	3. 7.65
F.T. Ch. Holway Gaiety	B	Crowell Gillie	Holway Flush of Yeo	Mrs J. R. Atkinson	Mrs J. R. Atkinson	25. 4.68
F.T. Ch. Palgrave Pinsley Link	D	Westhyde Metre	Eardisville Lyric	Mr K. J. Scandrett	Mr K. J. Scandrett	11. 6.67
F.T. Ch. Treunair Strathcarron Alexa	B	F.T. Ch. Treunair Texa	Stubblesdown Della	Mrs V. Cadell	Miss P. Macrae	1. 3.68
F.T. Ch. Claverdon Mighty	D	F.T. Ch. Holway Teal of Westley	Claverdon Holway Willow	Miss G. M. Knight	Dr N. Laughton	2. 6.67
F.T. Ch. Holway Barrister	D	F.T. Ch. Holway Zeus	F.T. Ch. Holway Flush of Yeo	Mrs J. Atkinson	Mrs J. Atkinson	22. 2.71
F.T. Ch. Palgrave Zilla of Ardyle	B	F.T. Ch. Palgrave Holway Folly	Palgrave Floss	Mr R. Taylor	Mr R. Stanwell	29. 7.70
F.T. Ch. Holway Jollity	B	F.T. Ch. Holway Westhyde Zeus	F.T. Ch. Holway Flush of Yeo	Mrs J. Atkinson	Mrs J. Atkinson	25. 4.68
F.T. Ch. Holway Spinner	D	F.T. Ch. Holway Westhyde Zeus	Holway Sparkler	Mr M. Dare	Mrs J. Atkinson	22. 6.70
F.T. Ch. Wadesmill Caesar	D	Vigilant of Yeo	Twinkle of Cavers	Mr & Mrs M. Wright	Mr Wright	17. 4.68
F.T. Ch. Holway Gorse	B	Crowell Gillie	F.T. Ch. Holway Flush of Yeo	Mrs M. Fielding	Mrs J. Atkinson	25. 4.68
F.T. Ch. Yarlaw Zip	D	F.T. Ch. Holway Westhyde Zeus	Culnor Belinda of Yarlaw	Mr G. Cheepe	Mrs R. Hutton	7. 4.71
F.T. Ch. Dowry of Maar	B	Irish F.T. Ch. Dorcas of Mohill	Pussywillow of Maar	Mrs Abel	Mrs Abel	29. 4.69
F.T. Ch. Volvo of Palgrave	D	Belway Vanguard	Hilost Peril	Mr E. Baldwin	Mr D. B. Kippax	2. 5.74
F.T. Ch. Holway Chanter	D	Palgrave Enchanter	Holway Sparkler	Mrs J. Atkinson	Mrs J. Atkinson	14. 3.75
F.T. Ch. Hilost Quibble of Castleshaw	B	Greenfoot Gambler	F.T. Ch. Holway Gorse	Mrs S. Buckley	Mrs Fielding	2. 6.73

Name	Sex	Sire	Dam	Owner	Breeder	Born
F.T. Ch. Lizzie of Ardyle	B	Claverdon Willie Winkle	Palgrave Zilla of Ardyle	Mr R. Taylor	Mr R. Taylor	22. 7.74
F.T. Ch. Brenjon Cleopatra	B	Sprig of Linswell	Hilost Quest	Mr J. Drury	Mr J. Drury	7. 4.76
F.T. Ch. Treunair Kelso	D	Palgrave Enchanter	Treunair Strathcarron Crion	Mr G. Roberts	Mrs J. Lumsden	6. 6.75
F.T. Ch. Holway Gem	B	F.T. Ch. Holway Westhyde Zeus	F.T. Ch. Holway Gaiety	Mrs J. Atkinson	Mrs J. Atkinson	2. 9.75
F.T. Ch. Greenfoot Dill	B	Heelook Cider	Westhyde Titania	Mrs C. Duff	Mrs M. Waters	11. 6.76
F.T. Ch. Ditchingham Tanner	D	F.T. Ch. Holway Westhyde Zeus	Albion Quest	Mr H. Frost	Miss P. Hudson	24. 7.76
F.T. Ch. Holway Calla	B	F.T. Ch. Holway Chanter	F.T. Ch. Holway Gaiety	Mr M. Dare	Mrs J. Atkinson	9. 3.77
F.T. Ch. Refley Candy	B	Walker of Palgrave	Refley Kim	Mr P. Allen	Mr J. Curtis	7.12.78
F.T. Ch. Little Marston Chorus of Holway	B	F.T. Ch. Holway Chanter	Belway Dove	Mr R. Atkinson	Mr M. Dare	9. 8.78
F.T. Ch. Ardyle Sioux	B	F.T. Ch. Holway Volvo of Palgrave	F.T. Ch. Lizzie of Ardyle	Mr R. Taylor	Mr R. Taylor	28. 4.79
F.T. Ch. Holway Dollar	B	Osmington Jacobus	F.T. Ch. Holway Gem	Mrs J. Atkinson	Mrs J. Atkinson	7. 5.80
F.T. Ch. Villa of Riversdale	B	Treunair Larras	Roxanna Sheldan Larksong	Miss J. Hunt	Mr A. Brind	10. 8.80
F.T. Ch. Holway Trumpet	D	Holway Barber	F.T. Ch. Little Marston Chorus of Holway	Mr R. Atkinson	Mr R. Atkinson	30. 5.81
F.T. Ch. Holway Grettle	B	Holway Riot	F.T. Ch. Holway Gem	Mrs J. Atkinson	Mrs J. Atkinson	3. 3.81
F.T. Ch. Standerwick Rumbustuous of Catcombe	D	Belway Flick of Flightline	Strathcarron Seil of Standerwick	Mrs W. Andrews	Miss J. Gill & Mrs D. Philpott	22. 4.82

F.T. Ch. Standerwick Roberta of Abnalls	B	Belway Flick of Flightline	Strathcarron Seil of Standerwick	Mr R. Burns	Miss J. Gill & Mrs D. Philpott	6. 5.80
F.T. Ch. Holway Denier	D	Osmington Jacobus	F.T. Ch. Holway Gem	Mrs G. Knox	Mrs J. Atkinson	26. 4.85
F.T. Ch. Standerwick Donna of Deadcraft	B	Golden Copper of Leeanchor	Standerwick Belinda	Mrs J. Hendry	Miss J. Gill & Mrs D. Philpott	
F.T. Ch. Holway Corbiere	D	F.T. Ch. Holway Denier	F.T. Ch. Little Marston Chorus of Holway	Mrs J. Atkinson	Mr R. Atkinson	30. 3.85
F.T. Ch. Holway Ruby	B	Holway Riot	F.T. Ch. Holway Gem	Mr R. Atkinson	Mrs J. Atkinson	20. 5.83

4. SHOW CHAMPIONS

(Those given in italics won their c.c.s before 1958, when the title was introduced)

(Sh. Ch.) Torrdale Kim of Stenbury	D	Torrdale Tinker	Torrdale Tiptoes	Mrs E. Minter	Mrs I. Parsons	26. 4.45
(Sh. Ch.) Tormist Marigold	B	Tormist Amber	Torrdale Lavender	Miss Burnage	Miss Burnage	17. 2.46
(Sh. Ch.) Nyda of Elsiville	B	Tim of Elsiville	Delilah of Elsiville	Mrs E. L. Ford	Mrs E. L. Ford	22. 3.45
(Sh. Ch.) Torrdale Maida	B	Torrdale Don Juan	Torrdale Honey	Miss J. Murray	Mrs I. Parsons	24. 4.47
(Sh. Ch.) Beauchasse Bergamot	B	Beauchasse Pioneer	Dorcas Leola	Mr W. D. Barwise	Mr W. D. Barwise	13. 7.45
(Sh. Ch.) Trooper of Matsonhouse	D	Stubbings Golden Dandylyon	Saffron of Heydown	Mrs Selwyn	Mrs Selwyn	12.12.41
(Sh. Ch.) Ophelia of Elsiville	B	Mazuel of Elsiville	Maria of Elsiville	Mrs E. L. Ford	Mrs E. L. Ford	17. 5.48
(Sh. Ch.) Roger of Rosecott	D	Dual Ch. Anningsley Stingo	Sally of Pinecroft	Miss R. Clark	Mr Nixon	9. 3.44
(Sh. Ch.) Happy of Peradenia	D	Major Dante	Beauty of Peradenia	Mr W. R. Jacobs	Mr W. R. Jacobs	6. 5.50
(Sh. Ch.) Sonia of Elsiville	B	Torrdale Laddie	Theurrech of Elsiville	Mrs J. Allwood	Mrs E. L. Ford	4.10.43
(Sh. Ch.) Anbria Andrew of Arbrook	D	Stubbings Golden Dandylyon	Honeyflower of Arbrook	Mrs G. Barron	Mrs M. Wills	16. 4.49

Name	Sex	Sire	Dam	Owner	Breeder	Born
(Sh. Ch.) Busbie Jewel	B	Ch. Alexander of Elsiville	Eileen's Pet	Mr Gemmell	Mr Gemmell	16. 8.50
(Sh. Ch.) Dorcas Always Pinkhill Rosa	B	Sinbad of Rookley	Stubbings Golden Jacosta	Mrs J. F. French	Mr R. Willis	20. 5.44
(Sh. Ch.) Sonnet	D	Ch. Torrdale Happy Lad	Dorcas Aurora	Mrs F. E. Borrow	Mrs F. E. Borrow	5. 2.49
(Sh. Ch.) Waterwitch of Stenbury	B	Ch. Boltby Skylon	Bewitching of Stenbury	Mrs E. Minter	Mrs E. Minter	24. 9.53
(Sh. Ch.) Annette of Westley	B	Ch. William of Westley	Ch. Sally of Westley	Miss J. Gill	Miss J. Gill	10.12.53
(Sh. Ch.) Halsham Honey	B	Sh. Ch. Major of Elsiville	Halsham Merrie Maid	Mrs I. Broomhall	Mrs I. Broomhall	9. 7.51
(Sh. Ch.) Pandown Poppet of Yeo	B	Ch. Torrdale Faithful	Ch. Fona of Maidafeld	Mrs W. H. Sawtell	Miss J. Murray	11. 5.54
(Sh. Ch.) Major of Elsiville	D	Ch. Alexander of Elsiville	Annabell of Elsiville	Mrs I. Broomhall	Mrs E. L Ford	26. 2.49
(Sh. Ch.) Heatherdrift Sonnet	B	Stubbings Duncan of Ipsden	Torrdale Sonnet	Mr F. Harris	Mr F. Harris	6.12.53
Sh. Ch. Stolford Joy	B	Brecklands Reporter	Brecklands Senoria	Mrs P. Robertson	Mrs P. Robertson	12. 8.56
Sh. Ch. Alresford Harringay (and Am Ch.)	B	Ch. Alresford Advertiser	Alresford Emblem	Mrs C. J. Rampling	Mrs L Pilkington	15.10.56
Sh. Ch. Danespark Angela	B	Danespark Gorse	Danespark Linda	Mr F. Dadd	Mr F. Dadd	20.11.56
Sh. Ch. Boltby Sugar Bush	B	Ch. Boltby Skylon	Boltby Gillrain Galalinda	Mrs R. Harrison	Mrs R. Harrison	14. 4.59
Sh. Ch. Gillrain Monty	D	Ch. Boltby Moonraker	Gillrain Susan	Mrs D. W. Gill	Mrs D. W. Gill	4.10.52

Name	Sex	Sire	Dam	Breeder	Owner	Date
Sh. Ch. Tingel Ripple of Arbrook	B	Arbrook Alresford Eclipse	Heatherbell of Arbrook	Mrs E. Southcombe	Mrs M. Wills	4.10.54
Sh. Ch. Watersprite of Stenbury	B	Ch. Boltby Moonraker	(Sh. Ch.) Waterwitch of Stenbury	Mrs E. Minter	Mrs E. Minter	8. 1.57
Sh. Ch. Whamstead Cavalier	D	Int. Ch. Jeanara's Blond Boy of Sektuny	Candy of Wham	Mrs D. Gostyn	Mrs D. Gostyn	1. 6.58
Sh. Ch. Boltby Syrian	D	Ch. Boltby Skylon	Boltby Gillrain Galalinda	Mrs R. Harrison	Mrs R. Harrison	14. 4.59
Sh. Ch. Janville Renown	B	Arlesford Illustrious	Feroce of Janville	Mrs J. Harrison	Mrs J. Harrison	31. 3.61
Sh. Ch. Broadwaters Camrose Tangay	D	Ch. Camrose Fantango	Carthew Gaiety Girl of Nayland	Mr J. Norman	Mrs A. Welch	16.11.58
Sh. Ch. Dellakcran Rose Bay	B	Boltby Thicka	Dellakcran Celandine	Mrs A. Gitins	Mr & Mrs N. Smales	15.11.59
Sh. Ch. Glennessa Waterwisp of Stenbury	B	Waterboy of Stenbury	Sh. Ch. Waterwitch of Stenbury	Wing-Cmdr J. Iles	Mrs E. Minter	8. 7.60
Sh. Ch. Waterwitchery of Stenbury	B	Ch. Boltby Skylon	(Sh. Ch.) Waterwitch of Stenbury	Mrs E. Minter	Mrs E. Minter	7. 4.58
Sh. Ch. Bridie of Shiremoor	B	Drofserla Chancery	Craignair Golden Lass	Mrs J. Raymond	Mr J. Raymond	8.10.60
Sh. Ch. Stolford Samala	B	Ch. Samdor Nimble Nick	Stolford Samantha	Mrs P. Robertson	Mrs P. Robertson	19. 9.60
Sh. Ch. Beauchasse Nous	D	Ch. Simon of Fionafield	Beauchasse Imprint	Mr W. D. Barwise	Mr W. D. Barwise	19.12.59
Sh. Ch. Contoul Robert	D	Ringmaster of Yeo	Contoul Melody	Mr M. Constable	Mr M. Constable	17. 4.60
Sh. Ch. Whamstead Emerald	B	Sh. Ch. Whamstead Cavalier	Whamstead Lavendar of Janville	Mrs D. Dawson	Mrs D. Gostyn	10. 1.60
Sh. Ch. Celandine of Carthew	B	Ch. Camrose Lucius	Deerflite Romance of Carthew	Mr D. B. Woods	Mrs A. Welch	14.10.57

Name	Sex	Sire	Dam	Owner	Breeder	Born
Sh. Ch. Gainspa Florette-of Shiremoor	B	Drofserla Chancery	Gainspa Glamour	Mr J. Raymond	Mrs E. J. Metcalfe	3. 1.61
Sh. Ch. Watersonnet of Stenbury	B	Waterboy of Stenbury	Sh. Ch. Waterwitchery of Stenbury	Mrs E. Minter	Mrs E. Minter	8. 7.60
Sh. Ch. Samdor Stolford Samarkand	D	Ch. Samdor Nimble Nick	Stolford Samantha	Mrs P. Robertson	Mrs P. Robertson	19. 9.60
Sh. Ch. Lindiskhan Suzanne	B	Boltby Sonja	Boltby Saara	Mrs J. Burnett	Mrs J. Hogg	26. 6.60
Sh. Ch. Anbria Laudable	D	Ch. Camrose Lucius	Ch. Miranda of Anbria	Mr A. R. Nicolle	Mrs G. Baron	2. 8.60
Sh. Ch. Alresford Purgold Tartan	D	Alresford Illustrious	Broadweir Damask	Mrs L. Pilkington	Mrs Alford	17. 2.62
Sh. Ch. Mangrove Anthia	B	Sh. Ch. Boltby Syrian	Danespark Coral	Mr W. C. Agar	Mr W. C. Agar	26. 2.64
Sh. Ch. Janville Yorkist	D	Janville Juan Junior	Janville Cabus Camillia	Mrs J. Harrison	Mrs J. Harrison	4.12.62
Sh. Ch. Gamebird Debonair of Teecon	D	Sh. Ch. Anbria Tantalus	Indian Ch. Mermaid of Anbria	Mr & Mrs J. Tiranti	Mrs S. Blackburn	29. 9.63
Sh. Ch. Deepleyvale Regency Cream	B	Wellhouse Janitor	Contoul Marilyn	Mrs E. R. Allen	Mr & Mrs Earsden	18.12.60
Sh. Ch. Danespark Dorinda of Fionafield	B	Sh. Ch. Beauchasse Nous	Sh. Ch. Danespark Angela	Mr J. Carney	Mr F. Dadd	13. 9.62
Sh. Ch. Oakwear Sally	B	Sh. Ch. Boltby Syrian	Sh. Ch. Dellakcran Rose Bay	Mr & Mrs P. Gittins	Mr & Mrs P. Gittins	26. 7.63
Sh. Ch. Gainspa Oonah	B	Gainspa Grenadier	Gainspa Daphne	Mrs Metcalfe	Mrs Metcalfe	21.11.62
Sh. Ch. Halsham Hifi of Yeo	D	Int. Ch. Figaro of Yeo	Sh. Ch. Pandown Poppet of Yeo	Mrs I. Broomhall	Mrs L. Sawell	1. 9.61
Sh. Ch. Peatling Stella of Teecon	B	Ch. Synspur Lunik	Tingel Mirage of Peatling	Mr & Mrs J. Tiranti	Mrs Pickard	18. 8.66

Name	Sex	Sire	Dam	Breeder	Owner	Date
Sh. Ch. Anbria Tantalus	D	Ch. Camrose Tallyrand of Anbria	Anbria Laurel	Mrs G. Barron	Mrs G. Barron	16. 9.61
Sh. Ch. Marcus of Hughenden	D	Glennessa Crofter of Empshott	Legend of Hughenden	Mrs M. Markham	Mrs L. Bacon	8.12.62
Sh. Ch. Amber of Milo	B	Int. Ch. Cabus Boltby Combine	Sh. Ch. Whamstead Emerlad	Mrs D. Dawson	Mrs D. Dawson	25. 8.66
Sh. Ch. Wenrad Crusader of Milo	D	Int. Ch. Cabus Boltby Combine	Sh. Ch. Whamstead Emerlad	Mr & Mrs J. Eastham	Mrs D. Dawson	7. 4.68
Sh. Ch. Camrose Psyche of Vennetry	B	Int. Ch. Cabus Cadet	Camrose Wistansy	Mrs J. Hurt	Mrs J. Tudor	11.11.65
Sh. Ch. Raynesgold Rifleman	D	Int. Ch. Cabus Boltby Combine	Raynesgold Glenessa Etoile	Mrs R. Rowe	Mrs R. Rowe	8. 3.67
Sh. Ch. Danespark Estelle	B	Danespark Waternewton of Stenbury	Danespark Dawn	Mr F. Dadd	Mr F. Dadd	11. 2.68
Sh. Ch. Apollo of Milo	D	Int. Ch. Cabus Boltby Combine	Sh. Ch. Whamstead Emerlad	Mr E. Hellawell	Mrs D. Dawson	25. 8.66
Sh. Ch. Mandingo Beau Legionnaire (& Irish Ch.)	D	Alresford Nice Fella	Lucky Charm of Yeo	Mr A. Baker	Mrs E. Harkness	8.12.66
Sh. Ch. Danespark Emile	D	Danespark Waternewton of Stenbury	Danespark Dawn	Mr F. Dadd	Mr F. Dadd	11. 2.68
Sh. Ch. Honeygold of Shiremoor	B	Axel of Shiremoor	Golden Katrina	Mrs E. Thane	Mr J. Raymond	4. 4.63
Sh. Ch. Sherrydan Wish Me Luck	B	Silas of Rosecout	Sherrydan Psyche-Belle	Mrs N. Blomfield	Mrs D. G. Brown	7. 3.63
Sh. Ch. Deerflite Rainfall	B	Raynesgold Rainaway	Deerflite Highlight	Mrs F. E. Borrow	Mrs F. E. Borrow	20. 8.66
Sh. Ch. Glennessa Emma of Fivewinds	B	Glennessa Grigore	Annabel Lee of Fivewinds	Mrs M. Iles	Mrs B. J. Jackson	26. 5.68

Name	Sex	Sire	Dam	Owner	Breeder	Born
Sh. Ch. Glennessa Leaderman	D	Glennessa Grigore	Heatherdrift Snowflake	Mrs M. Iles	Mrs M. Iles	29. 6.60
Sh. Ch. Gyrima Ariadne	B	Ch. Camrose Cabus Christopher	Sh. Ch. Romside Raffeena of Gyrima	Mrs M. Timson	Mrs M. Timson	20. 4.69
Sh. Ch. Cossack of Rachenco	D	Ch. Bellemount Contoul Commanche	Cheryl of Rachenco	Mrs S. M. Cochrane	Mrs S. M. Cochrane	27.12.69
Sh. Ch. Romside Raffeena of Gyrima	B	Camrose Imatomas	Romside Raffaela	Mrs M. Timson	Mr & Mrs I. Ferris	13. 1.66
Sh. Ch. Gainspa Fanfare	D	Int. Ch. Cabus Boltby Combine	Sh. Ch. Gainspa Oonah	Mrs M. Anderson	Mr E. J. Metcalfe	31.12.68
Sh. Ch. Crystal of Yeo	B	Int. Ch. Mandingo Buidhe Colum	Elmscrest Melody	Mrs L. D. Canning	Mrs R. K. Treasure	3. 3.68
Sh. Ch. Stolford Jasmine	B	Sh. Ch. Samdor Stolford Samarkand	Stolford Portir	Mrs P. Robertson	Mrs P. Robertson	9. 6.68
Sh. Ch. Raynesgold Renoun	B	Goldenpine Bracken	Raynesgold Ready Response	Mrs R. Rowe	Mrs R. Rowe	4. 8.71
Sh. Ch. Glennessa Petrushka	B	Glennessa Minion	Sh. Ch. Glennessa Emma of Fivewinds	Mrs M. Iles	Mrs M. Iles	4. 3.71
Sh. Ch. Gyrima Pipparetta	B	Ch. Camrose Cabus Christopher	Styal Sonnet of Gyrima	Mrs M. Timson	Mrs M. Timson	24. 4.70
Sh. Ch. Glenavis Barman	D	Ch. Camrose Cabus Christopher	Irish Ch. Mandingo Marigold	Mrs H. Avis	Mrs H. Avis	21. 8.71
Sh. Ch. Guelder of Rooftreetop	B	Ch. Camrose Cabus Christopher	Gilly of Rooftreetop	Mrs K. Honess	Mrs K. Honess	14. 5.69
Sh. Ch. Camrose Matilda	B	Ch. Cabus Janville Defender	Ch. Camrose Wistura	Mrs J. Tudor & Miss R. Wilcock	Mrs J. Tudor	4. 2.70

Sh. Ch. Concord of Yeo	D	Ch. Stolford Happy Lad	Ch. Deerflite Endeavour of Yeo	Mrs L. Sawell	Mrs L. Sawell	24.10.71
Sh. Ch. Brackengold Max	D	Glenavis Gary	Brackengold Ripple	Mr & Mrs R. Coward	Mr & Mrs R. Coward	10. 6.70
Sh. Ch. Happy Chance of Stolford (and N.Z. Ch.)	D	Ch. Stolford Happy Lad	Ormesby Tosca	Mrs P. Robertson	Mrs Sturrock	25. 7.72
Sh. Ch. Rossbourne Timothy	D	Rossbourne Osprey	Rossbourne Ripple	Mrs J. Burnett	Mrs J. Burnett	17.10.72
Sh. Ch. Milo Hollybush of Sansue	D	Ch. Sansue Camrose Phoenix	Sh. Ch. Amber of Milo	Mrs V. Birkin	Mrs D. Dawson	15.10.72
Sh. Ch. Gainspa Fiona	B	Int. Ch. Cabus Boltby Combine	Sh. Ch. Gainspa Oonah	Mrs Metcalfe	Mrs Metcalfe	31.12.68
Sh. Ch. Trident of Yeo Colbar	D	Sh. Ch. Concord of Yeo	Sweet Klarin	Mrs B. Keighley	Mr Miles	13. 3.73
Sh. Ch. Stenbury Seasonnet	B	Ch. Camrose Cabus Christopher	Ch. Nomis Portia of Stenbury	Mrs E. Minter	Mrs E. Minter	22. 2.74
Sh. Ch. Fleur of Milo	B	Ch. Sansue Camrose Phoenix	Sh. Ch. Amber of Milo	Mrs D. Dawson	Mrs D. Dawson	25. 8.71
Sh. Ch. Garbank Charming Cindy	B	Ch. Greenwards Latin Boy	Jasmine of Dowally	Mr J. L. Crosbie	Mr J. L. Crosbie	2.11.73
Sh. Ch. Rachenco Charnez of Gaineda	B	Ch. Camrose Cabus Christopher	Alexia of Tillwood Rachenco	Mrs M. Anderson	Mrs S. Cochrane	3.10.74
Sh. Ch. Stenbury Sea Laughter	B	Ch. Camrose Cabus Christopher	Ch. Nomis Portia of Stenbury	Mrs E. Minter	Mrs E. Minter	22. 2.74
Sh. Ch. Maresha of Pengelli	B	Golden Harvest of Pengelli	Baylems Heide	Mrs E. Allan	Mr D. G. Griffiths	25. 4.71
Sh. Ch. Lacons Enterprise	D	Ch. Camrose Cabus Christopher	Lacons Annaliesa	Mr J. Simister	Mr J. Simister	26. 1.74
Sh. Ch. Deerflite Paragon	D	Mandingo Beau Geste of Yeo	Sh. Ch. Deerflite Rainfall	Mrs E. Borrow	Mrs E. Borrow	31. 1.72

Name	Sex	Sire	Dam	Owner	Breeder	Born
Sh. Ch. Cyrima Moonstone	B	Sh. Ch. Nortonwood Faunus	Sh. Ch. Cyrima Pippareta	Mrs M. Timson	Mrs M. Timson	22. 3.75
Sh. Ch. Davern Josephine	B	Ch. Davern Figaro	Davern Gabriella	Mrs Beck	Mr & Mrs Lowe	29. 3.74
Sh. Ch. Teecon Knighterrant	D	Sh. Ch. Gambeird Debonair of Teecon	Sh. Ch. Peatling Stella of Teecon	Mr & Mrs J. Tiranti	Mr & Mrs J. Tiranti	22. 3.74
Sh. Ch. Lacons Candy Floss	B	Ch. Camrose Cabus Christopher	Lacons Annaliesa	Mr J. Simister	Mr J. Simister	13. 8.72
Sh. Ch. Camacre Golden Girl	B	Janacre Casanova	Celandyne Gaiety Girl	Mrs M. Weddell	Mr Edwards	4. 8.73
Sh. Ch. Janville Tempestuous at Lincheal	D	Deerflite Tradition of Janville	Janville Kristeen	Mrs L. Anderson	Mrs J. E. Harrison	24. 6.74
Sh. Ch. Nortonwood Canella	B	Ch. Cabus Caruso	Destiny of Milo	Mr & Mrs R. Bradbury	Mr & Mrs R. Bradbury	5.11.72
Sh. Ch. Bishopsgarth Felicity Girl	B	Janville Adjuant	Bishopsgarth Bonny	Mrs P. Wardale	Mr & Mrs R. Redmond	24. 8.76
Sh. Ch. Ninell Charade of Nortonwood	B	Sh. Ch. Nortonwood Faunus	Ninell Adelina	Mrs V. Jones	Mr & Mrs R. Bradbury	16. 6.75
Sh. Ch. Greta of Mytonvale	B	Sh. Ch. Nortonwood Faunus	Mytonvale Sophie	Mrs M. D. Guest	Mr E. Gompertz	11. 5.75
Sh. Ch. Stenbury Sea O'Dreams	B	Ch. Camrose Cabus Christopher	Ch. Nomis Portia of Stenbury	Mrs E. Minter	Mrs E. Minter	22. 4.77
Sh. Ch. Cattrysse Chevalier	D	Ch. Stolford Happy Lad	Cattrysse Amanda Jane	Mrs I. Holloway	Mrs I. Holloway	17. 9.74
Sh. Ch. Westley Tartan of Buidhe	D	Ch. Camrose Cabus Christopher	Ch. Westley Victoria	Miss L. Ross	Mr M. Philpott	5. 6.75
Sh. Ch. Rossbourne Harvest Gold	D	Sh. Ch. Rossbourne Timothy	Kingsburgh Bryony-Ann	Mrs R. Burnett	Mrs R. Burnett	22. 9.79

Name	Sex	Sire	Dam	Breeder	Owner	Date
Sh. Ch. Hingstondown Notoriety of Muskan	B	Sh. Ch. Brackengold Max	Hingstondown Lady Capulet	Mrs H. Lambshead	Mrs Sharp	29.12.76
Sh. Ch. Lindys Butterscotch of Melfricka	D	Sh. Ch. Lacons Enterprise	Lindys Violetta	Mr F. Hathaway	Mr & Mrs J. R. Anderson	9. 3.75
Sh. Ch. Dooneryan Snow Queen of Maridene	B	Styal Sabre of Dooneryan	Dooneryan Portia	Mrs D. Weir	Mrs J. Patterson	28.11.76
Sh. Ch. Portcullis Napoleon	D	Ch. Camrose Cabus Christopher	Portcullis Kittiwake	Mr R. Cooper	Mrs J. Parker	3.11.74
Sh. Ch. Zach of Dunblair	D	Raynesgold Right Royal of Fivewinds	Fivewinds Rosie	Mrs C. M. Hickinbottom	Mrs P. Palmer	20. 2.78
Sh. Ch. Styal Shakespeare	D	Ch. Nortonwood Faunus	Ch. Styal Susila	Mr & Mrs P. Pickard	Mrs H. Hinks	28.11.78
Sh. Ch. Muskan Miss Dior	B	Ch. Moorquest Mugwump	Sh. Ch. Hingstondown Notoriety of Muskan	Mrs H. Lambshead	Mrs H. Lambshead	15. 9.78
Sh. Ch. Gaineda Lost Heritage of Tarnbrook	B	Glennessa Escapade	Sh. Ch. Rachenco Charnez of Gaineda	Mrs S. Warren	Mrs E. Anderson	28. 9.78
Sh. Ch. Stolford Sugar Bush	B	Ch. Stolford Happy Lad	Guisnes Gretel	Mrs P. Robertson	Mrs P. Robertson	12. 9.75
Sh. Ch. Cyrima Oliver	D	Ch. Sansue Tobias	Cyrima Genevieve	Mrs M. Timson	Mrs M. Timson	29.11.75
Sh. Ch. Nortonwood Checkmate	D	Ch. Davern Figaro	Sh. Ch. Nortonwood Canella	Mr & Mrs R. Bradbury	Mr & Mrs R. Bradbury	25. 8.76
Sh. Ch. Davern Rosabella	B	Davern Jollyfella	Davern Fennella	Mr & Mrs C. Lowe	Mr & Mrs C. Lowe	21. 3.76
Sh. Ch. Rachenco Boomerang	D	Ch. Camrose Cabus Christopher	Alexia of Tillwood Rachenco	Mrs C. Cochrane	Mrs C. Cochrane	23. 5.76
Sh. Ch. Ninell Crusade of Dabess	D	Ch. Nortonwood Faunus	Ninell Adelina	Mrs R. Wilson	Mrs V. Jones	16. 6.75

Name	Sex	Sire	Dam	Owner	Breeder	Born
Sh. Ch. Glennessa Clare	B	Sh. Ch. Rossbourne Timothy	Sh. Ch. Glennessa Petrushka	Mrs M. Iles	Mrs M. Iles	1.10.76
Sh. Ch. Wedford Elderberry Tart	B	Ch. Camrose Fabius Tarquin	Wedford Buttered Bun	Mrs J. Baines	Mrs J. Baines	4. 9.77
Sh. Ch. Sansue Wrainbow	B	Gyrima Moonlord of Rockwin	Sansue Gillian	Mrs V. Birkin	Mrs V. Birkin	14. 8.77
Sh. Ch. Stolford Likely Lad	D	Ch. Stolford Happy Lad	Salora of Stolford	Mrs P. Robertson	Mrs P. Robertson	24. 3.78
Sh. Ch. Westley Munro of Nortonwood	D	Ch. Nortonwood Faunus	Ch. Westley Victoria	Mr & Mrs R. Bradbury	Mr M. Philpott	2.11.78
Sh. Ch. Davern Alpine Rose of Lacons	B	Sh. Ch. Lacons Enterprise	Sh. Ch. Davern Rosabella	Mr J. Simister	Mr & Mrs C. Lowe	8. 5.78
Sh. Ch. Kulawand Sandpiper	B	Lindys Starshine	Ninell Cascade	Mr & Mrs R. Lane	Mr & Mrs R. Lane	2.11.78
Sh. Ch. Pitcote Arcadian of Garthfield	D	Sh. Ch. Teecon Knighterrant	Singapore Ch. Lacons Edelweiss	Mr & Mrs J. Tiranti	Mrs D. Porter	1.10.78
Sh. Ch. Gyrima Wystonia of Camrose	B	Ch. Camrose Fabius Tarquin	Sh. Ch. Gyrima Moonstone	Mrs J. Tudor	Mrs M. Timson	17.10.78
Sh. Ch. Camrose Hardangerfjord of Beldonburn	D	Ch. Camrose Cabus Christopher	Sh. Ch. Camrose Matilda	Miss F. Weeks & Mrs A. Weeks	Mrs J. Tudor & Miss R. Wilcock	6.10.75
Sh. Ch. Melfricka Echo	B	Sh. Ch. Lindys Butterscotch of Melfricka	Melfricka Baggage	Mrs M. Hathaway	Mrs M. Hathaway	26. 3.78
Sh. Ch. Stenbury Sea Lace	B	Ch. Camrose Fabius Tarquin	Sh. Ch. Stenbury Seasonnet	Mrs E. Minter	Mrs E. Minter	1. 2.79
Sh. Ch. Sandusky Brigitta of Darris	B	Ch. Camrose Fabius Tarquin	Gyrima Rebecca of Sandusky	Mrs H. Morris & N. Day	Dr A. Morris	3. 4.79

Name	Sex	Sire	Dam	Owner	Breeder	Date
Sh. Ch. Verdayne Dandini of Davern	D	Ch. Brensham Audacity	Verdayne Charlotte	Mr & Mrs C. Lowe	Mrs G. Davie	21. 7.79
Sh. Ch. Deneford Amanda	B	Gaineda Top Flight	Rachenco Sweet Sue	Mrs L Graham	Mr S. Thane	12. 6.79
Sh. Ch. Fernavy Angelina	B	Gyrima Todmanton of Dabess	Rekion Frandan Clementeen of Fernavy	Mrs E. Ward	Mrs E. Ward	5.10.79
Sh. Ch. Portcullis Greetings of Gyrima	B	Sh. Ch. Gyrima Oliver	Portcullis Czarina	Mrs M. Timson	Mrs J. Parker	2. 8.79
Sh. Ch. Dabess Lindley of Honeyford	D	Gyrima Todmanton of Dabess	Fern of Dabess	Mr & Mrs J. Woodford	Mrs R. Wilson	23. 7.79
Sh. Ch. Rossbourne Harvest Gold	D	Sh. Ch. Rossbourne Timothy	Kingsburgh Bryony-Ann	Mrs J. Burnett	Mrs J. Burnett	22. 9.79
Sh. Ch. Braydon Classic of Garbank	B	Ch. Camrose Fabius Tarquin	Braydan Silver Jubilee	Mr J. Crosbie	Mrs M. Dick	20. 5.79
Sh. Ch. Linchael Delnoss	B	Ch. Camrose Fabius Tarquin	Rossbourne Angelene at Linchael	Mrs L Anderson	Mrs L Anderson	28. 5.80
Sh. Ch. Linchael Heritage	B	Sh. Ch. Janville Tempestuous of Linchael	Deerflite Destiny at Linchael	Mrs L Anderson	Mrs L Anderson	31. 1.80
Sh. Ch. Telmah Anabel of Beamsley	B	Ch. Nortonwood Faunus	Westley Larissa	Mrs J. Haigh	Mr & Mrs D. Hamlet	7. 7.80
Sh. Ch. Rossbourne Abbotsford Hope	B	Sh. Ch. Rossbourne Harvest Gold	Rossbourne Isha	Mrs J. Burnett	Miss P. Pape	28.10.80
Sh. Ch. Westley Simone	B	Ch. Nortonwood Faunus	Ch. Westley Victoria	Mrs V. Foss & Mr H. Troedsson	Mr M. Philpott	8. 5.81
Sh. Ch. Linchael Excelsior	D	Ch. Bryanstown Gaucho	Deerflite Destiny at Lincheal	Mr & Mrs A. Coopland	Mrs L Anderson	19. 9.81
Sh. Ch. Styal Symetrya	B	Sh. Ch. Westley Munro of Nortonwood	Ch. Styal Susila	Mrs H. Hinks	Mrs H. Hinks	10.10.81

Name	Sex	Sire	Dam	Owner	Breeder	Born
Sh. Ch. Rachenco Barbarella of Colbar	B	Ch. Camrose Fabius Tarquin	Alexia of Tillwood Rachenco	Mrs B. Keighley	Mrs S. Cochrane	19. 9.81
Sh. Ch. Kulawand Sandpiper	B	Lindys Starshine of Kulawand	Ninell Cascade	Mr & Mrs R. Lane	Mr & Mrs R. Lane	2.11.78
Sh. Ch. Horham Masterful Mistri	D	Sh. Ch. Stolford Likely Lad	Bell Blonde of Horham	Mr P. Hambling	Mr P. Hambling	4. 8.81
Sh. Ch. Camrose Frangipani of Beldonburn	B	Ch. Davern Figaro	Sh. Ch. Gyrima Wystonia of Camrose	Miss F. Weeks	Mrs J. Tudor & Miss R. Wilcock	23. 8.80
Sh. Ch. Stirchley Saxon	D	Ch. Nortonwood Faunus	Sansue Wanda of Stirchley	Mr & Mrs G. Hall	Mr & Mrs G. Hall	17. 8.83
Sh. Ch. Sansue Phoebe	B	Ch. Gaineda Consolidator of Sansue	Sh. Ch. Sansue Wrainbow	Mrs V. Birkin	Mrs V. Birkin	2. 2.80
Sh. Ch. Melfricka Kudos of Rossbourne	D	Sh. Ch. Rossbourne Harvest Gold	Sansue Angelina of Melfricka	Mrs J. Burnett	Mrs M. Hathaway	13. 4.80
Sh. Ch. Westley Sophia of Papeta	B	Ch. Nortonwood Faunus	Ch. Westley Victoria	Mr & Mrs P. Pickard	Mr M. Philpott	8. 5.81
Sh. Ch. Goldsheen Jade of Pondcroft	B	Loddonvale Lunar Eclipse	Goldsheen Duchess	Mr & Mrs A. Chalkley	Mrs N. Day	22.11.79
Sh. Ch. Styal Shelley of Maundale	D	Ch. Nortonwood Faunus	Ch. Styal Susila	Mr R. Taylor	Mrs H. Hinks	28.11.79
Sh. Ch. Chevanne Sugar & Spice	B	Ch. Styal Scott of Glengilde	Orchis Crystal Clear of Chevanne	Mr & Mrs G. Scragg	Mr & Mrs G. Scragg	6. 1.83
Sh. Ch. Lorinford Lancelot	D	Sh. Ch. Nortonwood Checkmate	Lorinford Playgirl	Mrs M. Everett-Monks	Mrs M. Everett-Monks	17.12.82
Sh. Ch. Sinnhein Minutemaid	B	Sh. Ch. Nortonwood Checkmate	Westley Matthia of Sinnhein	Mr & Mrs J. Clark	Mr & Mrs J. Clark	20. 7.82
Sh. Ch. Orchis Cherylee of Tasvane	B	Rachenco Spinner of Orchis	Rebas Carina of Orchis	Mr & Mrs D. Sterrett	Henderson	31. 3.81

Sh. Ch. Sansue Royal Fancy	B	Ch. Sansue Golden Ruler	Rossbourne Party Piece of Sansue	Mrs V. Birkin	Mrs V. Birkin	27. 3.85
Sh. Ch. Telmah Belinda of Dunbyan	B	Ch. Nortonwood Faunus	Westley Larissa	Mr & Mrs Stewart	Mr D. Hamlet	5. 5.82
Sh. Ch. Pengelli Keepsake	B	Ch. Gaineda Con-solidator of Sansue	Sansue Miss Muffet of Pengelli	Mrs E. Allan-Rossiter	Mrs E. Allan-Rossiter	14. 1.85
Sh. Ch. Elzac Amber of Beaconholme	B	Sh. Ch. Teecon Knighterrant	Beaconholm Bijou of Elzac	Mr & Mrs W. Holmes	Mrs Springer	26. 6.83
Sh. Ch. Melfricka Zed.	D	Ch. Styal Scott of Glengilde	Melfricka Jocasta	Mrs M. Hathaway	Mrs M. Hathaway	22. 7.84
Sh. Ch. Nortonwood Silvanus	D	Sh. Ch. Nortonwood Checkmate	Westley Sabrina of Nortonwood	Mr & Mrs R. Bradbury	Mr & Mrs R. Bradbury	1. 5.84
Sh. Ch. Brensham Endymion of Golmas	D	Golmas Guillermo	Camrose Fidelity of Brensham	Mr B. Catterall	Mrs M. Wood	29. 1.83
Sh. Ch. Linchael Cartier of Gloi	D	Ch. Styal Scott of Glengilde	Sh. Ch. Linchael Delmoss	Walker & Roberts	Mrs L. Anderson	6.11.82
Sh. Ch. Starlance Moonstone Meg	B	Amberland Black Sabre	Starlance Coffee 'n Cream	Mrs P. Beevis	Mrs Elkins	7.10.84
Sh. Ch. Amirene King Eider of Davern	D	Sh. Ch. Nortonwood Checkmate	Stalyhills Miss Avenger of Amirene	Mr & Mrs C. Lowe	Mrs M. Woods	15. 6.83
Sh. Ch. Rossbourne In love	B	Gaineda The Mahdi	Rossbourne Liana	Mrs J. Burnett	Mrs. J. Burnett	25. 3.83
Sh. Ch. Muskan Most Charming of Cracksavon	B	Ch. Gaineda Con-solidator of Sansue	Sh. Ch. Hingsdown Notoriety of Muskan	Mr & Mrs F. Comer	Mrs H. Lambshead	7.11.83
Sh. Ch. Westley Jacob	D	Sh. Ch. Lacons Enterprise	Ch. Westley Mabella	Miss J. Gill & Mr & Mrs M. Philpott	Miss J. Gill & Mr & Mrs M. Philpott	22. 3.84
Sh. Ch. Night Romance of Kenour at Chilzer	D	Sh. Ch. Westley Munro of Nortonwood	Thenford Georgette	Mrs E. Pope	M. Easterbrook	12. 4.84
Sh. Ch. Ipcress Apollo	D	Melfricka Xmas Wishes	Glengilde Barley of Ipcress	Mr & Mrs M. Brown	Mr & Mrs M. Brown	22. 6.85
Sh. Ch. Steval Melody Maker	D	Glennessa Escapade	Steval Harmony of Lonfir	M. Porter & V. Tregaskis	V. Tregaskis	29. 5.83

Name	Sex	Sire	Dam	Owner	Breeder	Born
Sh. Ch. Saucy Sue of Brekswood	B	Ch. Nortonwood Faunus	Brekswood Janine	Mrs P. & Mrs D. Rowark	Mr J. Horwell	

5. OBEDIENCE CHAMPIONS

Name	Sex	Sire	Dam	Owner	Breeder	Born
Obed. Ch. Castelnau Pizzicato W.D.ex., U.D.ex., C.D.ex.	D	Ch. Camrose Fantango	Castelnau Concerto	Mrs K. Needs	Miss M. Baker	23. 1.56
Obed. Ch. Nicholas of Albesdon	D	Stubblesdown Nerula	Judy of Eglesfield	Mr A. Frost	Mr A. Frost	17. 7.56
Obed. Ch. Golden Gift C.D.ex.	D	Ch. Camrose Tallyrand of Anbria	Linsun Sharon	Mr J. W. Burdett	Mr & Mrs Booth	6. 5.64
Obed. Ch. Nana of Bournemouth	B	Sh. Ch. Anbria Tantalus	Duchess of Wykeham	Mr R. J. Knight	D. I. Hadfield	1. 7.64
Obed. Ch. Golden Seeker	D	Blair Haig	Leygore Juno	Mr M. J. Allsopp	Mr A. Murray	11. 5.66
Obed. Ch. Melfricka Limelight	D	Ch. Camrose Fabius Tarquin	Melfricka Go for Gold	Mrs A. Richmond	Mr F. Hathaway	28.10.80
Obed. Ch. Kingsey Golden Lass	B	Temevale Foxtor of Empshott	Empshott Birthday Maid	Mrs V. White	Mrs Benham Crosswell	9. 9.81

BIBLIOGRAPHY

Charlesworth, W. M., *Book of the Golden Retriever*, 2nd Edition, Fletcher & Son Ltd., Norwich, 1947.

Charlesworth, W. M., *Golden Retrievers*, Williams & Norgate Ltd. 1952

Croxton-Smith, A., *Dogs Since 1900*, Andrew Dakers, 1950.

Dalziel, *British Dogs*, L. Upcott Gill, 1881.

Lawrence, Richard, *The Complete Farrier and British Sportsman*, W. Lewis, 1816.

Lee, Rawdon, *Modern Dogs*, Horace Cox, 1893.

Moxon, P. R. A., *Gundogs: Training and Field Trials*, Popular Dogs, 1952, Fifteenth edition, 1986.

Sharpe, R., *Gun Training by Amateurs*, Country Life, 1924.

Smythe, R. H., *The Anatomy of Dog Breeding*, Popular Dogs, 1962.

Shaw, Vero, *The Illustrated Book of the Dog*, Cassell, Petter & Galpin, 1882.

Stonex, Elma, *The Golden Retriever Handbook*, Nicholson & Watson, 1953.

Golden Retriever Club Yearbooks.
Golden Retriever Club of Scotland's Yearbooks.
Hutchinson's Dog Encyclopaedia.

INDEX

Page numbers in *italic* refer to the illustrations

250 INDEX

Dusk, 23
Dutch Kennel Club, 161

ears: American breed standard, 168;
    Canadian breed standard, 177–8;
    English breed standard, 63, 66;
    otitis, 205; trimming, 138
Eastern Counties Retriever Society, 27
Eccles, J., 27–8, 36–7, 41
Eccles, Mrs, 28, 36–7, 41
eclampsia, 198
eczema, 79, 198–9, 205
Edmay kennels, 186
Edwards, Mr, 187
Edwards, Mrs M.B., 35
eggs, 84, 109, 116
Eire, 158–60
elbows, movement, 75–6, 83
Elliott, Dr and Mrs M., 174
Elliott, Rachel, 16, 170
Elsiville kennels, 56
emphysema, 197
entropion, 95–6, 196, 199
Ericksson, Karin, 166
Escombe, Mrs B., 158
Escombe, Captain, 29
eucalyptus oil, 105
Evans, Dr L.M., 174
Evers-Swindell, L., 29, 35–6, 38, 41,
    171
Evers-Swindell, Mrs, 35–6, 38, 41, 171
exemption shows, 132
exercise: in-season bitches, 105; in-
    whelp bitches, 108, 109; nursing
    bitches, 118; puppies, 87; runs,
    129; stud dogs, 102
export pedigrees, 124
exporting puppies, 124–5
eyelids, entropion, 95–6, 196, 199
eyes: American breed standard, 168;
    Canadian breed standard, 177;
    cataracts, 96, 196; conjunctivitis,
    196–7; defects, 78; English breed
    standard, 63, 66; progressive
    retinal atrophy, 209

Faithful Sam, 22–4
faults: American breed standard, 170;
    Canadian breed standard, 179;
    English breed standard, 64–5
Feather Fetch kennels, 174
feathering, 74; trimming, 137–9
Featherquest kennels, 174

feeding: conditioning for shows, 135–
    6; constipation, 197; diarrhoea,
    198; in-whelp bitches, 108–9;
    nursing bitches, 116–17, 119;
    puppies, 81–5, 119–22, 123; stud
    dogs, 102
fees, stud, 106
feet: American breed standard, 169;
    Canadian breed standard, 178;
    English breed standard, 64, 73,
    73; pin-toes, 75; trimming, 139
fencing, runs, 128–9
The Field, 16, 17–18
Field Champions: American, 175;
    Canadian, 182
Field Trial Champions, 134–5, 154;
    Australian, 189–90; Indian, 185;
    New Zealand, 193
Field Trials, 142, 152–5; American,
    176–7; Australian, 190; Canadian,
    182; Irish, 160
Finland, 157
fits, 199–200
fleas, 88, 130, 199, 205–6, 207
Flinn, Mrs G.H., 174
floors: kennels, 127, 130; runs, 129
Ford, Mrs E.L., 56
Fordvale kennels, 56
forequarters: American breed
    standard, 168; Canadian breed
    standard, 178; English breed
    standard, 63–4, 67–9, 68, 69
Foster, B., 174
foster-mothers, 116
foundation stock, choosing, 94–6
Fox-Lowe, J., 36
Foxcote, 21
fractures, 200
France, 157, 162–3
Frantelle kennels, 172
Fraser, Colonel, 184
Fraser, Mrs P., 39
Fraser, Peter, 39, 50, 58, 158
French, Rev., 183
Fryckstrand, Henric, 166
Funtington kennels, 184

Gaineda kennels, 62
Gainspa kennels, 62
gait: American breed standard, 169–
    70; Canadian breed standard, 179;
    English breed standard, 64, 75–6
Gallop, Miss F., 187

Walker, Mrs Cyril, 39, 43
wasp-stings, 211
water, retrieving from, 149
water bag, 113, 114
Water-Spaniels, 19–20
Watson, Mrs H.M., 191
Wavertree Sam, 22–4, 34
Wayfarer's kennels, 181
weaning puppies, 118, 121–2
Webb, Miss M., 182–3
Webber, Mr and Mrs K., 187, 188
Weetabix, 121, 122
weight, breed standard, 74–5
Wentworth Smith, Major H., 36, 42–3
Wentworth Smith, Mrs M.K., 36, 62
Wessala kennels, 174
West Indies, 157
Westhyde kennels, 39, 62
Westley kennels, 163
wet eczema, 198–9
Weyland kennels, 39
whelping, 111–16; whelping boxes,
    120, 128; whelping quarters, 110–
    11, *111*, 128
Whinbrae kennels, 181
whip worms, 207–8
whistles, 142–3; training, 143–4
White, Mrs H., 191
Whythouse Rip, 188
Wilcock, Miss R., 50, 53, 58
Wild, Commander Frank, 182
Willan, R.T., 190–1
Williams, A.T., 27
Willoughby, Lt-Commander, 43
Willowglen kennels, 192

Wills, Mrs M., 55, 186
Wilshaw, Dr T., 32, 38, 43
Wilson, A.G., 181
Wilsonia kennels, 181
Windward kennels, 39
Winston, S., 38
Winston, Mrs S., 38, 48, 159
wire hound gloves, 140, 141
Wisdom, 23
Wood, Mrs M., 53
Wood, Miss V., 51, 57, 184
wood shavings, bedding, 130
wood-wool bedding, 116, 129–30
Woodbridge, Mrs M., 188
wooden kennels, 127–8
Woods, Mrs J., 60
Woolley kennels, 35
worming: bitches, 103, 108; puppies,
    83, 120, 121, 123
worms, 79, 83, 199, 202; hook worms,
    207; round worms, 206–7; tape-
    worms, 205, 207; whip worms,
    207–8
wounds, 211–12
Wright, Mr, 185
Wyn, Mrs D., 51, 61
Yellow Nell, 24, 26, 27, 34
Yelme kennels, 36, 62
Yeo kennels, 60–1, 163, 188

Zelstone, 23
Zettersténs, K.G., 166
Zoe, 21, 23
Zwang, M.C., 174